The
Nautical
Institute

SAFETY MANAGEMENT and its MARITIME APPLICATION

by

Chengi Kuo

**Second
in the series of
Maritime mf Futures**

Published by The Nautical Institute
202 Lambeth Road, London SE1 7LQ, England
Telephone +44 (0)207 928 1351   Fax +44 (0)207 401 2817
website: www.nautinst.org

Typeset by J A Hepworth FNI
1 Ropers Court, Lavenham, Suffolk CO10 9PU, England
email: javatony@uwclub.net

Printed in England by Modern Colour Solutions
2 Bullsbridge Industrial Estate, Hayes Road,
Southall, Middlesex UB2 5NB

ISBN 1 870077 83 0

Cover picture: The container ship *Hyundai Fortune*, which caught fire in March 2006. The suspected cause was fireworks stowed on or below deck. This provides a reminder that, when assessing risks, all links in the transport chain must be considered. (*picture courtesy of The International Salvage Union*)

FOREWORD

by Efthimios E. Mitropoulos,

Secretary-General, International Maritime Organization

Shipping makes international trade possible, while sustaining the world economy. A huge diversity of cargoes, such as liquids, bulk commodities, frozen and chilled food, finished products and vehicles, all need to be delivered in a safe and timely manner. Similarly, passengers who are increasing in numbers on ferries and cruise vessels expect their ships to be operated safely and efficiently.

It is the primary task of IMO to lay down global standards and the means of achieving them, so that personal injury, loss and damage are prevented and minimized and effective measures are taken to protect the marine environment.

Where transport is concerned, the public has the right to feel comfortable in the knowledge that it can rely on the operators, be they airline pilots, ships' officers or drivers of trains and buses. Because vehicles are moving, the threat of an accident is always there and so it is essential that all operators of transport systems achieve the highest practicable levels of competence if accidents are to be avoided.

Therefore, the Organization's main work is to facilitate the development, adoption and maintenance by its Member countries of an international regulatory framework to provide consistent and appropriate measures for the safe operation of ships.

Since its inception, IMO has introduced a comprehensive body of measures designed to achieve these aims. It is through these internationally-adopted instruments that IMO lays the foundation for a safety culture, as they are all interconnected and support a common purpose of safe and secure ship operations and protection of the marine environment.

In this context, this book by Professor Kuo is particularly welcome as he brings together in one volume the different approaches to maritime safety that have been developed in IMO and compares them with initiatives taken in the nuclear, chemical and offshore industries. He demonstrates, in an easily understandable way, the underlying principles and the fundamental role of management processes in safety systems.

As the author points out early in his book, safety is not an absolute concept and the levels chosen are based on shared values. It is for this reason that this book on maritime safety is so useful because it introduces safety concepts, explains safety terms and demonstrates how the different techniques can be applied to various situations.

Whether for students being introduced to the subject for the first time or experienced operators seeking greater awareness of complementary processes, this book provides a valuable basis that helps to reinforce that essential quality which is to be found in a safety culture.

PREFACE

Most of us are bought up in the belief that safety is something which has been achieved by the existence and application of prescribed rules and regulations which are regarded as correct. Furthermore, it is assumed that these rules and regulations have been prepared by responsible people with the appropriate expertise, knowledge and experience. This way of thinking is not surprising, since the role of rules, regulations or instructions has been ingrained in us from an early age. When we were young, it was our parents who prescribed the code of behaviour. When we were at school there were teachers who organised our learning process. In our working lives there are also managers who provide us with targets to be met and activities to be performed. In fact, there always seems to be someone telling us what to do. Indeed, on rare occasions when there is no one giving instructions some of us can be at loss as to the way forward.

Prescribed rules and regulations have played a significant role in ensuring the safety of ships and maritime installations and continue to do so. In a world that is increasingly more competitive, business survival requires innovation so that fresh ideas can be used to achieve safer and more cost-effective solutions. This in turn has exposed some of the limitations of the prescriptive approach to safety via the use of regulations. Part of the problem is that for the prescriptive regulatory approach to be effective, it requires past experience and a good understanding of how a ship or its equipment performs in various circumstances. This information is not available for new and extensively modified designs. More importantly still, the prescriptive regulatory approach assumes safety is something absolute, i.e. there is a unique solution or a common interpretation of safety for every device or situation. In practice, everyone has his or her own perception of what is safe and what is not safe.

It is the latter difficulty which led to the need to develop other methods to address the safety of new and more complex marine vehicles. When nuclear power stations were being considered, a prescriptive approach alone would not be effective as there was no past experience to guide those operating the installations : so a systems engineering approach was adopted. The chemical processing industry also adopted this approach after several major disasters. The term used to describe this approach is the goal setting approach or more familiarly the "safety case approach". Following the explosion of the steel jacket structure *Piper Alpha* in the North Sea, the UK offshore industry has opted for this approach. In the maritime industry, the safety case approach is also used when new designs and equipment are introduced. It is likely greater use will be made of this approach in the future as more innovative ideas are put into practice.

The main purpose of this book is to improve the understanding of safety from fundamental considerations and to assist with the application of safety management in practice. It is my hope that for those new to the subject this book will provide a firm basis for effective safety management. For those already familiar with the subject I believe they will find some fresh treatments that will inspire them to find alternative methods for addressing safety issues.

The book begins with a chapter on the nature of safety with special emphasis on its "non absoluteness" this is followed by a review of some available safety assessment methods. The next chapter starts with the traditional prescriptive regulatory approach before examining the existing treatment of safety in the maritime industry. Key safety terms are introduced before considering the safety case approach and its application to the maritime industry. Illustrative examples are used to show the differences between the prescriptive and safety case approaches and their interface. The next three chapters are devoted to explaining how management systems support safety, introducing the concept called the generic management system (GMS) for safety and showing how the GMS is adopted to apply the safety case approach.

The key reason for presenting the safety case approach in this manner is that the GMS methodology can be applied to anything that is not absolute such as quality, reliability, education and research. Thus once the capability is acquired in safety, the same skills can be applied to many other subject areas. The next five chapters address a safety scheme which consists of outlining methods for identifying the hazards, assessing their risk levels both qualitatively based on experience and quantitatively using available accident information, reducing risk and preparing for emergencies. It is useful to note that risk–based methods are given predominant attention.

The next four chapters deal with human related activities. Human factors and safety are given first and these are followed by considering the subject of safety culture. Since good leadership and effective teamwork can influence safety, the subjects are examined before devoting attention to some important issues which are related to safety but cannot be addressed fully in this book.

There are four appendices. The first appendix outlines typical examples on the role of management in safety and these examples were taken from assignments provided by those who attended my courses on safety management. The second appendix shows how safety management can be performed within a family home. The third appendix gives an illustrative example on how the prescriptive regulatory approach is used in a maritime activity. The last appendix provides a summarised version of a safety case for a high speed craft. There is a glossary of safety terms and a list of references is included.

In preparing this book I am most grateful to the valuable help given to me by many friends and colleagues. I would like to express my profound gratitude to Oleg Sukovoy, Simon Houison Craufurd, Julian Parker and Miriam Floyd for their help in the preparation of the script. Thanks are due to the following for their support and for providing me with useful information: Sandy Angus, Chris Cain, Wie Min Gho, David Harley, Andy Humphreys, David Percival, David Smith, Cheeweng Song, Kim Pong Tan, Zubinn Tan. I would also like to thank many of my students who have contributed to the materials given in the book through their comments, questions and suggestions and for letting me use their assignments to illustrate the various aspects of safety management.

Acknowledgments; I have used various pictures to illustrate this text which I have accumulated over a long period of time. I tried to acknowledge the source of as many as possible but some sources I have been unable to obtain, I hope that any individuals or organisations whose images I have used will appreciate this difficulty. However I do wish to thank all parties in this respect.

Chengi Kuo

May 2007

Glasgow, Scotland

CONTENTS

LIST OF FIGURES

Chapter 1

WHAT IS SAFETY?

1.1 Introduction

Safety is something that everyone seems to understand, but when you ask someone the question "What is Safety?" most are surprised that such an "obvious" question should be posed and very few can give a clear answer! Safety belongs to a family of items which are NOT absolute and this means that individuals have different perceptions as to whether a given activity is safe or not. It is for this reason that it is difficult to give a precise and generic definition.

The aims of this chapter are as follows:

(a)   To provide a background to safety issues.

(b)   To highlight the factors influencing safety.

(c)   To give two definitions of the term safety.

(d)   To explain what is understood by the term safety management.

1.2 The goal of the provider

In nearly all circumstances, safety is considered in the context of "doing something" or, more specifically, in the process of meeting an objective. For example, to go to work one usually has to make a journey, whether by bus, train or private car. Safety in each of these cases is examined in relation to cost, convenience and the likelihood and consequences of an accident leading to personal injury. Marine and offshore operations are no exception to this rule; their goal can be stated as follows:

> *"To be competitive in meeting the client's specifications with solutions that are cost-effective at an acceptable level of safety."*

In commercial operations "competitive" means "profitable", but in non-commercial activities the words "effective" or "viable" may be more appropriate as they have to take into account the specific objective of the activity concerned. This also implies that success in achieving the goal, in any project, depends on meeting four separate sets of criteria simultaneously, i.e.,

- Competitiveness
- Specification
- Cost-effectiveness
- Safety

The real challenge is to meet all four sets of criteria simultaneously in a balanced manner!

1.3 Safety and its interpretations

"Safety" is a very broad concept and the understanding of its actual meaning tends to vary widely. Popular interpretations of the term were collected over a four-year period from over 1,500 participants in ship safety workshops conducted in the UK, Europe, America, Canada and South East Asia. The most popular terms selected in the context of safety include:

- Training

- Design

- Culture

- Attitude

- Operation

- Human factors

- Procedures

- Communication

- Regulation

In fact, the word "safety" is used as if it is uniformly understood, but one can encounter great difficulty when seeking an explanation of what it actually means in any given context. Typical definitions include:

(a)   *Freedom from danger:* Concise Oxford Dictionary.

It should be noted that we can never have *complete* freedom from danger.

(b)   *Freedom from unacceptable risks/personal harm*, see Fido and Wood (1989).

It should be noted that the term "risk" is ambiguous.

(c)   *Not losing money*: Commercial statement.

The search for safety is often associated with the investment of money.

Questionnaires circulated to a wide spectrum of engineers in industry, in research and educational institutions have revealed the following attitudes regarding the features thought to be most closely associated with safety:

- Many practising engineers believe that safety is a matter of producing a design to satisfy rules and regulations.

- Operators regard safety as following operational procedures that are given by the management of the organisation.

- Most academics and researchers think that safety is achieved after performing a "risk analysis" of the situation or doing reliability studies.

There are many interpretations of the word "safety" and this has made it extremely difficult for those wishing to deal rationally with the subject. One thing is certain and can be definitively stated: "safety" covers more than engineering functions.

There are many instances where the causes of an accident have involved operational procedures, human errors and decisions taken by management and designers.

1.4   Lessons from marine and offshore disasters

The capsizing of the *Herald of Free Enterprise* and the explosion of the *Piper Alpha* disasters are selected as examples:

The *Herald of Free Enterprise* disaster
Background

The *Herald of Free Enterprise* was a triple screw Roll-on/Roll-off passenger and freight ship, built by Schichan Unterweser AG, Bremerhaven in 1980. The vessel was registered with Lloyd's Register and had a load line certificate valid until 25th March 1990. Her length was 131.9m overall and her breadth was 22.7m moulded. She had eight decks, with A deck being the topmost and H deck the lowest. G deck was the main deck and was enclosed by a full superstructure. This was an open vehicle deck with a single watertight door at the stern (clear opening: 8.5m x 4.73m) and double watertight doors at the bow (clear opening: 6.0m x 4.73m).

Courtesy of HMSO

Figure 1.1 Capsizing of the *Herald of Free Enterprise*

The capsizing

The *Herald of Free Enterprise* was operated by Townsend Thorensen Car Ferries Limited (a subsidiary of P&O) and its normal routes were Dover/Calais and Dover/Zeebrugge. At 18.05 hours on 6th March 1987 she left the inner harbour at Zeebrugge bound for Dover, with a crew of 80 on board plus 81 cars, 47 freight vehicles and approximately 460 passengers. There was a light easterly breeze but very little sea or swell. Four minutes after leaving the harbour she capsized. Complete sinking was only prevented by the fact the she was still in shallow water, but water rapidly filled her below the surface-level with the result that at least 150 passengers and 38 crew members lost their lives. The UK government ordered a Public Inquiry under the chairmanship of Justice Sheen, see Sheen [1987].

The capsizing was due to a number of factors acting together adversely. These factors included the following:

- *Trim Forward*: the loading facility at Zeebrugge required the ship to trim by the bow, i.e. the waves at the bow reached its upper area.

- *Open Bow Door*: with the bow doors not closed as they should have been, the vessel left the berth astern and turned to starboard at the end of the quay before proceeding seawards through the inner harbour.

- *Turning of Ship*: the vessel rapidly increased speed to more than 14 knots and entered the channel by turning to port. An angle of lurch very quickly reached 30 degrees and then gradually increased to 90 degrees as the vessel capsized.

Some important findings

The official investigation identified a number of corrective actions which should be taken. Immediate actions include:

- *Bow Door Monitoring*: Indicator lights should be fitted to all bow doors to show their operational state, e.g. "open" or "closed". Closed-circuit television is to be used for monitoring these doors.

- *Loading*: Draft gauges or indicators should be installed to provide a ready means of checking the load condition.

- *Life Saving Device*: Provision of emergency lighting, more accessible supplies of lifejackets, emergency escape apertures and other escape mechanisms are needed to increase life saving capability.

Lessons learnt

The key lessons learnt from this disaster were:

(a) Contribution of several factors: The capsizing of the *Herald of Free Enterprise* was caused by a combination of factors acting adversely and involving the bow door being left open, a low freeboard further reduced at the bow because of the forward trim, turning at near design speed just before the vessel capsized and the location of the ship's centre of the gravity, which is critical to the stability of the vessel.

(b) Management: The management system in operation was also an important factor. The inquiry found that there did not appear to be effective procedures for controlling the operation of the bow doors, monitoring operating conditions, ensuring correct manning levels and vetting job responsibilities.

(c)   Engineering: The basis of the Ro-Ro ferry design was questioned, in particular, the single-compartment standard for G-deck. There are no watertight bulkheads at all on this deck to prevent shipped water from spreading along the full length of the vessel, thus reducing its stability, greatly augmented by free surface effect. This is a common feature of most Ro-Ro designs.

(d)   Human factors: The findings of the inquiry demonstrated clearly the contributions of human actions, omissions and the decisions taken before and after the accident. These ranged from weakness in the management of safety to human errors caused by various factors, including a heavy work load.

The *Piper Alpha* disaster

Background

The *Piper Alpha* platform was owned by a consortium with Occidental Petroleum (Caledonia) Ltd as the operator. It was exploiting a reservoir covering an area of about 12 square miles, situated 110 miles north east of Aberdeen. It was a steel jacket, fixed to the sea bed by piles. The platform had facilities for drilling wells into the reservoir, extracting, separating and processing a mixture of oil, gas and water. An initial explosion occurred on the production deck of the platform at

Courtesy of HMSO

Figure 1.2 The explosion of the Piper Alpha platform

about 22.00 hours on 6th July 1988, followed by a fire at the west end. A series of smaller explosions followed the initial one. A major explosion at 22.20 was due to the rupture of a gas riser. This disaster resulted in 167 fatalities.

The UK Government ordered a Public Inquiry into the disaster under the chairmanship of Lord Cullen. Its findings — popularly referred to as "The Cullen Report" — were published in November 1990. All the recommendations made in the report were accepted by the Government.

Recommendations

A total of 106 recommendations were made, covering 24 areas, and it may be useful to consider some of them under separate headings, as follows:

(a) Safety Case: An operator of offshore installations should be required by regulation to submit to the regulatory body a safety case in respect of each of its installations. The relevant regulations should be analogous to the Control of Industrial Major Accidents Hazard (CIMAH) Regulations, see CIMAH (1984) and this was updated later in 2001.

(b) Auditing operators' management of safety: The operator should be required to satisfy itself that its safety management system is being adhered to and there should be regular reviews of the operator's audit.

(c) Permits to work: The "permit to work" procedure involves a permit being issued to a worker before a task is given the "go-ahead". This procedure should form a part of the company's safety management system.

(d) Fire and gas detectors and emergency shut-down: The installation of emergency shut-down valves on pipelines is one important requirement, which is expected to enhance safety.

(e) Evacuation, escape and rescue: The operator should be required to submit to the regulatory body for its acceptance an evacuation, escape and rescue analysis in respect of each of its installations. This would involve details of methods for dealing with various aspects of an emergency.

Lessons learnt

The main lessons learnt from the disaster are discussed under three separate headings, as follows:

(a) Special features of an offshore installation: On an offshore installation there is a total range of equipment needed for extracting oil from the wells, but the available space is limited: so the facilities have to be carefully laid out to make the best use of it. A typical installation would have between two and three hundred people working and living in this confined space. When an accident occurs, the emergency is more serious than at an on-shore installation, where people can escape to adjacent areas.

(b) Safety and design: The design goal of many of the earlier offshore platforms did not always give safety the attention it deserved. Efforts tended to be focused on making the best use of the limited space.

(c) Importance of management: Many of the failings, identified in this disaster, can be traced back to management decisions relating to safety, since it is the management that determines safety policy, allocates resources for training and implements the working practices. A poor safety management system will lead to low standards of safety.

Source: Cullen (1990).

1.5   Key lessons from accidents

It would be helpful to consider the overall lessons learnt from the accidents considered in the previous two sections.

The role of engineering

In the present context, engineering includes design, construction and commissioning. These all have an important part to play in ensuring safety. Design decisions, for example, can have a profound effect on the safety of a structure, particularly in the early stages of design, where the scope for introducing safety features is at its greatest. However, engineering alone cannot provide all the answers, e.g. a car cannot be designed to eliminate accidents altogether, because humans are involved. In addition, hardware solutions could well be very expensive, e.g., the introduction of devices to prevent excessive ship rolling motions.

The role of operations

Achieving "safe" performance of all the relevant activities in the operation of any system (particularly one which is very complex) requires the devising of correct procedures, followed by adequate personnel training. There is also a need to obtain and utilise feedback from experience.

The role of management

Management decisions were the most important aspects of the accidents considered. It is the management of an organisation that determines the policy, makes the decisions on a range of issues including expenditure and develops a safety culture within the organisation. It is the management which has to be committed to safety and to devoting resources to the achievement of the desired level of safety. People have an important role in ensuring safety.

Human factors

Human factors are concerned with personal capabilities and characteristics and their interface with various aspects of a system. Performance and safety are critically dependent on the contribution of human factors.

Clearly, the best solution for achieving an acceptable level of safety will depend on a balance of management, engineering and operations, which also takes the human factors fully into account.

1.6 Nature of accidents

While major accidents with multiple fatalities attract the most public attention and receive the largest efforts to avoid future occurrences, it has to be realized that those accidents are not random occurrences. Analyses of major accidents have shown that there are many contributing causes and one of the most critical relates to operational practices. Some of these practices have unsafe features embedded in them. For example, a company may have robust procedures for doing a given task but, in order to meet deadline pressures, short cuts are made routinely or sloppy performances are accepted. It may only be a matter of time before a series of negligent steps lead to a serious failure.

This phenomenon is well recognized and accident ratio studies have demonstrated that there exists a relationship between serious accidents involving fatalities and other dangerous incidents. In a UK Heath and Safety Executive publication [1997], the results of three accident ratio studies acquired from various industrial activities by Heinrich in 1950, Bird in 1969 and Tye-Pearson in 1974 were considered. Although the ratios themselves were different, the trend was very similar. Figure 1.3 gives the results of a typical set of data in the form of an accident ratio pyramid.

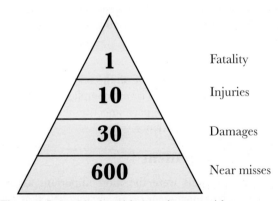

Figure 1.3 A typical accident ratio pyramid

The diagram gives the following message: For 1 fatal or serious injury there would be 10 minor injuries which are not considered serious. There would be 30 property damage accidents and 600 non-injury/damage incidents or "near misses". The maritime accident ratio pyramid will have different details but the same trend would apply. From the pyramid it can be deduced that the likelihood of major accidents can be reduced by eliminating or mitigating the number of minor accidents and near misses. It is therefore a good practice to encourage the reporting of near misses and to keep a record so as to monitor trends. The act of reporting also assists in preventing complacency. In parallel, it would be helpful to incorporate safe working practices as an integral part of developing a positive safety culture within an organization.

1.7 Defining the term "safety"

A definition of safety was proposed by Kuo (1990), as follows:

Safety is a perceived quality that determines to what extent the management, engineering and operation of a system is free of danger to life, property and the environment.

This definition was later modified with the addition of the word "human" before the perceived quality and it is now as follows:

*Safety is a **human** perceived quality that determines to what extent the management, engineering and operation of a system is free of danger to life, property and the environment.*

There are a number of words in this definition which need clarification:

- *Quality*: Safety is **not absolute** but an item which has to be specified according to given circumstances and can be continuously enhanced over a period of time, as a result of increased experience in new situations and advances in technology.

- *Human:* Accidents are caused, in most instances, by human actions such as ignoring good practices or disobeying essential instructions. In other words, safety is undermined by humans. However, it is also humans who can prevent accidents, either directly or indirectly through better understanding of the effects of their actions or the application of "common sense". Thus it can be stated that safety is underpinned by humans.

- *Perceived*: Perception of safety depends on actual circumstances, and the judgment, competence and experience of those involved in the situation. For example, a householder's decision to fit a double-throw lock to the outside doors will stem from his or her perception of the chances of being burgled and how far this lock will increase the security of the house.

- *System*: This term is used to represent any complete structure, such as a ship or semi-submersible, or a component of a ship, installation, process or project.

- *Management*: Coordinating resources and activities to meet a specific objective, which is implemented by the management of the organisation.

- *Engineering*: Many technical factors, including design and constructional methods, affect the system's performance.

- *Operation*: The operational aspect is important because even the most carefully thought out system could fail through incorrect operation.

- *Danger*: Hazards, which have high risk levels, are regarded as dangers.

- *Life*: The concept of safety is rightly associated with the protection of human life and human well-being.

- *Property*: The term "property" covers both the system of interest and other systems that may be endangered by it in any way.

- *Environment*: Marine failures, and others as well, can affect the environment in a most significant way, e.g., the grounding of an oil tanker can result in the spillage of a significant amount of crude oil.

It is because safety involves all these factors that the subject has to be dealt with in a systematic way.

While this definition is comprehensive, many people have found it to be difficult to remember and a more practical definition was therefore developed. The definition is given as follows:

> *A quality used by humans to judge a perceived danger.*

Two points should be noted. Firstly, the danger is perceived differently by each person. Secondly, humans use qualitative values for judging purposes.

1.8   Safety management

Having defined safety, it is now possible to explain what is meant by the term "safety management". Management, in a general sense, is concerned with the coordination of activities and resources to meet a specific goal. The choice of the goal will depend on the area of interest. Some typical examples are given here:

(a)   <u>Business</u>: The goal is to make a profit and, to do this, both human and non-human resources are needed. The former represents people, their expertise and experience while the latter involves finance, facilities and materials. These all have to be coordinated in the various activities to meet the goal.

(b)   <u>Information</u>: The goal is to make facts, figures, instructions, dates and knowledge available to those needing them in forms that are relevant, up-to-date and user friendly. The resources involve human skills and facilities such as computer hardware and software. The activities are coordinated to ensure that the goal can be met.

In the context of safety, the goal is the safety goal and the term can be defined as follows:

> *Safety management is the process which coordinates resources and activities to ensure that an acceptable level of safety is achieved for a situation or system.*

It should be noted that because safety is not something absolute a management system is needed in the process. The fulfilment of safety management and its application is the focus of the other chapters.

1.9 Conclusions

The main conclusions drawn are:

(a)   Safety is not absolute, is affected by management, engineering and operations and is dependent on human factors.

(b)   It is essential to have a good understanding of the term "safety" so as to determine its acceptable level.

(c)   Safety management is a process which coordinates resources and activities to meet the safety goals.

Chapter 2

SAFETY ASSESSMENT METHODS

2.1 Introduction

Safety is concerned with what harm can happen to people, damage to properties and impact on the environment when a task is being done. To manage this properly and effectively it is essential to have methods of assessing safety. Different types of methods are available to do the assessment and the choice of any one method will depend on the situation and the purpose in question. This, is turn, will determine the effectiveness of the chosen method.

The aims of this chapter are as follows:

a)   To outline the range of methods suitable for assessing the safety of various situations, activities and systems.

b)   To examine the areas of application for each of the methods and to identify its merits and drawbacks.

c)   To consider the methods from their practical application point of view.

2.2 Criteria for a successful method

To make a critical assessment of these methods, it is useful to devise a set of desirable criteria and the ones suitable in this case include the following:

•   The method should be able to provide an effective safety measure so that the application can lead to meaningful answers.

•   The thinking behind the concept can be readily understood by everybody.

•   There is scope for the user to play an active role and make a contribution if appropriate.

•   The steps involved are transparent and user friendly.

•   There should be flexibility in the way it can be applied but this should not be ambiguous.

2.3 Methods of assessing safety

There are many methods which can be used to assess the safety of a situation, activity, installation or system and a list of suitable ones is given here.

a)   *Informal guideline*: This method is considered in Section 2.4.

b)   *Formalized rules*: Highlights of this method are outlined in Section 2.5.

c)   *Prescriptive regulatory approach*: This method is examined in Chapters 3 and 4.

d) *Establishing equivalence method*: Highlights of this method are considered in Section 2.6.

e) *Risk based method*: Highlights of this method are considered in Section 2.7.

f) *Goal setting approach*: This approach, when applied to assessing the safety of a situation, activity or system is usually known as the Safety Case Approach or concept, and will be examined in the various chapters.

g) *Integrated safety approach*: Highlights of this method are considered in Section 2.8.

h) *Generic Management System (GMS) approach*: This method is a generalization of the safety case concept or goal setting approach and the key features will be found in the various chapters.

i) *A Special Assessment-Related Approach*: This approach was devised to use risk-based methods for developing prescriptive regulations. However, in many situations the method is regarded as a form of "maritime" safety case concept with special features introduced. Highlights of this method are examined in Section 2.9.

2.4   Informal guideline

Background

When an accident occurs it attracts attention. People directly involved will be concerned and seek ways to prevent any future re-occurrence or to minimise the harmful effects. When this happens, situations which involve a few persons or is so specialised it would be too difficult or costly or both to devise elaborate methods for dealing with safety, a more informal method would be adopted. It is this type of situation in which this approach is applicable.

Principle

The basic principle of this method can be stated as follows:

> *Safety is achieved by good practice in the form of informal guidelines prepared by persons or parties with interest in the welfare of everyone involved in the activity.*

Applicability

This method is generally used in leisure activities such as local yachting, small boats for fishing by individuals and pleasure craft involving fewer than eight persons.

Merits

The main merits are:

• Some people have given thought to safety.

- The guideline is particularly useful to those new to the activities.

- Some past experience is incorporated and appropriate guidelines can be given to any situation, activity or system.

Drawbacks

The main drawbacks are:

- It is unlikely to provide a consistent standard in that some informal guidelines would be very effective while others may not be more than a few words of general advice.

- Once established it would take time and educational effort to change to better guidelines.

Comments

It is useful to have some method of assessing safety even when few people are involved. An informal guideline would be a very good starting point.

2.5   Formalised rules

Background

For activities, equipment or facilities, which are popular or involve more users and people with varying amounts of experience, the informal approach would not be appropriate and there is the need to be more formal or organised. Furthermore, if the recommendations are to be adopted by many users, additional data, experience and methodologies are needed. In general, formalised rules would be devised for use and this would be more helpful.

Principle

> *Rules are drafted by organisations based on existing knowledge and past experience to help address safety and related issues in some specific situations and activities.*

Applicability

Safety associated with ship construction is published in the form of rules by the classification societies, such as the American Bureau of Shipping (2004) and Lloyd's Register of Shipping (2004), or the manufacturer of equipment such as machinery used on board ships.

Merits

The main merits are:

- Users would have available documents which are carefully prepared that can be used to address safety both directly and indirectly.

- A considerable amount of past operational experience is usually incorporated.

- Consistency can be achieved.

- Rules are regularly reviewed and improved or amended.

- Application of the rules would ensure that users will have insurance cover.

Drawbacks

The main drawbacks are:

- Users tend to rely on the information provided and would not be encouraged to think about safety.

- The rules tend to include mainly the knowledge and experience of the organisations and may not cover the entire scope.

- Rules do not encourage users to innovate or suggest radical improved alternatives.

- The reasoning behind the rules is sometimes unclear.

Comments

This approach is well established and is used in many situations. Its usefulness would be greatly enhanced by introducing a degree of flexibility.

2.6   Establishing equivalence

Background

Some rules or regulations are very restrictive in that only a single solution is given or prescribed, where there may be more cost-effective alternatives. Since rules and regulations are devised for general use they are not always relevant to the safety of a specific situation. One way out of this dilemma is to offer the users an alternative, in that they can propose another solution and demonstrate to the appropriate authorities that it is of equivalent standard or has equivalence (see IMO 2002).

Principle

> *The users of a new or alternative material or system are allowed to demonstrate to the authorities, by appropriate methods, that their proposed solution is equivalent to the existing approved solution or has equivalence.*

Applicability

This method is suitable for new materials or systems to be introduced into specific activities. An example would be to enable composite materials such as the Sandwich Plate System (SPS), which is made of a pair of steel plates with elastomer in between, to be used for shipbuilding (see SPS 2002). Regulations require the user to demonstrate that a structure made of SPS has fire equivalence to a steel structure with insulation material attached.

Merits

The main merits are:

- The method provides a way of introducing new solutions while retaining the majority of the existing requirements.

- The safety standard is maintained and sometimes even improved.

- Innovative thinking is encouraged.

Drawbacks

The main drawbacks are:

- Considerable thought and effort are needed by the users to demonstrate the equivalence.

- Extra cost and time are also involved.

Comment

This is a very useful tool for allowing the introduction of new approaches and for new methodologies and ideas to be introduced without changing the regulations. However, considerable effort and fresh approaches are needed to make the case.

2.7 Risk-based concept

Background

There are many things which can go wrong in any operation, activity or system. Some can lead to serious consequences and others may be more likely to occur. It would not be sensible, or cost-effective, to pay equal attention to all of them. It would be more logical to focus attention on the more serious ones and adopt a systematic and consistent way of addressing safety. The risk-based concept, or risk-based safety assessment method, is the one that can assist in achieving this goal.

Principle

For a given situation, activity or system, identify what aspects could go wrong and assess their significance and then focus on the ones which can have a major impact on safety.

Applicability

There are many situations in which this approach can be used and it is particularly suitable for assessing the safety of a new system, situation and activity where there is little or no background operational experience. Examples of application include the development of "new" regulations by the International Maritime Organization.

Merits

The main merits include:

- It is a more focused approach, with the emphasis on more significant problems.

- By having a systematic method of prioritising safety related issues and activities, better use can be made of resources.

- Some knowledge and working experience of this method can be very useful in addressing non-safety related situations as well.

Drawbacks

The main drawbacks include:

- The concept of risk will take time to be understood and applied effectively.

- Fresh thinking and attitudes must be developed in order to apply risk-based methods to practical problems.

Comments

The risk-based method is increasingly being used in many situations and a lot of safety management techniques have a risk feature. The challenge is to ensure that more people understand risk and its usage.

2.8   Integrated safety method

Background

The methods considered so far are dominated by technological features and experience has clearly shown that safety is dependent on what are called human factors and there is a need to develop a positive safety culture. It is therefore logical to find some way of linking the technological aspect to safety culture.

Principle

Safety techniques are woven into a safety culture to form the basis of a combined method for practical use.

Applicability

The method is ideal for situations where humans are dominant as, for example, small commercial operations like fishing or other offshore activities.

Merits

The main merits of this approach include:

- An attempt would be made to link the two important safety features together.

- Safety assessment takes into account the impact of human factors.

Drawbacks

The main drawbacks include:

- Human factors is a subject which can be very difficult to deal with in practice.

- There is a need for users to have expertise and experience in both technology and human behaviour, if successful application is to be achieved.

Comments

Potentially this concept is most valuable and there is an opportunity to integrate techniques such as the Generic Management System approach into the safety culture. However, before human factors are involved, it needs time to become viable.

2.9   Special assessment-related method

Background

In general, prescriptive regulations are introduced as a result of accidents. For example, the loss of the *Titanic* passenger ship in the Atlantic Ocean led to the Safety Of Life At Sea (SOLAS) regulations. The capsizing of the Ro-Ro passenger ferry, *Herald of Free Enterprise*, led to radical changes in the stability and safety of Ro-Ro passenger ferries. This reactive method was considered to be inefficient and undesirable, and a pro-active method seemed a better way forward.

This was actively pursued by the UK Maritime Coastguard Agency in the early 1990s and the UK delegation was able to persuade the IMO (International Maritime Organization) to adopt an alternative approach when new rules have to be devised. The name given to this approach is called Formal Safety Assessment (FSA), although it does not do assessment in the manner of the other assessment methods outlined in Section 2.4 to 2.8. However, FSA is included here because it is a special assessment-related approach.

Principle

The method consists of five steps, as follows:

Step 1:   Identification of hazards of an issue where new prescriptive regulations are needed.

Step 2:   Assessment of the risk associated with these hazards in order to establish their significance.

Step 3:   Suggest options for managing the identified risks.

Step 4:   Cost/benefit assessment of options from Step 3.

Step 5:   Selection of options based on the results.

Applicability

The initial idea was to use the FSA method to devise new regulations but some aspects of the five steps are used to assess the safety of a situation, activity or operation. In these cases, the latter three steps were modified. It will be noted that the name 'FSA' is used in safety assessment in other industries but with different emphases and for this reason it would be less confusing to call this approach IMO-FSA.

Merits

The main merits are:

* The approach is introduced for devising new regulations and thereby removes the "arbitrariness" concerning the development of prescriptive regulations.

* It encourages everyone in the marine industry to achieve an understanding of the term "risk" and adopt a risk based method in their work.

Drawbacks

The main drawbacks are:

* The subject is quite difficult, and there is confusion in the way the words 'hazard' and 'risk' are interchanged in Steps 2 and 3. For a discussion of these terms see Chapter 5.

* There is no management system in the approach and this is a fundamental drawback.

* Once the FSA method is adopted by IMO, it would be very difficult to modify it, even when there are worthwhile reasons for making an amendment.

Comments

It is a good idea for the marine industry to introduce a risk-based safety assement and to adopt some form of the safety-case concept. However, in the process of obtaining IMO acceptance, the approach does not address the basic need to have a management system to handle the five steps.

2.10 Conclusions

(a)   A range of methods is available for assessing the safety of a situation, activity or system with varying degrees of suitability for practical usage and care should be exercised in choosing the preferred method.

(b)   The prescriptive regulatory and safety-case approaches are most commonly used, but the other methods outlined in this chapter can also be effective in appropriate circumstances.

Chapter 3

PRESCRIPTIVE REGULATORY APPROACH TO SAFETY

3.1 Introduction

Safety has been treated in the maritime world by what is known as the Prescriptive Regulatory Approach (PRA), in which regulations are adopted to guide and control the suppliers of products such as ships and the operators of marine services. Thus an understanding of this approach will be useful in safety management.

The main aims of this chapter are:

(a)   To explain the basis of the prescriptive concept.

(b)   To outline the prescriptive regulatory approach for treating safety.

(c)   To examine the merits and drawbacks of the approach.

(d)   To consider issues relating to its practical usage.

3.2 The prescriptive concept

The prescriptive concept is very familiar to everyone as it is applied in many activities throughout one's life. There is usually someone telling others what to do both informally and formally via some regulations or laws. Informal prescribers include:

•   Parents to their children.

•   Teachers to their pupils.

•   Spouses to their partners.

The prescriptive process is best illustrated with the aid of an example.

Example 3.1: The application of the prescriptive concept can be worded in the following manner:

> *We would like to have a fruit cake after dinner and please buy one from a Marks and Spencer store.*

It is useful to recognise that there are two parts involved.

(a)   There is a requirement, which is "to have a fruit cake after dinner."

(b)   There is an instruction on how the requirement is to be met, i.e. buy the fruit cake from a Marks and Spencer store. In the UK, Marks and Spencer has a reputation for the quality of their food and some people would insist on buying a favourite item from that store and accept the standard without question!

Taking into account these issues, the prescriptive concept can be defined as follows:

One party prescribes both the requirement and how it should be met.

It should be noted that if the latter is not included in the instruction, i.e. to buy a tasty fruit cake from any store or supermarket instead of Marks and Spencer, then the process would not be considered as applying the prescriptive concept. In this circumstance the process would be called the "Safety Case concept or approach", i.e. the requirements are prescribed but the operator can use any suitable methods of solutions provided they can show to the prescribing authority how the requirements are satisfied. Further examination of this will be made later.

In more complex situations there could be a mixture of prescriptive instructions together with some degree of flexibility. In these circumstances, the process would still be regarded as applying the prescriptive concept.

3.3   The prescriptive regulatory approach

An extension of the prescriptive approach is to introduce regulations to define both the requirements and the methods to be used to obtain the solution. A possible definition of the term is expressed as follows:

One party prescribes the safety requirement, goal or standard, together with the method of achieving the solution in the form of regulations, often statutory, which have to be obeyed by the providers of products and services.

The prescribing body is usually some organisation with authority and examples are used here to illustrate the use of this approach.

Example 3.2:   The activity is associated with the ability to drive a car on the roads of a country such as the United Kingdom.

Regulatory requirement: The driver must have a valid licence to drive a car and the car must have insurance cover taken out for one's own car or paid to a car hire company.

Solution: The driver must pass a written test on the highway code from the Ministry of Transport that covers various aspects relating to driving on the roads. There is also a practical driving test over a designated route, conducted in the presence of an official examiner from an authority with responsibility for transport or road transport.

Example 3.3:   To gain a postgraduate degree (at Master's level) from a university in the UK.

Regulatory requirement: The applicant must have an undergraduate degree with a specific grade or equivalent qualification.

Solution: An applicant must fill a standard postgraduate application form giving personal information, academic qualifications and experience together with the names of referees. The admission decision will be that of the academic selector, based on the guidelines approved by the appropriate academic committee.

Example 3.4:   To build a ship for a ship operator.

Regulatory requirement: The ship should have sufficient strength to withstand sea loads, adequate stability and have facilities to safeguard life for those on board.

Solution: To meet the requirement, the shipbuilder has to satisfy a range of statutory regulations approved by the International Maritime Organization and classification society rules concerning the construction of merchant ships.

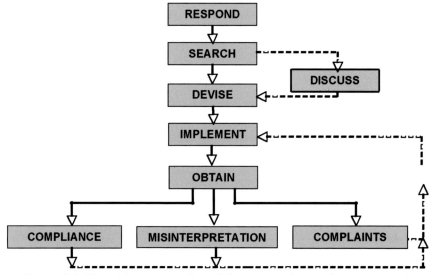

Figure 3.1 Pictorial representation of the prescriptive regulatory approach

The process of regulatory development consists of the following seven steps, as illustrated in figure 3.1:

(a)   Respond to an accident.

(b)   Search for similar regulations which can address the accident.

(c)   Devise new, or amend existing, regulations to prevent any repetition of the accident.

(d)   Circulate the proposals to stakeholders and incorporate any feedback as appropriate.

(e)   Implement the regulations in practice.

(f)   Respond to the following main comments:

- Compliance: This is an ideal response.

- Misinterpretations: This may be due to ambiguity or deliberate taking of possible alternative meanings.

- Complaints: The regulations may be considered to be too strict or add too much extra work. The user's trade organisation may take the lead in complaining, in order to force modifications to the regulations.

(g)   Modify the regulations: This is often a difficult process as the regulators have to obtain government approval for the changes.

3.4   Merits and drawbacks of the approach

The prescriptive approach or prescriptive regulatory approach is so well established that one tends to assume that it must be correct and have many merits. Therefore, when participants on safety management courses are asked to give a short list of the merits and drawbacks of the approach, they are always taken by surprise. However, after thinking for a while, there are no real difficulties in coming up with suggestions.

No.	Merit	Drawback
1	Clarity of acceptability	Can oversimplify the situation
2	Common standard	Can be outdated quickly
3	Standardisation	Complacency
4	Requirement clearly defined	Too restrictive
5	Legal protection	Inflexible
6	Incorporates past experience	Cannot cover all practical situations
7	Based on experience	Inhibits innovation
8	Meets expectations of most people	Reactive to accidents
9	Not subject to users' opinions	Does not cover all situations
10	Easy to implement	Can be too bureaucratic

Figure 3.2 The merits and drawbacks of the prescriptive regulatory approach

Thus as an exercise, participants on the courses are paired and then divided into two groups. Each pair is asked to write down one merit and one drawback of the prescriptive regulatory approach, on a transparency, before passing to the next pair to give their choices. To make the exercise more interesting, the next pair cannot suggest the same ones which have already been written down and they have to think up something different. In this way ten participants of one group would come up with five merits and drawbacks and ten participants in the other group would come up with a similar number. There are common choices, but a good range can usually be achieved. Figure 3.2 gives typical suggested examples of merits and drawbacks and it should be realised that the weighting given to each of them is not the same.

It is now useful to provide a list of key merits and drawbacks together with brief explanations of the prescriptive regulatory approach for treating safety.

Merits

- *A familiar concept*: Prescribing a code of behaviour is a straightforward and familiar concept that is "ingrained" in most of us. When we are young, it is parents who prescribe. At school it is the teachers. In higher education it is the academics and administrators. At work it is the line manager of the organisation and at home it may well be the spouse! This has led to a general belief that someone has to prescribe some rules and regulations.

- *Reference standards*: PRA would be recognised as giving a standard or level of safety and this is helpful in practical situations. The standards would normally be interpreted in the same way by all users, and people can be trained to meet the prescribed standards.

- *Past experience incorporated*: Regulations have been formulated as a result of accidents and, in this way, lessons from the past are incorporated into the regulations. Indeed, PRA is derived from accidents!

- *Suitable for routine activities*: PRA is suitable and useful for routine activities which have well-established patterns. It is also useful in situations where its behaviour is well understood and known.

- *Guidance for inexperienced personnel*: When new staff or less experienced personnel are first involved in an operation, it is very helpful to have prescribed regulations as a guide until they gain sufficient experience and can appreciate the value of the guidance. For example, for operations in nuclear submarines, PRA is essential.

Drawbacks

There are key weaknesses requiring attention and these include:

- *Devolved responsibility*: It is the prescribers who have the responsibility and users simply have to comply with what is required. It has been suggested that users always have responsibility, but if an accident occurs and prescriptive regulations were met, the responsibility would be on the prescriber. More importantly, there is no "ownership" by the users of the regulations.

- *Cost implications not fully considered*: Regulations are devised in the "best" interest of people's safety by those involved and little thought is given to the cost to users in complying with the regulations. Often, the solution may not be the best way forward to ensure a better safety standard. An example is the introduction of double hull tankers for preventing oil pollution. Its cost-effectiveness still has to be verified.

- *A management system is not explicitly used*: The question of having to use a management safety system will be examined later but it is sufficient to state here that a management system is needed for treating anything which is not absolute, such as safety.

Other drawbacks of the prescriptive regulatory approach include:

- *Unsuitable for new developments*: PRA stems from past accidents, i.e. it is reactive instead of proactive, and cannot be used in fresh situations in which there is little background data or experience about its operation.

- *Inhibits innovation*: When there is something quite different, e.g. new concept, and existing regulations cannot cope with the situation, people tend to be put off taking the matter forward.

- *Difficult to keep up to date*: Prescriptive regulations are often statutory, i.e. they have been put into law, and updating them can be a very long process. This is particularly true when technological changes are so rapid!

- *Possibility of imbalance*: When a major accident occurs, there is a tendency to focus all attention on preventing its re-occurrence. As a result, many of the steps introduced may make the situation worse for other types of ships, as it is believed that a "good" safety feature for one ship should "automatically" be of benefit to all ships!

3.5   Practical application

The prescriptive regulatory approach is used in many situations although it has significant drawbacks. It is therefore useful to decide when to use the prescriptive regulatory approach and when not to use it. As a guide, the following situations will find the method valuable:

(a)   Routine situations and activities

When routine situations and activities are well established and understood, the prescriptive regulatory approach would be most suitable. Examples include:

- Stopping the car at a road junction when a red traffic light is displayed.

- Having no smoking or ignitable materials on a person while working on board oil tankers.

- Following sea lanes in restricted waters.

- Wearing survival suits while flying to an oil installation in a helicopter.

(b)   Introducing inexperienced staff to new jobs

People new to a job are unlikely to have as much confidence as more experienced staff and the prescriptive regulatory approach can be very useful as a "back-up" at the beginning. This will help those people until experience is gained. Examples include:

- Regulations which require specific procedures to be followed when performing welding repairs on board a ship.

- The time to be spent by the personnel on board in a "temporary safe haven" of an offshore installation until they are rescued.

It should be noted that, for new situations and activities, it will be essential to use alternative methods.

3.6   Conclusions

The key conclusions to be drawn are:

(a)   The prescriptive regulatory approach is based on the principle that both the requirements and the method of solution are prescribed and written in the form of regulations and the providers must comply with them if they wish to provide products and services to the public.

(b)   The prescriptive regulatory approach is the most commonly applied method for treating safety because its basic concept is familiar to everyone from an early age.

(b)   The main weaknesses of the prescriptive regulatory approach are that responsibility is vested in the prescribing authority and that a management system is lacking.

Chapter 4

MARITIME REGULATIONS AND THEIR APPLICATION

4.1 Introduction

In the previous chapter the regulatory approach to safety was examined from the point of view of the concept and the process before identifying its merits and drawbacks. This chapter considers the important features of maritime regulations and explores significant developments in this area and their practical application. It is useful to note that the prescriptive regulatory approach generally defines both the safety requirements and how the regulatory process should be adopted, i.e. the solution should follow the prescribed methods. However, in many circumstances, the methods of solution can be ineffective, inefficient or inappropriate. For these reasons, a refinement has been introduced which still has the safety requirements defined prescriptively but allows any suitable method to be used for deriving the solution. Sometimes this latter approach is called the "goal setting" approach.

The main aims of this chapter are:

(a)   To highlight the background to maritime regulations.

(b)   To outline the main types of regulations and their key features.

(c)   To consider changes in regulatory emphases.

(d)   To examine significant developments and their implications.

4.2 Background to maritime regulations

Regulations are the means by which governments manage the risk of the hazards encountered by the public. Transport, which can be considered as a "mobile" hazard, has been in the forefront of regulatory control. For example, all drivers and pilots have to be qualified and their vehicles have to be safe to operate.

In shipping, government intervention was applied early to the certification of masters and officers and later, when steam was introduced, such intervention was also applied to marine engineers. The foundering at sea of so many ships with a corresponding loss of life and cargoes in the nineteenth century, led to the introduction of load lines to ensure adequate buoyancy and freeboard.

The loss of the *Titanic* led to the international convention on Safety of Life at Sea (SOLAS) which required all passenger vessels to have adequate lifesaving equipment for everybody on board. Horrendous ship fires gave rise to regulations concerning improved fire protection, and the practice of pumping sea water into crude oil tanks to ballast tankers when returning to the load port was changed with the introduction of segregated ballast tanks, so reducing the level of pollution when the ballast was discharged prior to loading.

From these few examples it can be seen that regulations tend to be reactive to accidents. They are implemented through enforcement, which aims to ensure compliance through inspections, surveys and — in the case of negligence — prosecution.

Most activities within shipping are well prescribed by regulations governing the human, technical, and environmental dimensions of sea transport and become part of any safety management system. However, new challenges — such as the reduction of sulphur emissions from ships — are likely to be achieved through a variety of strategies where target emission values are set and the industry is given choice in the optimum solution for any particular ship or trade.

4.3   Types of safety regulations

There are many safety regulations with varying degrees of importance and applicability. It is therefore helpful to group or classify them in some way, so as to assist in gaining an understanding of their role and application. The suggested classification involves the following groups:

(a)   International regulations

Regulations in this group have international implications in that they affect ships which operate in international waters. They stem from the International Maritime Organization via conventions, protocols and resolutions and are processed through the various committees.

(b)   Regional regulations

These regulations have been devised by one or more countries and the requirements have to be satisfied by ships entering the regional waters and, generally, there is a correlation with international regulations.

(c)   Flag State regulations

Under international law, it is the flag State which regulates all the ships registered in the country of the flag. Some of the regulations can be similar to international and regional ones but others are specific to the flag State.

(c)   Port State regulations

Following the investigation of many marine accidents involving sub-standard ships, coastal states introduced their own inspection regimes which are co-ordinated via memoranda of agreement between neighbouring coastal countries. Port State Control is the process by which a nation exercises authority over foreign ships when these ships are in waters subject to its jurisdiction.

As can be recognised, ship operators may have to satisfy all of these groups of regulations although, in practice, it is the international and flag State regulations which are most relevant. The former apply to all ships while the latter are associated with the State in which the ship is registered. In addition, flag States recognise each other's regulations and this in turn makes things less onerous.

It is worthwhile mentioning that there is another group of non-mandatory rules which are crucial in support of the practical implementation of the above mentioned regulations. These are the rules of classification societies, e.g. Lloyds Register of Shipping, Det Norske Veritas and the American Bureau of Shipping, which are used in ship construction. In theory, it is possible to build ships without using the rules of classification societies but, in practice, use could then not be made of the experience acquired over many years and insurance cover would not readily be obtained.

4.4 International regulations

The most important organisation for maritime activities in an international context is the International Maritime Organization or IMO as it is usually called. Some information on the history of the IMO can be found on its web site (see IMO 2006). It is useful to highlight the key activities of IMO under the following headings:

(a) *Historical background*

In the past, shipping nations devised regulations for use by ships registered under their own flags. Bearing in mind that shipping is a hazardous activity and safety at sea is something well recognised by the shipping industry, the suggested idea was to develop international regulations that could be followed by all shipping nations. The idea was implemented in the mid-nineteenth century, when maritime treaties on safety were adopted by the major shipping nations. In the twentieth century, several countries promoted the concept that a permanent international organisation should be established to enhance maritime safety. The concept only became feasible with the establishment of the United Nations itself. In 1948 an international conference, held in Geneva, Switzerland, adopted a convention to formally establish the Inter-Governmental Maritime Consultative Organization (IMCO), but it did not come into force until 1958. IMCO was situated in London with a small staff and meetings took place two to three times per year. With the growth of world trade and shipping activities, the name of IMCO was changed to the International Maritime Organization (IMO) in 1982. It now has a permanent building in London and has a membership of 167 member states in the year 2007.

(b) *The role of IMO on safety*

There are three principal objectives for IMO and these can be summarised as follows:

- To provide a machinery to facilitate cooperation between governments or governmental regulators and to harmonise practices relating to technical matters of all kinds affecting shipping engaged in international trade.

- To encourage and facilitate the general adoption of the highest practical standards concerning maritime safety.

- To achieve efficiency in navigation and prevent and control marine pollution from ships.

In general, the achievement of these objectives is done via regulations. The earlier tasks for IMO included producing a new version of the international convention for the Safety of Life at Sea (SOLAS).

In addition, IMO addressed issues concerning marine pollution via the Convention for the Prevention of Pollution from Ships in 1973 and modified by the protocol of 1978. These are now referred to as MARPOL 73/78.

Two initiatives in the 1990s relating to maritime safety which deserve mention are:

- The introduction, on 1 July 1998, of the International Safety Management (ISM) code. This will be considered later.

- On 1 February 1997, the 1995 amendments to the 1978 International Convention on Standards of Training, Certification and Watchkeeping (STCW) for seafarers came into force. Again, these will be considered later.

In the 2000s the most significant developments have been concerned with the security of international shipping and goal based standards.

(c)   *Summary of IMO structure*

For an organisation with 167 member states involved in international activities, addressing many issues including maritime safety, it is useful to have an appreciation of how IMO is organised to carry out its various functions. The structure is now summarised.

- Assembly

  This is the highest governing body of IMO and it consists of all member states. The assembly meets every two years to make key decisions, e.g. voting the budget.

- Council

  The council is elected by the assembly for two years. Its key function is to implement the policies and work programme from the assembly, i.e. Council effectively approves IMO activities. There are two categories of council members and each has representatives from 10 states, determined by the largest interest in shipping and seaborne trade respectively. There is also a third category with 12 states providing representation for major geographic areas.

- Maritime Safety Committee (MSC)

  This is the highest technical body in the IMO and it consists of representatives from all member states. The MSC considers all matters within the IMO's terms of reference concerning safety.

- The Marine Environment Protection Committee (MEPC)

  The MEPC is empowered to consider any matter within the IMO's terms, i.e. methods concerned with the prevention and control of pollution from ships.

Reporting to these two committees there are subcommittees for detailed consideration of specialist topics e.g. fire protection, training, design and equipment, maritime law, civil liability and others.

4.5 Key international regulations

There are many international regulations relating to maritime safety and the following deserve highlighting:

- Safety of life at sea (SOLAS) convention.

- Prevention and control of pollution from ships (MARPOL) convention.

- International safety management (ISM) code.

- Standards in training, certification and watchkeeping (STCW) convention and code.

Information and details on the above can be found in various references. In this section brief attention is focused on their backgrounds, the objectives and main features.

(a)   SOLAS regulations

Safety of life at sea has always been a most important issue ever since ships were used to carry passengers and cargoes, but it was only after the sinking of the passenger ship *Titanic* that formalisation began. The *Titanic* sank on 12 April 1912 with the loss of 817 passengers and 673 crew on her maiden voyage from Southampton to New York. This led to calls for unifying separate safety agreements relating to ship safety, e.g. mutual recognition of certificates of survey and a more coordinated approach to the safety of life at sea. The first conference on safety of life at sea was held in late 1913, with representatives from 16 countries. The meetings lasted ten weeks. The outcome would have been known as SOLAS 1914, but never came into force because of the outbreak of the First World War. The main emphasis was placed on ways of preventing a similar accident, with attention being given to ship construction, e.g. watertight subdivision, stability after damage, life-saving equipment, e.g. provision of lifeboat capacity, navigation and communication from ships.

For further details, see (1915). After the war the shipping industry took some time to return to the subject of safety and it was only in 1929 that the second international conference was held. It addressed more fully issues relating to safety of life at sea and was attended by 18 countries. The meetings lasted seven weeks. The convention signed by the delegates to this conference contained proposed rules and principles for international observance under the following headings:

- Construction of passenger ships.

- Life-saving equipment of all ships.

- Radio-telegraphy (communication).

- Navigation.

- Safety certificates.

The implementation of the convention became known as SOLAS 1929, see Abell & Daniel (1930) for further details.

The third international conference on safety of life at sea was held in 1948 with representatives from 30 countries. The main purpose was to review the SOLAS 1929 convention in the light of the experience gained and scientific advances made over the intervening years. The work of the conference followed a similar pattern to the second conference and considered issues under the same headings. For further details, see Daniel (1949).

The next conference took place in 1960 with representatives from 55 countries. The issues that prompted the conference were the development of the inflatable liferaft and the introduction of ships using nuclear power plants. In addition, the increased frequency of ship collisions raised concern because this feature was not included in the previous SOLAS conventions. This led to the revised SOLAS 1960 and further conferences took place in 1974, 1990 and 1995, with significant amendments made regularly. The latest version of SOLAS regulations are given in IMO [2004].

(b) *MARPOL regulations*

The growth in the demand for oil as the principal energy source in the second half of the 20th century led to the construction of more tankers and, often, very large ships to transport crude oil from onshore and offshore wells to the refineries and users. This in turn increased maritime traffic and the emergence of a new problem called pollution. Marine pollution can occur in a number of ways with the most significant being the following:

- Runoffs from land into rivers and adjacent seas.

- Collision between ships.

- Grounding.

- Discharging of oil cargo tank washing in the sea.

- Disposing of engine room wastes into the sea.

The first is not maritime, but very significant, the next two causes are safety related and generally receive wide media attention but contribute a small percentage of total marine pollution. It is the latter two causes which make the rest of the total. To address the four latter problems, an international convention for the prevention of pollution from ships took place in 1973 and was modified by a protocol in 1978. These outcomes became the main regulations for dealing with pollution and are commonly known as MARPOL 73/78. The regulations cover not only accidental and operational oil pollution but also pollution into the sea caused by chemicals, goods in package form, sewage, garbage and air transmission. Later, IMO was given the task of devising and establishing a system for providing compensation to those who had suffered financially as a result of pollution. For details of the regulations see IMO (2006).

(c)   ISM Code regulations

In the 1989s, there were a number of major maritime accidents, involving significant number of fatalities, e.g. capsize of the Ro-Ro ferry *Herald of Free Enterprise* in March, 1987. In the offshore industry, there was the explosion of the steel jacket oil production installation *Piper Alpha* in July, 1988. The dominant cause of these accidents was the failure of management. It is the management of an organisation which defines the safety goals, develops a safety culture and assigns resources to ensure focused safety training is given to everyone in the organisation.

In 1989, IMO adopted a resolution in the form of "Guidelines on Management for the Safe Operation of Ships and for Pollution Prevention". The main objective of the guidelines was to provide a management framework for the proper development, implementation and assessment of safety and pollution prevention. The provisions were directed at those responsible for the operation of ships. After some experience in the use of the guidelines, IMO adopted in 1993 the International Management Code for the Safe Operation of Ships and for Pollution Prevention. It is known as the ISM Code. In 1998 the ISM Code became mandatory for ship operations.

The ISM is a short document with the following sections:

- Preamble.
- General.
- Safety and environmental protection policy.
- Company responsibility and authority.
- Designated person(s).
- The master's responsibility and authority.
- Resources and personnel.
- Development of plans for shipboard operation.
- Emergency preparedness.

- Reports and analyses of non-conformities, accidents and hazardous occurrences.

- Maintenance of the ship and equipment.

- Documentation.

- Company verification, review and evaluation.

- Certification, verification and control.

It will be noted that the ISM Code does not prescribe what method must be used to achieve the requirements and no specific management system is mentioned in the document. It will be noted that a management system is required, however, for effective safety management.

(d) STCW Conventions

The International Convention on Standards of Training, Certification and Watchkeeping for Seafarers (STCW) was first held in 1978 and was the first to establish a minimum standard or better for the training of, and certification of ship's officers.

In 1995 major amendments were made to the convention of 1978 and an STCW Code was produced which was made up of two parts. Part A is mandatory and contains eight chapters and addresses issues such as standards of qualifications for masters and officers in the deck department in Chapter II. Part B contains recommended guidance which is intended to help parties to implement the convention.

There are two aspects of STCW 95 which deserve brief comment. Firstly, Chapter I dealt with a number of general issues that have significant implications. For example, the concept of port State control, in which the port State can detain a ship for deficiencies in meeting the regulations of the code, e.g. certificates are not in order. Others include the use of simulators for crew training and the prevention of fatigue for watchkeeping personnel.

Secondly, not all countries were willing to be party to the convention, and a special feature required the contents of the convention to be obeyed by ships of non-party countries while visiting ports of countries who are parties. A major change was the authority given to verify the training providers in all countries where such facilities exist. The STCW Convention is currently being revised again at the time of writing.

4.6 Regional regulations

International regulations can be regarded as directives given by IMO to member states. They could then "fine tune" them in order to meet a flag State's specific requirements. Sometimes a group of countries have similar problems and a more coordinated approach would be more beneficial than each flag State acting on its own. This is true when there are already formal arrangements for the groups of nations to function in a cooperative manner. For example, the European Union (EU) has, in 2006, 25 members and it has regulations for maritime activities including maritime safety. Normally, maritime activities would tend to interface well with international regulations.

From time to time, one or two major maritime accidents occur and maritime safety raises its profile under media and public pressure. These types of situation often lead to calls for regional regulations to "safeguard" the maritime interests of the community. An example to illustrate what has happened would be to use instances of maritime accidents in EU waters.

In December 1999, an old oil tanker *Erika* broke up and sank off the French coast. Three months later the commission of the Council of The European Parliament proposed a directive and two regulations. The directive seeks to introduce a community monitoring, control and information system for maritime traffic. The proposed regulations involved setting up a compensation fund for oil pollution in European waters and forming a European Maritime Safety Agency. Realisation of these proposals was hastened by the accident to the oil tanker *Prestige* in November 2002 off the coast of Spain.

In exceptional circumstances, the regulations of a coastal State can have significant international implications. The best example is the Oil Pollution Act of the USA. In response to the grounding of *Exxon Valdez* in Alaska in 1989, the US Congress passed legislation known as the Oil Pollution Act of 1990 or OPA90. The guidelines introduced include:

(a) *Prevention involving the following:*

• Double hull requirements for tank vessels by the year 2015 in US waters.

• Access to national records before issuing or renewing a merchant mariner's licence.

• Permit US coastguard to take appropriate routine legal action against polluters.

(b) *Preparedness for oil polluters require:*

• Area committees and contingency plans.

• Vessel and facility response plans.

(c) *Liability and compensation:*

• National pollution funds centre to manage oil spill liability trust fund.

• Vessel owners or operators to establish and maintain evidence of adequate insurance.

(d)   *Response via the formation of:*

•   Response management system.

•   National strike force trained to deal with major spillage.

The OPA90 applies to oil tanker vessels entering the USA and hence it is a coastal State regulation, but since the USA is at present the largest oil importer the law effectively covers most ship operators. For example, any shipping company wishing to transport oil with the possibility of going into USA waters must upgrade its ships to double hull standard. For these reasons, ship operators must be aware of the existence of regional regulations.

4.7   Flag State regulations

The name of this section would suggest that the regulations are concerned with specific countries and this is precisely what is intended. Different countries have their own regulations, often in existence long before international harmonisation, to deal with maritime matters concerning their own ships or ships flying the country's flag. Generally, maritime safety is dealt with by an agency of the national government. For example, in the UK it is the Maritime and Coastguard Agency (MCA) which is an agency of the UK government department responsible for maritime transport. The agency has the role of implementing and enforcing the regulations and punishing those companies or individuals for negligence or non-compliance. The important safety-related activities include:

•   Surveys of passenger ships to ensure conformity to regulations and issuing of passenger vessel safety certificates.

•   Checking that life saving appliances (LSA) are built to LSA regulations and are in working order.

•   Flag States generally delegate their statutory surveys and inspections to the classification societies which have a world wide network of offices with surveyors. The classification societies themselves would be audited by the flag States in order to verify that they perform the work competently.

4.8   Port State control

Port State control is a method of checking the successful enforcement of the provisions of various international conventions covering safety, work conditions and pollution prevention on merchant ships when ships visit the waters of the coastal State. The first regional agreement to set up an inspection regime covering Europe and the north Atlantic was in 1982. Similar agreements exist in Asia, South America and the Caribbean.

During the early phase of implementation, 25% of all ships visiting the port States were inspected. This process was restructured in 2000 with a more focused approach on targeted vessels. These are ships with a poor past record of failing inspections or ships which are registered by countries and surveyed by organisations with a reputation for being less rigorous in upholding basic standards.

The results of port State inspections are posted on the EQUASIS web site called www.equasis.org. It shows all the ships detained for serious deficiencies. There is no charge for using the service but all the users must register before gaining access to the database. In this way, Equasis provides a powerful method for cargo owners to check for any major deficiencies before chartering or booking a ship for transporting their cargoes.

4.9   Changes in regulatory emphases

(a)   Background

The basic principle behind the prescriptive regulatory approach is to devise regulations which can be prescriptively applied, i.e. safety regulations are mandatory and the methods of meeting the safety requirements are prescribed. This approach works well for routine tasks with few unknowns. However, with rapid technological developments, this approach may not be suitable for all situations. In Chapter 3, the drawbacks of the prescriptive regulatory approach were considered. There are two possible methods for dealing with the problem. One method is to put in extra effort into developing fresh prescriptive regulations to keep pace with technological advancement. This method is neither practical nor realistic. The other method is to refrain from prescribing the solution but to allow users to propose solutions and to demonstrate their appropriateness from basic principles or scientific reasoning/ proof. In a number of situations this latter method is the only feasible way forward. It is useful to note that this method can be regarded as a form of goal setting approach which can lead to the safety case concept. The method can also be viewed as a variation of the equivalence approach. Examples will now be used to illustrate this change of emphasis.

(b)   Evacuation from High Speed Craft (HSC)

For a high speed craft to be economically viable, it has to achieve high speed, operate cost-effectively, deliver the payload and satisfy appropriate safety requirements. High speed craft designers tend to use lighter materials for construction; for example, the use of aluminium in place of steel. However, to meet safety requirements using conventional lifeboats would compromise its capability of carrying the desired payload.

Thus in the IMO's International Code of Safety for High Speed Craft, lifeboats for passenger and crew evacuation is not a mandatory requirement. Instead, the operators of the high speed craft have to show that the system they use can achieve the same safety standard as a lifeboat or better. Thus, instead of using heavy lifeboats and their associated handling equipment, HSC use inflatable chute systems such as a Marine Escape System (MES). The approach is given in the High Speed Craft Code, see IMO (1996).

(c)   Fire regulations for composite material

Fire is a hazard which is well recognised in maritime activities and the regulations are strict and explicit. The regulations are written for materials such as steel and insulation requirements are clearly stated. With advances in technology, new materials have been developed with comparable or better strength than steel plate stiffeners and are lighter in weight, lower in cost to manufacture, easier to use and do not corrode so rapidly. Under strict SOLAS regulations, these innovations could not be used for building ships. At the same time, to amend the rules to cater for all composite materials would make regulations highly complicated and more difficult to use.

The way to overcome this difficulty is to ask the user of the new material to demonstrate from fundamental considerations if the material can have "equivalence to steel", as given in the amendments to Part II of SOLAS regulations. It should be noted that the concept of equivalence is used in many activities; for example, a university admits students to postgraduate courses with requirements which would be worded in the following manner: "The candidate should have an Honours Degree in Engineering or Science or an equivalent qualification." What this means is that an Ordinary Degree in Engineering plus several years of relevant work experience would be considered as an acceptable entrance requirement.

An example of an "equivalence application" is the use of the Sandwich Plate System (SPS) to build ships in place of conventional steel. SPS is a composite material made up of steel, elastomer and steel with a typical thickness of 10mm-25mm-10mm for the three components respectively. For SPS to meet SOLAS fire regulations it has to achieve equivalence, e.g. the temperature of the surface of the SPS exposed to fire of specific intensity should not fail at a given temperature after 60 minutes. From fundamental considerations it is possible to show that the requirements are met and SPS has been used in the engine room of a number of Ro-Ro ships, see Kuo-Sukovoy (2004) for further details.

(d)   Maritime security

Ships have been subjected to attacks by pirates and terrorists but following the destruction of the twin towers in New York on 9 November 2001, the USA introduced via IMO proposals for new security measures on merchant ships. This is a typical situation which requires international collaboration if the solutions are to be effective. For this reason IMO took the initiative to devise an international approach to maritime security. The convention on security is called the International Ship and Port Security Facilities code or ISPS code. This was implemented by means of an amendment to SOLAS 1974. For further information see The Nautical Institute (2005).

The important feature of the ISPS is that ship operators have to comply with security standards but can adopt their own methods of achieving the desired level of security, i.e. ship operators are given the opportunity to adopt the most appropriate approach without having to follow a prescribed method of meeting security requirements. An effective method of treating security is similar to the basic considerations and techniques given in Chapters 5 to 14 of this book.

4.10 Significant regulatory developments

(a)   Some major developments

There are many maritime regulatory initiatives concerning safety and just a few of them will now be highlighted under the following headings:

- Application of risk based methodology.

- Commercial and military safety standards.

- Goal based standard (GBS).

(b)   Application of risk based methodology

As discussed in Chapter 3, the prescriptive regulatory approach is devised for regulations to be obeyed without question, i.e. there should be a clear "yes" or "no" in the decision making process. However, in a safety context this is not always possible because safety is not absolute, but is governed by personal perception. As technologies advance and new ship concepts are developed, the limitations of the prescriptive regulatory approach are becoming noticeable. It is therefore helpful to seek ways of benefiting from recent scientific advances and use them to enhance the application of the prescriptive regulatory approach.

The most obvious choice is to use risk-based techniques to improve the formulation of new regulations. The subject of risk-based techniques is examined in more detail in Chapters 5, 9, 10 and 11. It is sufficient to state here that a risk-based method involves the following steps when an activity, task or project is being considered from the risk point of view:

Step 1: Identify hazards associated with the activity.

Step 2: Assess the risk level of the hazards or their significance.

Step 3: Make decisions based on the results obtained.

In many instances, when new regulations are being formulated, some form of the risk-based approach is also used.

(c)   The approach of navies to safety

In the past, the navies of the world tended to develop their own regulations, essentially prescriptive. This applies in particular to safety. As technologies advance, the military is facing new challenges in keeping up to date, often with reduced resources. To overcome this problem, navies have increased cooperation between each other, sharing information and adopting techniques used in the commercial industries such as marine and offshore. For example, in the safety context, the UK's Royal Navy's approach for assessing the safety of warships and their equipment in non-combat activities is to specify their own safety standards. Evidence is gathered for preparing a "Safety Case" and safety case reports are produced to specify the safety standards at any given point in time in the life-cycle of the ship or equipment. As can be seen, this is very similar to what is required in the UK offshore industry. In addition, many navies have fully embraced the safety management approach which is the main topic of this book.

(d)   *Goal based standard (GBS)*

In recent years, IMO has been actively debating an approach which is known as goal based standard (GBS). Reports published to explain what GBS is, tend to be dominated by how the organisations believe GBS could be used in their sphere of activity, before giving the main components of GBS. It is helpful, therefore, to outline a possible explanation of what IMO members had in mind from a historical perspective.

In the early days, ships were built as prototypes and put to sea in accordance with specified performance criteria, e.g maximum speed, fuel consumption, etc. The oceans were effectively used as a laboratory, the results obtained and lessons learnt being gathered for refining future designs. This evolutionary approach worked when changes were small and technological advancements were slow. The situation altered radically as demand for larger tankers and advances in computer technology made the evolutionary approach unsuitable. The move was made to design ships from first principles, i.e. to estimate the loads expected and calculate the structural response. To avoid undetected mistakes creeping into the process, some extra margins were added to improve safety, e.g. plating thicknesses were increased. The standards for shipbuilding were (and continue to be) led by the classification societies. However, classification societies are commercial organisations, competing for business in the maritime market, and standards of ships are not uniform across all the classification societies. This in turn resulted in IMO stating four basic principles of GBS as follows:

- Broad, over-arching safety, environmental and/or security standards that ships are required to meet during their life-cycle.

- The standard to be achieved by the requirements applied by class societies and other recognised organisations, administrations and IMO.

- Clear, demonstrable, verifiable, long standing, implementable and achievable, irrespective of ship design and technology.

- Specific enough in order not to be open to differing interpretations.

As can be seen, this is a very demanding requirement and IMO then suggested a five-tier framework for GBS new ship construction standards to which the first three are IMO specifications, i.e.

Tier 1:   Goals (to be achieved).

Tier 2:   Functional requirements (e.g. structural strength).

Tier 3:   Verification process (e.g. prescriptive rules of classification societies are in accordance with GBS).

The other two tiers cover:

Tier 4:   Prescriptive regulations and class rules.

Tier 5:   Industry standards and code of practice to be used as appropriate.

The application of the framework will then result in individual ships being constructed while meeting the goal based standard.

It is difficult to provide comments on GBS until there is a worked example. The process requires a management system to guide and drive it and such a management system, e.g. called a GBS Management System, would be similar to the methodology given in this book.

4.10 Conclusions

Based on the issues discussed in this chapter, the following conclusions are drawn:

(a)   There are many safety regulations of varying degrees of significance and a useful way of acquiring an appreciation of their roles and applications is to consider them under the groupings of international, regional, flag and port State regulations.

(b)   The major international regulations stem from the International Maritime Organization (IMO) with the safety of life at sea (SOLAS) convention having a major influence. However, unilateral regulations can also have global impact, such as the Oil Pollution Act of 1990 (OPA90) from the United States.

(c)   Enforcement of safety standards is done by port State control whereby coastal states inspect foreign ships visiting their ports to ensure that the regulations of the international conventions are properly complied with.

(d)   In the past, maritime safety has been treated entirely through the prescriptive regulatory approach for all activities, but today, due to the changing nature of maritime activities, to enable ships and their equipment to meet standards equivalent to the prescriptive regulatory requirements, new methods have been developed which are based on sound fundamental, scientific and technological considerations.

Chapter 5

UNDERSTANDING KEY SAFETY TERMS

5.1 Introduction

Safety is a subject in which the terminology has not yet been "standardised", so that the same words may not have the same meaning to the majority of people working on the subject. Indeed, it is only recently that professionals have begun to differentiate between the words "hazard" and "risk". The reason is that in everyday language there is a tendency to use "risk" to mean both hazard and risk! This chapter defines the key terms in order to try to achieve consistency.

The main aims of this chapter are as follows:

(a)   To outline the key terms used in safety management.

(b)   To provide definitions of the terms hazard, risk, risk assessment and risk levels.

(c)   To explain the differences between tolerability and acceptability.

5.2 Why understand safety terms?

It may seem obvious that there should be a need to understand safety terms, but in many subjects practical application may not require an in-depth understanding of the terms so long as proper usage is achieved. However, in the case of safety there are some good reasons for having an understanding or a good appreciation of the meanings of the key terms. The reasons are summarised as follows:

•   The terms are often used in a confused way and can be inconsistent. Correct understanding is essential for effective safety management.

•   It helps communication on safety matters.

•   It is of long term benefit to the safety profession if there is consistency in the use of the terms as this will help win the support of those not so closely involved.

5.3 The term "hazard"

The term "hazard" is usually associated with danger to personal wellbeing, damage to property such as the ship, its cargo and its equipment, or harm to the environment. This has led to a popular definition:

The potential to do harm.

Sometimes this is worded as a cause with potential to do harm. While this definition reflects the above situation it is less applicable in more general situations. Other suggestions include consequences of harm. It should be borne in mind that a hazard is associated with something going "wrong" when doing a task, or meeting an objective. For this reason a generalised definition is given here:

> *A hazard is something that can lead to an undesirable outcome in the process of meeting an objective.*

In the safety context, something which brings about an undesired outcome would involve:

- Injury to personnel.

- Damage to property.

- Harm to the environment.

- A combination of any of these three.

In the generic sense, "something" can be physical, mental or any other form. It is therefore helpful to use examples to illustrate the use of this definition.

It may be helpful to think of hazards as barriers or obstacles that prevent the objective being met fully or even partially.

Example 5.1: The objective is to get to a meeting at 14.00 by car. Something or a hazard can be:

(a) Heavy traffic at a road junction.

(b) Car breakdown on the way.

(c) Running out of petrol on the journey.

(c) Searching for a key document before the scheduled starting time.

(d) Getting lost en route, taking a wrong turning.

It will be noted that none of these are safety related but they can cause delay in reaching the destination and are hence an undesired outcome.

However, it is not difficult to find some safety hazards as well:

(e) Collision with another car.

(f) Tyre blow-out at high speed.

(g) Skidding on a wet surface.

Example 5.2: The objective is the efficient and safe operation of a Ro-Ro passenger ferry between two ports. Something or a hazard which could prevent the objective being met include:

(a) Engine failure.

(b) Collision with another ship.

(c) Being hit by a large wave.

(d)   Dense fog en route.

(e)   A lorry falling over on deck.

(f)   An outbreak of fire in the lounge.

All the above have safety implications for an undesired outcome.

5.4   Risk and its interpretations

The term "risk" has been given many interpretations and some typical examples are given here:

•   Chances of encountering harm.

•   The same meaning as hazard, i.e. two different words with the same meaning.

•   Danger.

•   Seriousness of a failure.

None of these are correct and it is useful to start from basics by considering an example.

Example 5.3:   In this example, attention is given to a pedestrian wishing to cross a road. The objective is to cross the road without being injured by a car. Three types of road are under examination:

(1)   A city centre high street, where the traffic can be heavy but the speeds of cars and buses is relatively slow.

(2)   An urban clearway with a dual carriageway and where there is less traffic, but with cars and buses travelling at higher speeds.

(3)   A highway which allows cars to travel at the national speed limit, e.g. 70 mph in the UK.

Bearing in mind that being hit by a vehicle while crossing a road is a hazard, it is an undesired outcome when trying to achieve the objective of crossing the road. It is useful to consider both the chance of a pedestrian crossing the road and the seriousness of injury if hit by a car.

One good way of doing this is to plot each scenario on the graph of seriousness of injury (C = consequence of being hit) and the chance of someone crossing the road and being hit (P = probability of occurrence). The results are illustrated in figures 6.1a to 6.1d, where C is along the vertical axis and P is along the horizontal axis.

For the city centre high street, scenario 1 in figure 5.1a (overleaf) indicates that more people will cross this street and the consequence of any accident would be low.

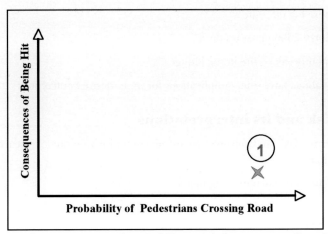

Figure 5.1a Consequences and probability graph for one type of road crossing

For the urban clearway, where traffic speeds are higher, fewer people would cross the road and any injury would have more serious consequences. Scenario 2 would be on the left of scenario 1 and at a location that is higher, see figure 5.1b.

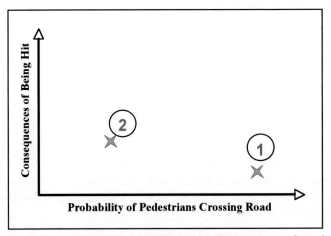

Figure 5.1b Consequence and probability graph for two types of road crossing

In scenario 3, very few people will attempt to cross the highway. However, if the person crossing the road is hit by a vehicle travelling at speed, the injury would be very serious and could lead to death. The location of the scenario would be towards the left hand side and at a higher point along the seriousness axis, see figure 5.1c.

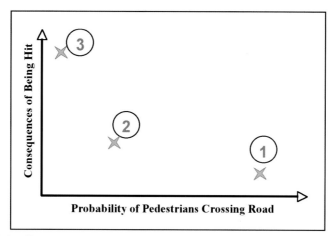

Figure 5.1c Consequence and probability graph for three types of road crossing

By joining the three points together, a curve looking something like the one given in figure 5.1d is shown.

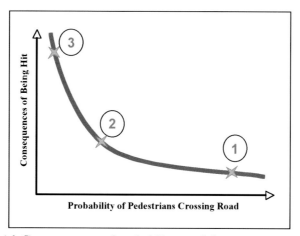

Figure 5.1d Consequence and probability graph in a curve representation

It can be seen that the consequence is inversely proportional to the probability of occurrence, and a popular relationship is

$$C \; \alpha \; \frac{1}{P} \; = \; \frac{\text{Coefficient}}{P}$$

By letting the coefficient be denoted by the letter "R" and by re-arranging, the relationship becomes

$$R = C \times P$$

Where C is the consequence of the hazard and P is the probability that the hazard would occur. What this means is that risk measures the significance of a hazard with the two parameters of C and P. There are two points worth noting:

(a) *Other expressions for the relation*

Other possible relations: In the example, P is inversely proportional to C, but in practice there could be any relationship within the general expression of

$$C \quad 1/P^N$$

and possible indices can be N=2, N=0.8, N = 1.5.

(b) *Role of parameters*

Both C and P are functions of many parameters, e.g. human factors, engineering, management, operation and time. Taking the probability of occurrence,

$$P = f_p (H, E, M, O, T)$$

Where f_p is a probability function, the probability will vary and hence the risk value, depending on these parameters.

In the selected example, the following variations are possible:

- H (Human Factors):   How alert one is at the time, mood, etc.

- E (Engineering):   Fitness, footwear for coping with road conditions, etc.

- M (Management):   Judgement on the relative speed of cars, distance to be crossed, etc.

- O (Operation):   Traffic density, environmental conditions prevailing, visibility, etc.

- T (Time):   Midday, rush hour, midnight, etc.

Thus it is useful to give a formal definition of the term risk:

> *Risk is a measure of the significance of a hazard involving simultaneous examination of its consequences and probability of occurrence.*

It is useful to note that since the risk of a hazard is dependent on two parameters it would be incorrect to draw a conclusion on only one of the parameters. For example, the consequence of an accident may be extremely serious but if its likelihood of occurrence is extremely small, the risk would be different to that in which the accidents are both very serious and likely to occur.

5.5   Risk assessment

To determine the value of risk it is essential to analyse the situation, estimate the magnitude and draw a general conclusion. This process comes under the name of "risk assessment". The definition given to risk assessment may be as follows:

> *Risk assessment is the process that determines where a hazard will be located on a risk scale which normally comprises of intolerable, tolerable and negligible regions.*

The approaches used to estimate risks come under the following names:

*   Qualitative approach: In this approach, use is made of the past experience of the team doing the work and the levels are represented by a small number of discrete values. The information is expressed in the form of a matrix, commonly known as a risk matrix, in which consequence is along the columns and probability of occurrence is listed in rows. This approach is examined in Chapter 9.

*   Quantitative approach: In this approach, simulation methods are used to model consequences and fault tree or event techniques are used to estimate the probability of occurrence. It also makes use of statistical information relating to frequency of accidents, etc. The approach is examined in Chapter 10.

*   Combined approach: In this approach, both of the two previous methods are used, with the former giving a rough guide, while the latter is used for specific hazards needing further investigation.

Here is a brief examination of the three risk regions:

(a)   *Intolerable risk region*

Hazards with an intolerable risk level should be reduced by appropriate means, e.g. engineering and management methods. If it is in the design stage, the project may have to be modified or abandoned if the risk cannot be reduced cost-effectively.

(b)   *Tolerable risk region*

Hazards in this region are tolerable and, since the approaches used to estimate the risk do not give precise answers, it is essential to give attention to those in the boundary between the intolerable and tolerable regions. What this means is that consideration should be given to ways of reducing the risk level of hazards in the tolerable region. However, it is necessary to establish whether this reduction can be done cost-effectively and the term As Low As Reasonably Practicable (ALARP) has been adopted to make this assessment.

(c)   *Negligible risk region*

The hazards in this region have a low risk level and generally there is no need to take any action to reduce their level. However, hazards interact with each other and this in turn can lead to a higher risk level. For this reason, re-assessment should be performed periodically.

Example 5.4:   Injury to personnel on board passenger ships may adopt the following classification:

- Intolerable risk region: Death/serious injury of 1 case per 100.

- Tolerable risk region: Death /serious injury of 1 case per 1000.

- Negligible risk region: Death/serious injury of 1 case per 10,000.

The time unit is left open for the user to choose, e.g. 100 passengers, travel-hours or sea days. It should be noted that the boundaries between the regions are defined by society at a given point in time and they may change with time. For example, what was a tolerable risk level 50 years ago on board ships would probably be regarded today as having an intolerable risk level.

5.6   Tolerability and acceptability

So far the term tolerable, or more correctly tolerability, is used to assess the risk level. There is also a decision to be made with respect to whether the risk level is acceptable or not. It is therefore essential to have a good grasp of the meaning of the terms "tolerability" and "acceptability".

It is useful to point out that "tolerability" and "acceptability" are not the same, although they are often used in practice as if they have the same meaning. In the context of the risk level of a hazard, the two terms have the following roles:

- Tolerability involves a classification.

- Acceptability involves a decision.

An example is used here to illustrate the two terms.

Example 5.5:   In this example it is assumed that a young and ambitious professional couple is inviting the boss of one spouse to their flat for a VIP dinner. The wedding gift white tablecloth is being used for the first time and a special meal has been cooked for the occasion. Three types of drinks are being served.

Spillage of drinks on this lovely tablecloth would be a hazard. The risk in this case involves determining the probabilities of spillage and their consequences. For the three glasses, the chances of spilling the drinks are the same and the focus for risk would be on the consequences. The hosts classify the spills with the following tolerability scale:

- Permanent damage, e.g. red wine, as the stains cannot be removed completely. Risk is therefore regarded as intolerable.

- Recoverable damage, e.g. lime juice, as the stains can be removed and the appearance of the tablecloth would be almost the same as new. Risk is therefore regarded as tolerable.

- No damage, e.g. clear water, which will have no effect on the tablecloth once it is dried. Risk is therefore regarded as negligible.

The question of acceptability if the spillage occurred will depend on the perception of the hosts. For the house-proud spouse only clear water is acceptable. The other spouse is easy going and finds all three scenarios acceptable as long as everyone has had an enjoyable evening and a good impression has been made.

As a follow up, the hosts can have a number of options over the differences in implementing acceptability and these are:

- Going to a restaurant – less appealing and more expensive.

- Putting a plastic sheet over the tablecloth – less attractive but can overcome the spillage problem.

- Serving only clear water – this is only a realistic option if the guests do not take alcohol.

In the context of society, organisations and individuals, it is useful to give formalised definitions to these two terms:

Tolerability:

Willingness to consider living with a situation in order to secure certain benefits by devising or using a risk scale.

Acceptability:

Making a conscious decision on a situation based on the available information relating to the perceived risk involved.

Tolerability is a scale which can be devised by one of the following methods:

(a)   Devised by practitioners or their associations:

A group of practitioners can establish a scale which will be interpreted in the same way in practice by everyone in the group. Alternatively, the trade association of the practitioners may provide a recommended guideline based on the collective experience of their members.

(b)   Provided by a government agency:

The tolerability scale may be published by a government agency to which all practitioners must adhere if they are to be allowed to offer their facilities and services to the public.

(c)   Adopted by individuals from personal standpoints:

Individuals can have a tolerability scale to a given activity that is determined personally. For example, an individual keen on rock climbing may well decide on the following:

- Intolerable: Rock climbing without a harness.

- Tolerable :   Rock climbing with a harness.

- Negligible: Watching rock climbing.

Acceptability, on the other hand, is a decision taken with the tolerability scale used as a broad guide. Influential factors on whether something is acceptable or not include:

- Personal attitude.

- Whether real choice is available.

- Trading the risk of doing the activity against the reward to be gained.

6.7   Decisions on acceptance

It is useful to note that there are situations with hazards having intolerable risks which are accepted and situations with hazards having tolerable risk which are not accepted. Typical examples of the former include:

- It is too expensive to change an already built system, even if one of its hazards has an intolerable risk level.

- The job has exposed the individual to extreme pressures that could lead to illness and make the risk intolerable, but there is no immediate practical alternative so the intolerable risk is accepted.

Typical examples of the latter include:

- One has serious doubts about the location of a hazard in the tolerable risk region and based on past personal knowledge and experience it should be in the intolerable risk region and hence the reason for not accepting the decision.

- Due to personal belief and past experience, one would only save money in a building society, because it is the "only acceptable" form of investment and not government bonds, shares or other "safe" investments, even if they have tolerable risks.

6.8   Conclusions

The main conclusions to be drawn are:

(a)   It is helpful to interpret hazard in a broad context as it enables wider application.

(b)   Hazards have various risk levels and each should be assessed by a combination of qualitative and quantitative methods.

(c)   It is useful to understand the meanings of the terms "tolerability" and "acceptability" so that their difference can be appreciated.

Chapter 6

SAFETY CASE APPROACH AND MARITIME INDUSTRY

6.1 Introduction

In Chapter 3 the principles of the prescriptive regulatory approach were outlined and this was followed in Chapter 4 with an examination of the use of the approach in addressing maritime safety. However, it was also noted that the prescriptive regulatory approach is effective for treating the safety of routine and well understood situations but not for new or extensively modified ones. Since the maritime industry is continuously evolving in response to competition in the transport industry there needed to be other approaches and the goal setting approach which involves the preparation of a safety case has been adopted in other industries to replace or supplement the prescriptive regulatory approach. It is often known as the "Safety Case Approach". However, before outlining the latter approach it would be helpful to understand the key safety terms which have been considered in Chapter 5. The purpose of this chapter is to give some background information on the safety regime being operated in the offshore hydrocarbon industry, examine the process of preparing safety cases while explaining why it is relevant to the maritime industry.

The specific aims of this chapter are as follows. :

(a)   To explain the relevance of the safety case approach to maritime activities.

(b)   To consider the relationship between the safety case approach and the prescriptive regulatory approach.

(c)   To examine the basis of the safety case approach and its merits and drawbacks.

(d)   To give some background information on the safety regime and to use the UK safety case regulations for offshore installations to highlight key issues involved

(e)   To consider the preparation of a safety case and the use of a safety template.

6.2 Why consider the safety case approach?

It is useful to begin by asking the question:

What is the relevance of the safety case approach to the maritime industry?

There are three main reasons why the maritime industry and shipping should have some knowledge and acquire expertise in this approach and these will now be given under the following headings:

a) *Essential for technological advancement*

It is often not appreciated by those outside the maritime industry that it had to innovate in order to survive in the intense competition which include operations in an international context and other forms of transport such as aircraft. It is interesting to use some examples to illustrate these innovations. The shipbuilding industry was one of the very first to use computer aided design and production techniques and robot welding. In shipping the introduction of super tankers or Very Large Crude Carriers required a major technological step forward. In more recent years, high speed Ro-Ro ferries with speeds of over 40 knots have become popular for carrying passengers and vehicles. With the increased emphasis on the importance of safety, it would not be possible to use the prescriptive regulatory approach, for the reasons given in Chapter 3, to judge the safety of these innovations. Thus, the safety case approach based on setting the safety standard or goal to be achieved offers the only sound method of judging the safety of these novel vessels and activities.

b) *Ships working on offshore projects*

At present the shipping industry does not demand operators to use the safety case approach but the regulatory bodies would indirectly welcome shipping companies to use such techniques to assess the safety of more novel designs. However, the UK offshore industry concerned with hydrocarbon activities require safety cases to be prepared by the operators of offshore installations and the operators of ships which serve the offshore organisations. This in turn means that if a shipping company wishes to compete for work in the offshore industry it has to be able to prepare safety cases. Since the offshore industry does provide a valuable market, those shipping companies wishing to bid for business will have to acquire the skill and experience in applying the safety case approach.

c) *Acquiring new capabilities*

In order to be able to implement safety management of an installation, a ship or a system it is necessary to apply the safety case approach. This in turn requires those involved to have a good understanding of management and management systems as well as risk based techniques. These are fresh skills for a large number of those working in the maritime industry and the benefits in having these skills and experience would serve maritime personnel well because the same know-how can be applied in many other applications, e.g. addressing quality and reliability issues in an organisation.

d) *Special applications*

In special circumstance, for example, the military world safety is very important and it has to be treated in a manner that is appropriate to its activities. It would not be possible to employ the civilian prescriptive regulations and it would be very costly to devise, maintain and apply it own regulations. In these situations the safety case approach offers a suitable methodology that can also be interfaced with the prescriptive regulatory approach. It will be noted that in UK Ministry of Defence dealing with navy vessels, it is now the normal practice for the project teams to prepare safety cases for the naval vessels and their equipment. When extensive re-fit tasks have been performed on a ship, a fresh safety case has to be prepared.

6.3 The relation with the prescriptive regulatory approach

It is important to distinguish clearly between the two approaches because some people have the impression that the safety case approach is another form of 'prescriptive regulatory approach' that happens to be the "flavour" at the moment. For this reason it would be helpful to highlight the relationship between the two approaches using illustrative examples so that the differences and interfaces can be appreciated. Their definitions and the situations where they are most effective for safety assessment would then be given.

Example 6.1   This example uses the same theme as that given in Example 3.1 but the instruction is expressed in the following two forms, illustrated in figures 6.1 and 6.2 respectively, to show the difference between the prescriptive and safety case approaches:

Form 1: We need a cheesecake for dinner. Buy one from Marks & Spencer

Figure 6.1 Illustration of the prescriptive approach

Form 2: We need a cheesecake for dinner. Buy a tasty and high quality one from any shop.

Figure 6.2 Illustration of the safety case approach

As stated already, Form 1 can be regarded as applying the prescriptive approach because both the need and the solution are prescribed. Form 2 can be regarded as applying the safety case approach because the need is prescribed but the solution is not. This allows flexibility and enables the purchaser to choose any suitable cheesecake which in his or her judgement can satisfy the requirement. However, to support the choice, a justification case would need to be made to demonstrate that the cheesecake brought is tasty, high quality and to the likings of everyone. This in turn requires the purchaser to do some thinking before making the decision.

Example 6.2   This example is used to illustrate the interface between the safety case approach and the prescriptive approach. The theme is the same as that given in Example 6.1 and the form of the instruction is illustrated in Figure (6.3) and is now expressed as follows:

Form 3: We need a cheesecake for dinner. Buy a tasty and high quality one from any shop. Remember it should NOT contain any nuts.

Figure 6.3 Illustration of the safety case approach with a prescriptive element

This form of instruction can also be considered to be applying the safety case approach in the same way as Form 2 of Example 6.1 but there is a prescriptive element in the solution, i.e. the purchased cheesecake should be nut free. What this means is that it is possible to interface prescriptive features within the safety case approach. This interface overcomes the incorrect belief that in applying the safety case approach there cannot be any prescriptive element present.

6.4 The safety case approach and its key features

One possible definition of the term is expressed as follows:

> One party prescribes the safety requirement, goal or standard while allowing any appropriate method to be used by the provider of products and services to obtain the solution. The adopted method, however, has to be justified scientifically for meeting the goal.

It will be noted that in this approach the method of solution is not prescribed and the provider can select any appropriate method to obtain the solution provided it can justify that the safety requirement has been met. The approach is most suitable for new or extensively modified ships, situations or systems.

To discover the key merits of the safety case approach, and in a similar exercise to that described in Chapter 3, the participants, grouped in pairs, are asked to write down one merit and one drawback on a transparency before passing onto the next group to give fresh choices. Typical suggestions are given in Figure (6.4). It will be noted that the weightings given to the merits or drawbacks are not the same.

No	Merit	Drawback
1	A pro-active approach	More efforts are needed
2	Essential for innovation	Need knowledge and skill
3	Involve stakeholders	End point is not obvious
4	Flexible in addressing safety	Must have support information
5	Focus on specific situations	May not be universally recognised
6	Examines all "angles"	Hard to show the goal is achieved
7	Encourage thinking about safety	Each case is unique
8	Technique has wider applications	Can be very time consuming

Figure 6.4 Some suggested merits and drawbacks for the safety case approach

It is now useful to give a list of key merits and drawbacks together with brief explanations of the safety case approach for treating safety.

Merits

(a)   A proactive approach: It can be stated that the approach is a proactive one, i.e. it is not devised based on response to an accident, but instead it is sets out to meet a goal by whatever the method that would be most suitable for the system or situation under consideration. This is a positive way of addressing safety.

(b)   User ownership for safety: In applying the safety case approach the provider or user is more actively involved and would have taken on the main safety responsibility for the products and services. The prescribers continue to have a role but it is less than that in the prescriptive regulatory approach.

(c)   Widening the horizon: By seeking alternative methods of addressing safety, new ideas have to be generated which ensures the thinking process is activated. This in turn would encourage giving consideration to many possibilities and leading to solutions which may not necessarily be better but would offer wider choices and stimulate fresh safer ideas.

(d)   Ideal for new systems and activities: The safety case approach is based on systems engineering which involves seeking answers to relevant questions, reasoning, assessing the derived solutions and making decisions. It is most suitable for assessing the safety of new systems or new activities where there is little past operational experience. This is essential for ensuring technological innovations can be made.

(e) Enhanced safety understanding: Having to think more about the safety of the ship and their equipment would help those involved to acquire a better understanding of the issues concerning not only safety but other aspects of these facilities. This can assist in examining safety with a fresh prospective and in turn help to improve overall safety of items under consideration.

Drawbacks

(a)   Additional efforts are needed: Since the user or provider has the flexibility in choosing the method of solution instead of following a prescribed route, there will be extra work for both the users and the prescribers to be done. For example, the justification for selecting a specific approach and the solutions obtained prepared by the former have to be examined on an individual basis by the prescribers.

(b)   Demonstrating the meeting of the requirement: Since the providers have been given the flexibility to use any method to meet the requirement or standard, it is necessary to demonstrate that the derived solution does satisfy the goal. This can be hard as the end point may not be obvious and how well a case is made can be subjective.

(c)   Comparison challenge: Since the derived solutions may vary widely it can be difficult to compare the effectiveness of the solutions directly using standard method. Instead, judgement has to be made on an equivalent basis and this can lead to disagreements. At international level it is expected that different countries will satisfy the goal by different methods and the comparison can be very hard to make.

(d)   Increased educational and training efforts: The safety case approach requires increased knowledge in addition to what is given in the present education and training programmes, i.e. those involved have to have a better understanding of management system and risk based techniques. Additional time and resources are needed to ensure the understanding and skills are acquired.

6.5 The safety regime

In the earlier days of offshore hydrocarbon development, safety was treated by the prescriptive regulatory approach which has been examined in Chapter 3. The limitation of this approach stemmed basically from the fact that safety is not something absolute and is dominated by human factors. After the disaster of *Piper Alpha* in the North Sea in 1988, the UK safety regime changed to that based on goal setting principles following the publication of the Cullen report, see [Cullen 1990].

The goal setting approach which is developed from systems engineering, was first used to deal with the safety of nuclear power generation installations. This was a logical way forward because little operational experience was available on these installations and the only suitable method available was to examine safety from fundamental considerations. Later the same approach was adopted also in treating the safety of chemical installations. As far as it is known, it was the UK Health and Safety Executive which first implemented the safety case concept formally to offshore hydrocarbon exploration and production activities although similar methods have been used in countries such as Norway.

As explained earlier, in this safety regime, the safety standard sought is prescriptively defined but the operators can use their own preferred methods for demonstrating that the safety standard has been met in the safety case prepared. It is therefore not surprising the forms of the safety cases can very considerably depending on what safety standards are specified and what methods are used by the operators. For example, the required standard in one activity may be confined to safety issues only, while in another activity the standard could include environmental impact, hence one can expect different safety cases being produced.

The output from the application of the safety case concept is a document, sometimes called the safety case report, which provides information relating to the safety of an activity such as the operation of an offshore installation. The contents of the information should be such that it gives confidence to both the duty holder (the person responsible for the operation of an offshore installation in the organisation) and the prescribing body (in the UK it is the Health and Safety Executive — HSE) that the duty holder has demonstrated the ability and means to control the risks of major hazards effectively.

The safety case is regarded as a "live" document in that it is time sensitive with respect to the life-cycle of the installation. For example, in the design phase the safety case report will address the safety issues of the design and in the operational phase the safety case report will address the safety of the installation's operations. In order to provide an understanding of the basic issues concerning a safety case the next section will consider the key features of UK Offshore installation (safety case) regulation 2005, see [OSCR 2005].

6.6 UK approach to safety in the offshore industry

Following the public inquiry into the *Piper Alpha* disaster in the North Sea, the Cullen report made a long list of recommendations. The central theme was that the operator or owner of every offshore installation associated with hydrocarbon activities in UK Continental Shelf will be required to prepare a safety case and submit it to UK HSE for acceptance.

This requirement is applicable to all installations involving both fixed platforms and mobile vessels. The requirement was first published in the form of safety case regulations in 1992 and revised over the years with the latest regulations presented in the report called "The Offshore Installation (safety case) Regulations 2005" and it came into force on 6 April 2006. The key features of the Regulations will now be considered under the following headings.

(a)   The prime aim of the regulations

The prime aim of the Regulations can be stated as follows:

> *To ensure that the risk of major hazards are reduced to a tolerable level in order to safeguard the health and wellbeing of the work force employed on the offshore installations or in related activities.*

(b)   Setting of safety standards

The Safety Case Regulations 2005 does not set standards for controlling the risk level of major hazards or accidents and these are set by another set of prescriptive regulations:

- Offshore installations (Prevention of Fire and Explosion, Emergency Response) Regulations 1995, see [PFEER 1995].

- Offshore Installations and Wells (Design and construction, etc) Regulations 1996, see [DCR 1996].

- Health and Safety at Work etc Act 1974, see[HSW Act 1974].

The operators have to meet the requirements of these regulations and a safety case therefore must demonstrate that the duty holder has put in place arrangements which, if implemented, are capable of achieving compliance with the legal objectives.

These arrangements include ensuring that management systems for addressing health and safety are in place and operate as they should, having available proven methods for reducing risk levels of the major hazards and controlling them effectively.

(c)   Acceptance of safety cases

The safety case regulations demand that the safety case is submitted to HSE for acceptance and it is therefore useful to understand what is meant by the word 'acceptance'. In the present context, acceptance means that the HSE is satisfied with the duty holder's approach to meeting safety needs. In practice, this means that HSE 'accepts' the validity of the described approach as being capable, if implemented as described, of achieving the necessary degree of risk control. It should be noted that HSE does NOT confirm the outcome of that approach.

It will be noted that when HSE is making an acceptance decision the key criterion is concerned with whether a safety case contains sufficient information for appropriate safety decisions to be made. This in turn will lead HSE to choose whether to examine certain elements of a specific safety case in greater depth. A degree of flexibility in the assessment process is therefore introduced. Further information on the list of principles needing to be addressed to ensure the safety case includes sufficient relevant information and the thinking behind the HSE's approach to assessing safety cases, can be found in [APOSC 1995].

It can be seen that the process of achieving acceptance initially can be quite difficult and to overcome the difficulties it is the usual practice for duty holders and HSE assessors to work together to enable the safety case submissions to become acceptable. Once the safety case receives acceptance the duty holder has the responsibility to ensure that the installation is operated in the way as described in the documents.

(d)   *Important changes in regulatory requirements*

There have been several changes made between the Regulations of 1992 and the Regulations of 2005, and key ones include the following:

- Resubmission of safety case: A safety case, once it has received acceptance, will last a life time and this replaces the 3 year up date requirement. However, the duty holder has to perform a ' thorough review' at five yearly intervals or as directed by HSE.

- Design phase: The design safety case has been replaced by a simpler design notification which does not need the acceptance of HSE.

- Abandonment phase: In the Regulations 1992, an abandonment safety case is needed before starting to decommission a fixed installation. The Regulations 2005 asks the duty holder to revise the safety case, giving details of each phase of the decommissioning process and submit it to HSE for acceptance.

- Risk reduction: The earlier safety cases have been asked to include a demonstration that the risk levels of major hazards are ALARP (As Low As Reasonably Practicable). Instead the Regulations, 2005 require the safety cases to demonstrate that the risk level of major hazards have been assessed and evaluated and the 'relevant statutory provisions' will be compiled with. This means that the reduced risk level may not necessarily be ALARP.

6.7 Preparing a safety case

When a safety case is being prepared, it is useful to ask how one should go about doing the task. One must first of all bear in mind the background to the regulatory requirements and the fact that the duty holder has been given the freedom to adopt any appropriate methodology to establish that the identified major hazards with intolerable risk associated with the operation of the offshore installation can be reduced to a tolerable level and can also be controlled effectively. The flexibility given by setting a goal instead of prescribing a solution can make life more demanding in that there is no fixed or unique method of preparing the safety case. To a large extent the choice is decided by the emphasis and experience of the team preparing the safety case. This situation in turn has led to several usable methods and two of them will be highlighted and examined in Chapter 9. It is useful to remember that the team in question has to select which method it would like to adopt as the basic idea of the goal setting approach encourages people to think about safety and use their own preferred solutions to derive and meet the required safety standard and requirements.

There is no formal specification on the format of the safety cases and the duty holders can adopt whatever format they wish to use. Earlier safety cases were fairly unstructured and very hard to follow and they also varied greatly in length and size. As experience has been gained over the years, users of the safety cases, e.g. HSE assessors and team members of duty holders, have found it helpful when the documentation for the safety case showed clearly the presence of the following main features:

- An executive summary giving the main contents of the safety case.

- Factual information about the installation, e.g. principal dimensions, structural arrangement and size.

- Environmental conditions in which it is operating.

- The management system used to co-ordinate activities and resources to meet the safety standard.

- Technical demonstration that the safety requirements have been met or provided for and details on how hazards are identified, their risks assessed and selected risks reduced as appropriate and how to deal with the emergencies.

Of course, in addition to these features the arguments presented and support information should be written clearly and succinctly with emphasis on reader friendliness. There should be sufficient relevant details for convincing the users of the safety cases.

6.8 The use of a safety case template

The process in preparing a safety case can be complicated and extensive efforts are needed. In most offshore companies there are a limited number of people with the necessary knowledge and experience to prepare the safety cases and as the goal setting approach offers flexibility and options it can make the preparation more demanding. Thus the concept of developing a safety case template is very appealing. Indeed, the International Association of Diving Contractors (IADC) has been promoting the use of a safety case template for a number of years. It has been designed to assist the operators of the mobile offshore vessels, see IADC [2006]. So far the idea has the support of contractors working in West European waters and IADC is hoping to offer the template to the international offshore community.

There are several merits in this approach and the key ones include:

- More effective use of resources: Fewer staff or people need to be trained to reach a competence level so that they can prepare safety cases effectively.

- Increased efficiency: With a template fewer mistakes are likely to be made and the task would be completed in shorter time.

- Assist in developing staff: Using a template gives confidence to those with little previous knowledge of the subject and limited experience.

- Provide basis for comparison: It would be easy to compare the safety cases obtained for similar mobile offshore vessels doing closely related jobs.

There are also drawbacks and the most important ones include:

- Opt out thinking about safety: Once a template is available for 'copying' there is a tendency to stop individuals from thinking about safety. Experience has shown that when students are provided with solutions to problems via worked examples, some are good at applying the knowledge with fresh data in examinations but they may have little real understanding of the basic methodology and its usefulness for solving other problems. Similar outcomes can also occur from using templates.

- Accepting template unquestioningly: Once a template is established the users tend to believe it must be correct and would use it even when some aspects are not applicable to the situation in question.

In spite of these drawbacks it is worthwhile remembering the usefulness of the safety case template.

6.9 Conclusions

Based on the points considered in this chapter, the following conclusions are drawn.

a) The safety case approach is based on the concept that the safety requirement or standard is prescribed by an organisation with statutory authority but the method of meeting the requirement can be selected by the provider who must show that the solution obtained can satisfy the goal.

b) The safety case approach has several merits and the most important ones relate to the provider or user having ownership of the safety. It is also a proactive approach which can ensure that technological innovations can be realised.

c) The safety case approach, which requires operators to prepare safety cases to demonstrate that the risks of the major hazards have been reduced to tolerable risk levels and can be controlled as proposed, provides a flexible method of addressing the safety requirements. The method is most suitable for assessing the safety of new and extensively modified ships, situations or systems.

d) The work associated with the preparation of a safety case can be demanding and in order to improve efficiency the idea of using a safety case template can be helpful provided that team members involved have gained a good understanding of safety fundamentals.

Chapter 7

MANAGEMENT SYSTEMS AND SAFETY

7.1 Introduction

A management system is the essential requirement for treating safety which is not absolute. The concept of having a management system may puzzle those who are technologically educated but they actually apply an informal management system in their everyday activities. Since a management system has a critical role in safety management, as well as in many other activities, situations and systems, it will be examined next.

The main aims of this chapter are as follows:

a)   To describe the basis of a management system (MS).

b)   To outline the key components involved.

c)   To use an illustrative example to show its usage.

d)   To discuss the role of the management system and safety.

7.2 Management and management systems

The goal of management can be stated as follows:

To coordinate activities and resources to meet an objective.

Activities can range from planning and scheduling through searching and hiring of experts to how the team members will work together. Resources include human skills and experience, facilities, equipment, and funds. Typical examples of objectives in a general context can be as follows:

•   To increase output by 10% over the next twelve months.

•   To achieve a 15% reduction in cost over the next three months.

It is useful to explain the relationship between "management" and "management system". The goal of management is given above and to perform the tasks effectively a logical and systematic approach is needed. A management system can assist in the coordination when a non-absolute item is involved. Thus it is appropriate to define a management system as follows:

A structured arrangement which is needed to ensure effective co-ordination of resources and activities to meet the objective.

In a safety context the objectives may be as follows:

•   To meet the safety target with 10% less "lost time" injuries.

•   To maintain the safety standard with 5% less funds.

7.3   Basis of a management system

It is useful to begin with an example. In this case a young man, called Sandy, has to buy a birthday gift for his wife. The principal steps can typically be the following:

- Decide on what would be the most appropriate gift, taking into account what has been given before and what is sought.

- Organise the purchase by giving attention to where the gift can be purchased, the price, availability of the product and the related issues.

- Make the purchase at the preferred shop.

Figure 7.1 (a)

A gift for the wife

Figure 7.1 (b)

Choosing a gift

Figure 7.1 (c)

Do shopping

Figure 7.1 (d)

Assess reception

Figure 7.1

Pictorial representation of an informal management system

Figure 7.1 (e)

Review lessons learnt

- Measure how the gift is received by the recipient, the quality of the gift and the service provided by the staff of the shop.

- Review the lessons gained, the appropriateness of the gift, its reception, value for money and the choice of shops for future reference.

It will be noted that this is an informal management system and it is possible to rewrite the steps in the following form:

S1: *DEFINE*:   the goal and criteria for success.

S2: *ORGANISE*:   the task, via careful preparation.

S3: *IMPLEMENT*:   the decision in practice.

S4: *MEASURE*:   the performance and procedures.

S5: *REVIEW*:   the results obtained and compare with benchmark.

The previous steps are illustrated in figure 7.1, which shows Sandy realising that it is his wife's birthday (figure 7.1a). He then considers a number of choices (figure 7.1b), before getting money and going to the shop to make the purchase of a gift (figure 7.1c). Sandy can imagine three possible receptions to his gift – unhappiness with his choice, a neutral reaction, or absolute joy with the gift (figure 7.1d). Once he has given the gift, regardless of the actual reception, he is thinking about next year (figure 7.1e). His choice is to overcome a poor reception or to do even better.

The traditional method of illustrating these steps is given in figure 7.2.

It will be noted that while the arrangement will ensure the goal is fulfilled, there is no scope for refinement or adjustment.

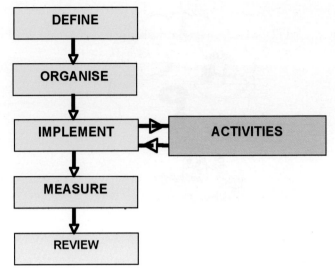

Figure 7.2 Conventional representation of a management system

A better representation is to place the five elements of the Management System on a revolving circuit so that feedback can be introduced, see figure 7.3.

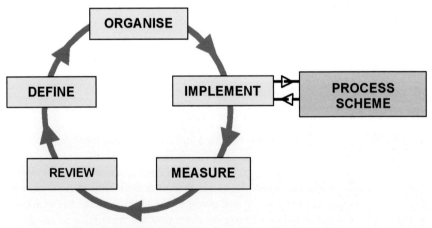

Figure 7.3 Ideal representation of a management system

In this way it will ensure that improvement is continuous and iteration can be introduced to adjust the goal, e.g. since safety is not absolute the correct safety level for a system at a given time can only be derived via some iteration. It will be noted that the term process scheme is used to replace activities in the latter figure (7.3) to indicate that one can implement any set of activities or a combination of activities, methods and decisions.

There are several reasons for having an MS and the key ones are:

a)   Safety is NOT absolute, in the same way that a business activity is not absolute. There is no right or wrong, except by determining how closely the goal has been satisfied. A management system is needed to assist in reaching the correct balance, i.e. checking whether the goal is too demanding or too lenient.

b)   Some form of iteration is needed in order to achieve the balance and an MS allows this to be done effectively.

c)   In a management system, the components lie on a circuit and enable improvements to be achieved continuously. Improvement does not, however, mean making increasingly more demanding requirements but a more cost-effective achievement of the goal.

7.4   Key components of an MS

The five basic elements are now considered, under the following main headings.

Element 1:   DEFINE

The role of this component is to define the safety objectives, such as to minimise human error in ship operations and to establish performance criteria, such as a 10% reduction in lost time injuries should be achieved.

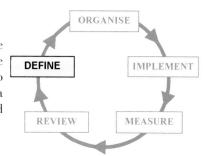

Element 2:   ORGANISE

This component represents the preparation to be done to ensure the goal can be achieved and involves such tasks as: a) Acquiring the necessary resources for the work, e.g. availability of experts and experienced personnel. b) Examining the activities, e.g. working methods, time scale. c) Assigning safety responsibility to people, e.g. team leader, duty holder.

Element 3:   IMPLEMENT

This component would implement in practice a process scheme (PS). i.e. a series of functions arranged in a logical sequence, and in the case of safety the scheme would be the "Safety Scheme". Typical contents of a safety scheme would consist of the following:

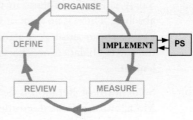

- Identify hazards relating to the activity or system under consideration.

- Assess the risk levels of the hazards by various methods.

- Reduce the risk levels of selected hazards with high risk levels.

- Prepare for emergency situations.

- Provide deliverables and outputs.

Element 4:   MEASURE

This component has the task of measuring how well the criteria, defined earlier, have been met and whether the cost involved is acceptable. Examples of the former include checking whether risks are within the specified level and examples of the latter would be whether the risk reductions were value for money.

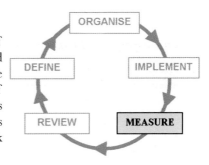

Element 5:   REVIEW

This last component would review a range of issues such as:

- The lessons learnt, e.g. whether major hazards have been identified and their risk levels have been reduced cost-effectively.

- Comparison with benchmark, e.g. does the safety level compare well with industrial standards.

- Effectiveness of the process itself, e.g. is the scheme logical and has it incorporated all the key items.

Once these issues are addressed, the next step is to feedback to the DEFINE component. In this way improvement would be continuous as the cycle is repeated (see figure 7.4).

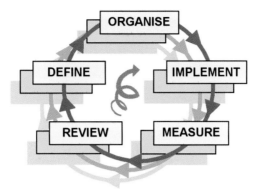

Figure 7.4 The MS sketch shows continuous iteration and improvement

7.5 The role of a management system in safety

The role of a management system (MS) is to implement a scheme and in the case of safety, it is the safety scheme. A typical safety scheme would contain the following main components:

- Hazard identification.

- Risk assessment.

- Risk reduction.

- Emergency preparedness.

The management system is retained in the same form but will define the safety standard or goal and performance criteria used to organise the resources and work to ensure the safety goal can be met. It is after this step that the Safety Scheme is implemented. The results should be measured against performance criteria and reviewed to ensure that the lessons learned can be fed back into the system.

7.6 An illustrative example

To demonstrate the application of the management system, an example of an everyday situation will be used to illustrate the steps involved.

The background to the situation is summarised under the following headings:

- A flat or apartment in the city centre is located on the second floor. It is rented by a postgraduate student while doing research at university.

- There are two large public rooms and four bedrooms, plus a kitchen.

- The condition of the flat is such that it could do with some repairs and a fresh coat of paint.

- Heating and cooking are by gas.

- The property is sublet to three other young persons, who have little previous experience in living away from home and in a rented place.

- The owner is conscious of safety and has asked his tenants to give attention to the safety of the flat. After discussion, they decided to devise a safety management system.

The summarised version of the MS for safety, produced by these young people, is given here:

Element 1: **Define**

Typical goal and criteria can be as follows, e.g.

- *Goal*: Relaxed and safe living.

- *Criteria*: There should be no injury to people living in the flat or to their visitors. Care should be taken to minimise damage to the property and a no smoking policy is also agreed.

Element 2: **Organise**

The activities involved in organisation include, e.g.

- An inspection was performed to ensure the smoke and fire detectors were in working order and an alarm system has been installed.

- Each tenant was given the responsibility to check their own rooms and the public living area on a regular basis.

- There would be monthly meetings that would include an item on safety related matters.

Element 3 :**Implement**

The safety scheme by carrying out the following:

Step 1 *Hazard identification*: Typical examples include:

Ref No.	Hazard
H1	Faulty wiring
H2	Gas leak
H3	Burst pipe
H4	Slip in the bath
H5	Break drinking cups

Step 2 *Risk assessment*: The agreed risk for each hazard is given here:

Ref No.	Hazard	Risk
H1	Faulty wiring	Tolerable
H2	Gas leak	Intolerable
H3	Burst pipe	Intolerable
H4	Slip in the bath	Negligible
H5	Break drinking cups	Tolerable

Step 3 *Risk reduction*: e.g. for Hazard H3, the methods of reducing the risk level would involve lagging the pipes, ensuring the flat temperature was maintained at a comfortable level at all times and regular checks being made in cold periods of the year.

Step 4 *Emergency preparedness*: For the case of burst pipes, there should be training given to everyone on how to deal with such an occurrence. The contact telephone numbers of plumbers should be readily available, as well as other useful information.

Element 4: **Measure**

There are a number of ways to measure performance, e.g.

• Number of instances which required attention over periods of three months.

• Number of situations where decisions were ignored, forgotten or not followed.

• The frequency of maintenance on specific equipment such as the cooker.

• Questionnaire for everyone to fill in.

Element 5: **Review**

Review can be performed in the following manner, e.g.

• The experience gained in sharing the flat.

• Explore scope for improvement.

• Compare safety standards with similar flats owned by friends in the city.

7.7 Conclusions

The main conclusions to be drawn are:

(a) Everyone uses some form of an informal management system in their daily activities but the steps must be formalised for recognition and effective application.

(b) In linking a management system with a process scheme, a flexible and versatile method is available to address any feature that is not absolute.

(c) By arranging the elements of a management system in a circular form, iteration can be initiated and improvement would be continuous.

Chapter 8

GENERIC MANAGEMENT SYSTEM (GMS) FOR SAFETY

8.1 Introduction

Safety has been treated by what is known as the prescriptive regulatory approach, which was considered in Chapter 3. Since the approach relies extensively on past experience, it would not be suitable for new and more radically modified ships, offshore installations or systems.

There is, therefore, a need to adopt an alternative approach and the safety case approach or concept was selected because it has been used for assessing the safety of nuclear installations, chemical plants and offshore installations for hydrocarbon production. The main features of the safety case approach can be found in Chapter 6. However, for reasons to be examined later in greater detail, a generalised approach is more appropriate and this, in turn, led to the Generic Management System (GMS) approach which starts from fundamental considerations.

The aims of this chapter are:

(a)   To explain how safety can be examined from basic considerations.

(b)   To outline the basis of the GMS approach.

(c)   To examine some key features of GMS for safety and its link with the safety case approach.

8.2 The need for a fresh methodology

In Chapter 2, when the approaches to be used in dealing with safety were examined, it was noted that the traditional method was to adopt the prescriptive regulatory approach in which the regulations are prescribed by the authority. Further considerations to this latter approach were given in Chapter 3. This method makes extensive use of past experience, gained from accidents, in the formulation of the regulations. While there are a number of merits in this approach, one of the drawbacks relates to its inappropriateness for dealing with the safety of new situations, activities, installations, ships or systems. This was highlighted when ship regulations were used for dealing with the safety of offshore installations built for oil and gas production in the early 1970s. It was soon recognised that the existing regulations were not applicable to new situations. Likewise, the introduction of high speed craft in the early 1980s also pushed the International Maritime Organization (IMO) into devising new safety regulations.

How one deals with completely new situations is a challenge not only limited to the marine industry but also to other activities. For example, when the first nuclear power station was being considered, there was no past experience to act as a guide.

At the same time, it is not possible to wait until some experience is gained before its introduction. For these reasons there was a need to devise a fresh methodology to address these types of situations. The approach adopted was based on the thinking derived from systems engineering, and is applicable to many situations.

In the safety context, the approach begins by setting a target safety level and then starts from fundamental considerations. The latter involves asking a set of basic questions, before transforming them into tasks that would provide answers to the safety level being sought. The approach is given the name "Goal Setting" and in applying it to safety it has been called the "Safety Case Concept". The operator of an offshore installation has to submit a safety case to the appropriate regulatory body to show how safety is being managed. It is intended that in preparing the case the operator's team would also clarify their own thoughts on the treatment of safety.

It will be noted that when the safety case is developed in a safety specific manner the methodology becomes specialised. To achieve greater flexibility, the approach has been generalised using a management system and given the name "generic management system" or GMS approach. For safety application it becomes GMS for safety.

8.3   Safety of a novel system

In order to illustrate the situation in the marine world, an example is used to illustrate the dilemma with respect to safety standards. The idea of benefiting from the presence of lower resistance in the layer between the sea surface and the bottom surface of a craft moving a metre or so above, has led to the development of a craft called Wing in Ground (WIG). An artist's picture of a WIG craft is shown in figure 8.1. There is little operational experience. It travels at a high speed, around 100 knots, and has limited manoeuvrability. No regulations exist for dealing with its safety.

Figure 8.1 An artist's impression of a WIG (wing-in-ground) craft

Some suggested ways forward include:

- Modifying the existing High Speed Craft Safety Code. WIG is different to conventional high speed craft and it is difficult to justify using that code.

- Using aircraft regulations. Since the WIG operates above sea surface, it resembles an aircraft and the similarity makes this approach a possibility. Yet WIG is not a conventional aircraft.

- Adopting hovercraft regulations. The principle of a hovercraft is quite different to WIG and it requires a lot of imagination to be able to bridge the gap.

Thus, when an eight-seat WIG was built and planned to be used on a route between Cairns and the Greater Barrier Reef in Queensland, Australia the above mentioned methods were rejected. It was necessary to start from basics to assess how the safety of this craft can be addressed from fundamental principles.

8.4   Safety from fundamental considerations

There is a set of five questions that can be asked about any situation, activity or system in order to provide better understanding of its performance. These are:

Question 1:   What is the objective?

Question 2:   What is needed to achieve the objective?

Question 3:   What tasks must be done in practice to meet the objective?

Question 4:   What methods are used to check the objective is met?

Question 5:   What scope is there for improvement?

These five questions can be generalised as follows:

Q1: DEFINE   : The objective and criteria.

Q2: ORGANISE   : The resources and activities.

Q3: IMPLEMENT   : The tasks in practice to ensure the objectives are met.

Q4: MEASURE   : The results and the process against criteria.

Q5: REVIEW   : The lessons learnt and the experience gained.

It will be noted that the five questions are similar to the main elements of a management system, and tasks to be implemented will determine the issue to be addressed. For example, in a safety context, the objective is the safety standard and the tasks to be implemented would be related to safety.

8.5   The GMS approach

The GMS approach is a versatile method for managing a situation, activity or system so that the objective can be achieved effectively. The core is the basic

GMS unit which can be reproduced to as many levels as required. The GMS unit is made up of two interlinked parts, i.e. the management system (MS) and the process scheme (PS), see figure 8.2.

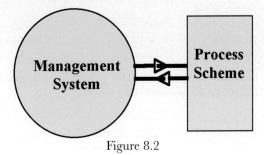

Figure 8.2

The basic GMS unit

The main MS elements are as follows:

- DEFINE   :   The objective and performance criteria.
- ORGANISE   :   The resources and plan to ensure that the goal can be met.
- IMPLEMENT   :   The plan in practice, via a process scheme.
- MEASURE   :   The results by independent methods.
- REVIEW   :   The lessons learnt during feedback.

The process scheme can be selected to deal with a specific theme and, in the present circumstance, the process scheme becomes the safety scheme which will be examined in the next section. By combining the MS for safety and the safety scheme, the GMS for safety is given in figure 8.3.

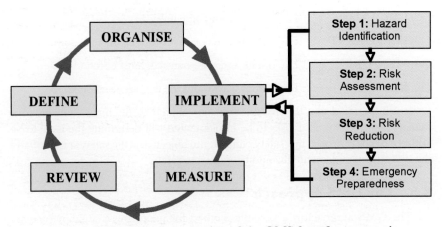

Figure 8.3 Pictorial representation of the GMS for safety approach

It will be noted that each of the components of the safety scheme can be linked to a GMS unit at a lower level so that the focus would be on the specific component in question. It is this property of the GMS unit that enables a complex situation, activity or system to be managed effectively.

8.6   The safety scheme

The four main components of the safety scheme are:

- Hazard identification.

- Risk assessment.

- Risk reduction.

- Emergency preparedness.

These components are shown on the right hand side of the sketch given in figure 8.3. It is useful to state the role of each component, while further examination can be found in Chapters 10 to 14.

(a)   Hazard identification

The goal is to identify the presence of hazards and put them into meaningful lists for various sub-situations, sub-activities and sub-systems. This can be further divided into different types of hazards, as for example, engineering. The methods used include a) Brainstorming, b) What If? and c) HAZard OPerability (HAZOP). This component is illustrated in figure 8.4 and further details can be found in Chapter 10.

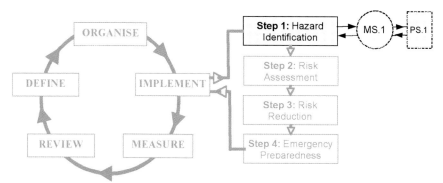

Figure 8.4 Highlighting hazard identification in the GMS for safety approach

(b)   Risk assessment

The goal is to locate the hazards on a risk scale based on the hazard's risk level. The risk scale is normally made up of three regions called intolerable, tolerable and negligible risk regions. To do this it is necessary to estimate the consequence (C) and the probability of occurrence (P) of a situation, activity or system. The methods used can be:

- Qualitative methods: Using past experience and a risk matrix devised for the situation, activity or system.

- Quantitative methods: Modelling consequences and analysing the probability of occurrence.

- Combined methods : Results from the qualitative method are used as a guide, examining available accident statistics before using quantitative methods and drawing generalised conclusions.

This component is illustrated in figure 8.5 and further details can be found in Chapters 11 and 12.

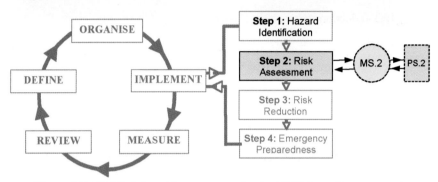

Figure 8.5 Highlighting risk assessment in the GMS for safety approach

(c)   *Risk reduction*

The goal is to reduce the risk levels of the hazards in the intolerable region to tolerable risk region and, for those hazards in the tolerable region, further risk reduction should be done if cost-effective.

The basic approach is to reduce the consequences, the probability of occurrence or both. The methods used include management based, engineering based, operation based and a combination of previous three. This component is illustrated in figure 8.6 and further details can be found in Chapter 13.

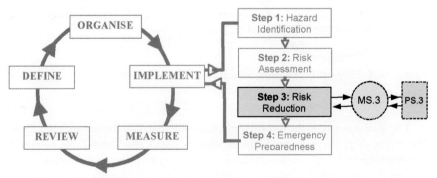

Figure 8.6 Highlighting risk reduction in the GMS for safety approach

(d)   *Emergency preparedness*

The goal is to be prepared to take the most appropriate action in the event that a hazard becomes a reality so as to minimise its effects and, if necessary, to transfer people from a location with a higher risk level to one with a lower risk level. The method of solution is to devise plans to deal with the results of specific hazards, and use computer simulation to study people movement, to gather data from practical exercises and to train crew in crowd management. This component is illustrated by figure 8.7 and further details can be found in Chapter 14.

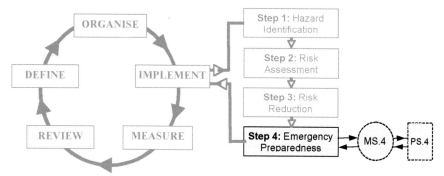

Figure 8.7 Emergency preparedness in the GMS for safety approach

8.7   The merits of the GMS approach

The merits of the GMS approach, when applied to safety, can be summarised as follows:

- It is devised specially to treat a non-absolute item such as safety and it possesses a generic management system which is versatile for use in effective safety management.

- The safety scheme can take on any appropriate form to fit with the situation, activity or system under consideration, i.e. it can have more than the four components given in this chapter.

- Each individual component of the safety scheme, e.g. hazard identification, can have a GMS unit linked to it, see figure 8.8.

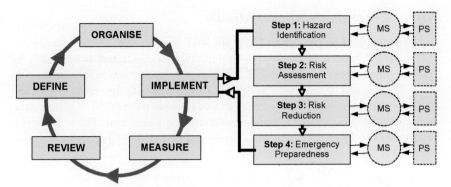

Figure 8.8 The GMS for safety showing other levels

8.8 CONCLUSIONS

(a) When the generic management system (GMS) approach is used in the safety context it provides a more flexible way of treating safety with a management system linked to the safety scheme.

(b) The management system provides direction, strategy and drive for implementing the safety scheme as well as measuring performance against criteria and allows for reviews to take place.

Chapter 9

THE GMS APPROACH AND THE SAFETY CASE CONCEPT

9.1 Introduction

The purpose of this Chapter is to explain the two methods for preparing a safety case before showing the relationship between the GMS for safety and the safety case approach. The reasons why GMS for safety approach is adopted are also given. Two examples will be used to illustrate how a safety assessment is performed.

Thus the aims of this chapter can be stated as follows:

(a)   To outline the two methods for preparing a safety case.

(b)   To relate the GMS for safety with the safety case approach.

(c)   To explain why GMS for safety is selected for safety management.

(d)   To present the main stages in doing a safety assessment.

(e)   To demonstrate the application of the main stages of safety assessment with the aid of two illustrative examples.

9.2 Two methods for preparing a safety case

To prepare a safety case of an activity, an installation or a system a number of methods can be adopted but there are two main methods as mentioned in Chapter 6. For ease of explanation these methods will be given the following names:

•   The technology driven method.

•   The management system driven method.

An examination of the bases of these two methods will now be given.

(a) The technology driven method

The starting point of this method is to form a team responsibility for doing the work. Team members generally have a balance of expertise and experience in various aspects of the offshore installation's operations including safety. The team would then go about gathering the basic information about the offshore installation, its activities and the environmental conditions associated with the operation. The central focus involves the following four tasks:

•   <u>Task 1</u>: Identify the hazards associated with the operation of the installation. The process is performed using the suitable techniques and some of them will be examined in Chapter 10. The outcome of this task would be a list of hazards.

- Task 2: This task involves assessing the risk levels of all hazards identified based on the experience of those working on the project and by using the popular risk matrix. Chapter 11 gives more details about this approach. The initial outcome of this task would be to assign a risk level to each of the identified hazards. The hazards are usually classified into regions by their risk levels and the popular practice is to put them into three regions with intolerable, tolerable and negligible risk levels.

  It is the first region that is of greatest interest, i.e. the hazards with intolerable risk levels. These hazards are usually given the name "major hazards" and would have to be reduced and controlled. To check the classification is reasonable, often a quantitative risk assessment is done on these hazards and the techniques for doing this is summarised in Chapter 12. Thus the outcome of this task would be the same list of hazards as identified from Task 1 but each will now have a risk level assigned

- Task 3: Using the outcome of Task 2, efforts will be devoted to reducing the intolerable risk level of hazards to a tolerable level by lowering the consequence or severity, by minimising probability of occurrence and by using a combination of the two previous approaches. To check the results are appropriate with respect to the legal requirements, it is helpful to verify if the risk has been reduced to as low as reasonably practicable or ask if the risk is ALARP. Further discussion can be found in Chapter 13.

- Task 4: Even when Task 3 has been done correctly there is always the possibility that an accident would occur due to a variety of reasons. For example, interaction between two or more hazards which each has a tolerable risk level may lead to a higher risk level. It has also to be remembered that safety is dominated by human factors and can be undermined by human errors. For this reason special attention must be given to preparing for emergencies so that when an accident does occur the actions taken would be able to minimise the adverse effects on the people and the environment. Further examination of emergency preparedness can be found in Chapter 14.

On completion of these four tasks, often called "Risk Management Process" or "Risk Assessment", a management system would be introduced for controlling the major hazards so that the regulatory requirements would be satisfied. It will be noted that the form of the management system can vary widely. A document would then be prepared for submission to the appropriate authority concerned and for use by the duty holder's team in their work. The approach is regarded as technology driven because the four tasks are essentially technical ones which are done first without the need to know the overall objective in advance or the suitability of the performance criteria to be met.

(b) The management system driven method

This method uses a management system as the driving force for the preparation of the safety case. The form of the management system is similar to that described in Chapter 7 and the five elements are located on the circumstance of a circuit and have the following roles:

- Element 1: Define

  The process begins by defining the objectives, e.g. safety standard, and the performance criteria, e.g. there would be no hazards with intolerable risk levels. In this way the team is clear in what it is trying to achieve.

- Element 2: Organise

  The next element would be concerned with organising the work that covers planning, work method, co-ordination of activities and resources, target dates, etc. It should be noted the team members would also gather the basic data about the installation and the operational environment separately or as a task of the organisation element.

- Element 3: Implement

  On the completion of these two elements, the next element of this management system would implement a safety scheme which is made up essentially of the four tasks described in the technology driven approach, i.e. identify the hazards in the operation of the installation, assess the risk level of the hazards, reduce the risk of hazards with intolerable risk level to tolerable level and prepare for emergency in the event an accident is realised.

- Element 4: Measure

  The next element would measure the results obtained against the performance criteria so as to establish to what extent the objective have been met.

- Element 5: Review

  Based on the outputs of the previous element, a review is done that includes benchmarking against the treatment of safety in other industries, consider the lessons learnt and explore scope for improvement. On completion of this element all the experience gained would be fedback to the starting point for use in refining the elements of the initial safety case for future applications.

In this approach, the improvement is continuous and iteration is introduced for refinement so as to cope with the non-absolute characteristics of safety. This approach enables the team to focus on the work with a clear sight of the objective and also allows the main features to be summarised in a document while putting the details in the appendices or supplementary reports.

9.3 The significance of the difference

From the previous section, it can be seen that the technology driven method can be used with the conventional safety case approach while the management system driven methods would be used with the GMS for safety. Both methods have similarities and one key difference is the order in which the safety case is being prepared.

The important question to be asked relates to whether this difference is significant. Before answering this question, it is interesting to give the experience of the head of safety in a large UK governmental organisation. He noted that the same contractor was doing projects for the reliability, quality and safety divisions. Each division had a series of tasks to be done and each had suggested how it wanted the tasks to be controlled or managed. The staff of the contractor were doing their very best to keep everybody happy.

On closer examination, he discovered that the specific details of the tasks were different but control or management aspects were almost identical and instead of taking advantage of this feature, the divisional requirements made everything very complicated. He then drafted a note that advocated "integrating management" and circulated this informally to a number of people for comments. When he was shown the GMS approach with the common management system implementing various specific process schemes, he remarked that this is the obvious way to achieve better co-ordination of efforts, consistency and effectiveness. This means that the same management system would be capable of implementing a reliability scheme, a quality scheme and a safety scheme.

It would be useful to summarise the key feature of the two methods. The technology driven method will address the technological issues first and they would influence the way the situation is to be controlled or managed. The management system driven method is much more flexible as it uses the same management system for implementing any scheme. This is turn ensures better interfaces with all the schemes of an organisation that can range from business and design schemes to safety and quality schemes. It is for the above reason that this book will use GMS approach to meet the safety requirement and for preparing the safety cases.

9.4 Performing a safety assessment

It will be useful to explain how the safety assessment of a new situation, activity or system is performed. The actual process usually follows three stages as follows:

Stage 1: Establishing the safety requirement

In all circumstances the first task is to define the safety requirement. A typical requirement can be stated as follows:

> *To ensure that the operation of a ship, system or activity achieves an acceptable level of safety.*

Stage 2: Acquiring safety support information

To meet the safety requirement, a large quantity of information relating to safety has to be acquired and it can cover the complete life-cycle of the ship. It would be used to make a full case so that the ship, equipment, situation, activity or system can meet an acceptable safety level for a given operating environment. The key information can be summarised using a ship example under the following headings:

a) Characteristics of the ship: These include the principal dimensions, displacement, facilities on board, in what operating class it is, general arrangement plans and other design data such as its structural strength. The information would provide a full specification and description of the ship.

b) The operating environment: The conditions the ship has been designed to operate in, including both the internal and external environment. Examples of the former include: the number of crew members, procedures for operations on the bridge, communication arrangements and engine room operating procedures. Examples of the latter would include areas of operation, routes, weather conditions and significant wave heights.

c) Safety management and justifications: Under this heading the information would include:

- Defining the safety standards to be met and performance criteria.

- Organising resources and activities to enable the objective to be met, such as scheduling, planning and maintenance.

- Implementing a safety scheme that is applicable to a specific phase of the ship's life-cycle. The actual tasks include identifying the hazards, assessing their risk levels and reducing the risk levels of those hazards with intolerable risk levels, plus preparing for emergencies when an accident actually occurs.

- Measuring the results obtained so as to verify that the performance criteria are met.

- Reviewing the whole process in order to coordinate the lessons learnt and quantify scope for improvement.

(d) Cover the range: The previous step should be performed for all phases of the ship's life-cycle, i.e. design, procurement, construction, operation, refurbishment and decommissioning.

Stage 3: Outlining the safety status

As can be seen from Stage 2, a large quantity of information would be acquired from each phase of the ship's life-cycle. At a given time, specific information may be needed to provide relevant evidence on the level of safety and a report would be prepared to demonstrate that the required safety standard has been achieved. The report is normally called "The Safety Case Report" and would be given a date to indicate the time when it was prepared. In the offshore industry, safety case reports are needed for the design, operational and decommissioning phases. The safety case reports are generally structured in such a way as to ensure consistency. For example, the main elements of the management system are present in all reports but the details would be different for the design and decommissioning phases.

The arrangement is illustrated in figure 9.1 in which the three stages are referred to as follows:

Stage 1:   The need   —>   Safety requirement

Stage 2:   The support information   —>   Safety case

Stage 3:   The status   —>   Safety case report

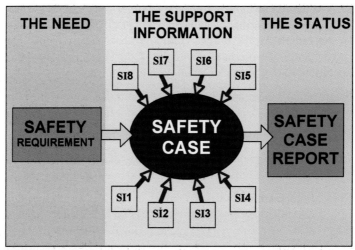

Figure 9.1 A sketch representing the key stages of safety assessment

9.5   Illustrative example for a laptop computer

The application of the three stages can be illustrated by examining the safety of a laptop computer. The three stages are:

Stage 1: The need

The safety requirement can be stated as follows:

> *To procure a laptop computer with an acceptable safety standard for use in performing daily work.*

The owner is a professional engineer who will be using the laptop in her office, at her home and taking it with her for business trips. The safety requirements are related to her need.

Stage 2: *The supporting information*

The laptop computer is to be used in many countries. The supporting information relating to safety has to meet the requirements of various countries. The safety information can be examined under the following headings:

(a)   Specification of the laptop: The specification defines the characteristics of the computer and would include the following items:

- Physical dimensions: Weight and size.

- Power requirements: Voltage and current.

- Built-in modem: Type, function, etc.

- Communication features: System, protocol, speed, etc.

- Hardware: Items in the personal computer.

- Software: Computer programs pre-installed.

- Features: Memory, power, disks, displays.

(b)   Operating environment: The environmental requirement for operation covers ambient temperatures, relative humidity and altitude. Operations must not cause harmful interference and should be able to deal with interference received.

(c)   Safety management and justification: A number of items relating to safety include:

- The equipment has been tested and found to comply with the limits for a class B digital device and meeting the US FCC roles. The product conforms to the CE-mark in accordance with related European directives. It satisfies Japanese regulations, carries the industry of Canada certificate and meets the safety conditions for use in Australia and New Zealand.

- Guidelines on the proper use of a computer include: avoiding stress and strain injuries, keeping the computer away from heat sources, not using the computer near liquids or corrosive chemicals and not blocking the vents.

- Advice on seating, posture, lighting and placement of the computer.

- Providing advice on the handling of computer parts, including: modules which can become hot with use, battery pack removal and disposal and memory cards.

- Warnings regarding damaged power cables which could cause fire or electric shock and the dangers of removing power plugs with wet hands.

Stage 3:   The status

In this example, no safety case report would be produced but the safety aspects would be contained in the owner's handbook. Typical guideline statements would include that the laptop computer should avoid coming into contact with water and how the battery should be handled and disposed of after it has reached the end of its useful life. The information provided would be specific to the laptop computer and a date of issue would be given to indicate the status at the time.

9.6   Illustrative example for a high speed ferry

In this example, the safety of a high speed Ro-Ro ferry is considered. The ferry had a major re-fit and its safety was to be examined. The highlights of the three stages are now given:

Stage 1:   The need

The safety requirement can be stated as follows:

> *To demonstrate that, following a major re-fit, the risk level of hazards are tolerable and negligible and As Low As Reasonably Practicable (ALARP).*

Since the vessel follows the high speed code of the International Maritime Organization, safety has to be examined from basic considerations.

Stage 2:   The supporting information

The ferry operates on a route from the UK to The Netherlands, and the safety requirements are those from the UK. The safety information can be examined under the following headings:

(a)   Specification of the ferry: The specification defines the main characteristics of the ferry and includes the following:

- Principal dimensions: Length, beam, depth, draft, etc.

- Design features: Speed, carrying capacities, displacement, etc.

- Classification: The class in which the vessel is classified and hence the structural strength.

- General arrangement: The layout of the vessel with drawings of each deck.

- Machinery: The type of main and auxiliary machinery, power output, control method.

- Propulsion system: The type of water jets used, the number of units, power output, etc.

- Equipment on board: The availability of key equipment on board, including life saving appliances and fire fighting equipment.

- Experimental results: Performance predictions using model experiments.

- Stability of the vessel: The ferry's initial and damaged stability calculations.

- Other features: Additional information which can provide a better description of the vessel.

(b) Operating environment: This involves both internal and external environments which include:

- External environment: Weather conditions; sea states and significant wave heights for the route.

- Internal environment: The activities on board the ferry that range from the embarkation and disembarkation of passengers to handling of supplies between the shore base and the vessel. In addition, operational procedures for dealing with the restaurant and entertainment activities.

(c) Safety management and justification: The items of information relating to safety include the following:

- The method of dealing with safety: The management system and the safety scheme.

- Define element: Defining the objective and performance criteria for the ferry.

- Organise element: Devising methods for effective coordination of resources and activities, e.g. scheduling, working arrangements and allocation of responsibilities.

- Implement element: Linking to the safety scheme, which involves components identifying the hazards, assessing their risk levels and reducing selected risk levels and preparation for emergencies. These would be considered later.

- Measure element: Measuring the results in order to check that the performance criteria are satisfied.

- Review element: Gathering the lessons learnt, comparing with the benchmark and refining before the output results and iterating as appropriate.

- Hazard identification component: Various techniques can be used to identify the hazards present for various aspects of the vessel, e.g embarkation and disembarkation of passengers and vehicles, machinery, lounge and leisure areas and bridge operation, acquiring a list of hazards which can affect personal wellbeing, property damage and the environment.

- Risk assessment component: Examining each hazard for the consequences and the likelihood of occurrence points of view and placing each on a tolerability scale.

- Risk reduction component: Reducing the risk level of specific hazards with an intolerable risk level, by addressing both the consequences and the probability of occurrence, using a combination of management, engineering and operational methods.

- Emergency preparedness component: Being prepared to deal with the situation when an accident occurs, e.g. fire on the car deck and having contingency plans ready to put into action.

Stage 3:   *The status*

A safety case report would be provided for the re-fit activity of the Ro-Ro's life-cycle. Documents of the safety case vary in style, emphasis, details and presentation. A readable one may include the following:

- An executive summary: A brief outline of the ship or system being considered, its operating environment and key features of the safety case scheme. The length is usually around two to three pages.

- Main text: A description of the ship, the environment in which it operates, elements of the management system and components of the safety scheme, e.g. hazard identification, risk assessment, conclusions and recommendations. The text is written clearly and concisely with a length of around 20-30 pages.

- Details: Detailed information is usually given in the appendices and can be several hundred pages long. For example, the full list of identified hazards may be given in an appendix.

9.7   Other applications of the GMS approach

By formulating the specific safety case concept as a special situation of the Generic Management System methodology, i.e. GMS for Safety, it is now possible to see the versatility and flexibility of the GMS approach. For safety, the GMS for Safety is made up of a GMS unit composed of a management system and a safety scheme, see figure 9.2.

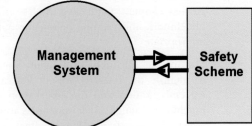

Figure 9.2 The GMS for safety

For any other situation the same pattern can be followed with the scheme changed to suit the non-absolute item in question. Thus for design, the GMS unit would have a management system and a design scheme, see figure 9.3.

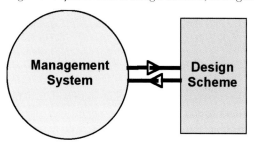

Figure 9.3 The GMS for design

It will be noted that the MS would have the same elements but the design scheme can have components which are appropriate for design (see Kuo 2003). In the same way, the following non-absolute items can be readily addressed:

(a) Quality: This is not an absolute item as quality relates to the standard met as defined by specified requirements. A quality product is one which most closely fulfils the specification. Thus GMS for quality would be an effective method of meeting the requirements.

(b) Research: This is another activity which is not absolute and often one cannot define the end point accurately, although what is wanted is well established. Once again, GMS for research would be a useful way to deal with research and its application. It can ensure a balance between practical need and achievable research advances. An example of GMS for research usage is given by Kuo (2005) for the development of the innovative structural material, called the Sandwich Plate System, for shipbuilding and ship repair. GMS for research is illustrated in figure 9.4.

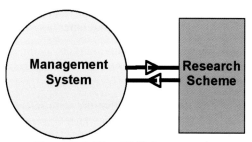

Figure 9.4 The GMS for research

(c)   Teaching: Effective teaching requires an understanding of how students acquire knowledge. A well known Chinese proverb on teaching puts the situation as follows:

If you tell me — I forget.

If you show me — I remember.

If you involve me — I learn.

This in turn makes teaching a non-absolute item and, to achieve effectiveness, a management system is needed. The teaching scheme can take any form depending on the subject and teacher. Attention needs to be given to performance criteria and how they should be measured and reviewed.

There are many other items which for which a GMS unit can be used. Initial studies have involved GMS for environment as a method of verifying environmental impact of a system and GMS for reliability as a way of assessing the reliability of a system. Other areas where GMS can be used include the International Maritime Organization's method of developing prescriptive regulations called Formal Safety Assessment or FSA (see Chapter 2). These five steps are not meaningful unless there is a management system in place for the implementation, and a GMS for FSA by Kuo (2002) was suggested at a Conference on FSA in September 2002. In 2005, IMO was actively debating the introduction of Goal Based Standard (GBS) for ships with the aim of raising the standard of ships. Although many features are considered, it is most likely that to implement the goal based standard a management system is needed and a GMS for goal based standard would be the most effective way forward.

9.8   Conclusions

The main conclusions to be drawn are:

(a)   The Generic Management System approach provides a versatile and flexible method of addressing safety and other non-absolute items.

(b)   The GMS for Safety gives the same outputs as the safety case concept but is more logical because it starts with the management system before implementing a safety scheme

(c)   For ship safety, it should be noted that the term safety case represents the supporting safety related information which is assembled throughout the ship's life-cycle, and the safety case report outlines the safety status for a given phase or situation of the ship at a given date.

Chapter 10

HAZARD IDENTIFICATION TECHNIQUES

10.1 Introduction

Hazard identification is the first element, or Step 1, of the Safety Scheme and is illustrated in figure 10.1.

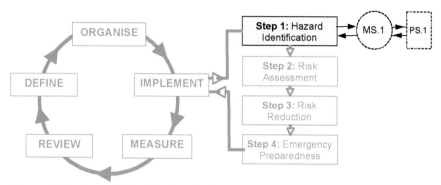

Figure 10.1 Hazard identification in the context of the GMS for safety diagram

In any situation, activity or system there are many hazards that can prevent the objective being achieved cost-effectively or achieved at all. To identify these hazards, it is useful to have a number of techniques which can assist in finding them efficiently.

The aims of this chapter are therefore as follows:

(a)   To outline the various types of hazard present in a situation, activity or system.

(b)   To explain the basic principle adopted in hazard identification.

(c)   To highlight popular methods of making the identification.

(d)   To show their uses with the aid of examples.

10.2 What is a hazard?

People generally associate the word "hazard" with the potential to do harm and the word harm is used in a broad context, from personal injuries to impact on the environment. In practice, it is more helpful to adopt a generalised definition:

> *A hazard is something that can lead to undesired outcomes or harm in the process of meeting an objective.*

This definition is applicable to any activity, situation, operation or system and the merits of this flexibility will be appreciated later.

In the safety context, the undesired outcome could be:

- Injuries to personnel.

- Damage to property.

- Pollution of the environment.

- A combination of previous three.

It will be helpful to use some examples to clarify the term:

Example 10.1

This relates to the operation of a Ro-Ro passenger ferry between two ports. The objective is to carry passengers safely between these ports and on schedule. Possible undesirable outcomes include:

- Fire occurring on board, leading to injury to personnel and damage to the ship.

- Collision with another vessel outside the harbour area at one port, leading to damage to the vessel, delay in fulfilling the schedule and danger to the life of all on board.

- A very high wind, causing the ferry to delay her departure by half a day, leading to the programme running behind schedule.

In this example, the occurrence of fire, collision with another ship and poor weather conditions are hazards, because they are likely to lead to an undesired outcome in terms of injury to personnel, damage to property and delayed departure. The first two are safety related hazards. In practice, it is necessary to determine the importance or risk level of each identified hazard.

Example 10.2

There is a hole in the road, and the question is whether such a hole is, or is not, a hazard. On the basis of the definition given above, two possible outcomes are:

- The hole is in a road which is in regular use. Its existence could lead to personal injury and damage to a vehicle. In this case the hole is a hazard.

- The hole is located in a road no longer used by people or vehicles. Its existence does not lead directly to any undesirable outcome, hence it may not be regarded as a hazard. Alternatively, it is a hazard with very low significance.

It will be noted that for a golfer, the hole on the green would not be a hazard since the aim is to hit the ball into the hole with as few shots as possible!

Example 10.3

This example is concerned with investing a sum of money with the aim of increasing its capital value over a period of five years. The following choices are possible:

a) Invest the amount in a UK government security such as National Savings Certificates, where the capital is returned after the specified period together with accrued interest. There is a government guarantee in this case.

b) Turn to the stock market and invest the amount in the shares of some well established company, where both large gains and large losses are possible.

Both choices are hazards in this case but have different significance on risk levels. In (a) the initial capital is protected, but the potential gain depends on the interest rate operating during the specified period. It tends to be lower on government securities than on some other forms of investment and can be regarded as undesirable. (b) would be a calculated gamble, leading to either high profit or great loss. It is not recommended to anyone who cannot afford to lose the initial capital. In other words, investment in shares is a hazard because it can lead to an undesirable outcome.

10.3 Hazard identification

The role of hazard identification is to find out what aspects can go wrong in a situation, activity or system. These occur in a random manner and various techniques are used to identify hazards and organise them into a hazard list which may be further divided into various types of hazard. Figure 10.2 illustrates the process of hazard identification that produces a hazard list.

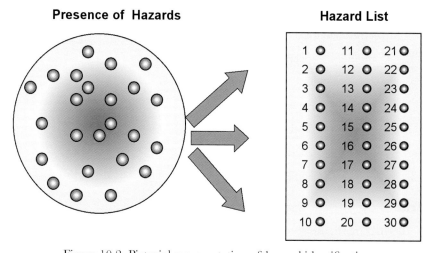

Figure 10.2 Pictorial representation of hazard identification

10.4 The basic principle of hazard identification

In the course of any activity we are exposed to many hazards, some of which may be very serious, although others may not result in any harm. To help us make a balanced judgment on a given situation it is useful, wherever possible, to identify what could go wrong before deciding on the action that needs to be taken. To determine what can go wrong, the following should be applied:

Step 1: Understand what the desired or planned path should be for meeting the objective and the associated assumptions.

Step 2: Identify possible deviations from the planned path, preferably by involving colleagues with a range of expertise, experience and outlook.

Step 3: List all the possible deviations in writing, so that there is a record of the items identified.

Application of this principle can be illustrated by means of the example of someone planning to travel from home to work.

The first step is to decide on the available modes of travel, e.g. walking, private car or public transport. One then has to define the time and cost constraints and from these parameters to consider the safety of each mode of travel. The next step is to identify the hazards involved with each of the identified travel modes.

Travel by Private Car

The hazards include:

*   Collision with another car whilst in motion.

*   An accident caused by a stationary vehicle.

*   Injury to a pedestrian.

*   Electrical failure.

*   Committing a speeding offence.

*   A punctured tyre.

*   Poor visibility due to fog.

*   Ice on sections of the road.

*   Running out of petrol.

*   Increased stress on personal health.

Travel by public transport

The hazards in this case include:

*   Injury caused by getting on or off the vehicle.

*   An accident to the vehicle.

*   Missing a connection.

*   Exposure to viruses from other passengers.

- Loss of personal possessions.

Walking

In this case the hazards include:

- Personal injury caused by a vehicle on the road.

- Exposure to exhaust fumes.

- Illness caused by adverse weather conditions.

In these examples the hazards can be identified by individuals, but more effectively by a group or team. It is particularly valuable to have a team for complex situations, activities and systems.

10.5 Popular techniques

The basic principle of this group of techniques is to provide a systematic approach for identifying potential hazards in complex systems. These techniques are based on a combination of applying past experience, accepting what is obvious, preparing a checklist of items that can go wrong in an activity and cross-referencing with an established database of hazards. Many techniques can be used for hazard identification and similar methods are often known by several different names. The most popular are the following:

(a) Checklist: Prepare a list to check which items could go wrong and the ways this could happen.

(b) Brainstorming: In this approach, a team generates a target number of hazards orally during an agreed period of time and these are written down for discussion when time is up. A list of hazards is then prepared.

(c) HAZOP: Shortened from HAZard OPerability is a technique that uses guide-words in order to study deviation from the design objective of a system and its components.

(d) What If?: Here, a list of potential hazards is produced for a system or subsystem, by asking "What If?" something does not work as planned. The approach can also be used as a follow-up to a brainstorming session, when a list of hazards has been compiled.

(e) SWIFT: The term stands for Structured What If? Techniques and it can be regarded as an extension of the What If? method, but performed in a structured manner.

(f) FMEA: Failure Mode and Effect Analysis is similar to HAZOP except that the emphasis is on identifying hazards via an examination of the failure mode.

It will be noted that, with the exception of the brainstorming and 'What If?' approaches, these methods have been developed for identifying the hazards of hardware systems, e.g. equipment, ships, plant and installations. However, there is a limit to the applicability of these methods, since human factors play a very important part in safety.

10.6 The brainstorming approach

This method involves the generation of ideas over a specified period by a group of people with different interests, expertise and experience. The approach is now used in many contexts, ranging from the search for new markets by a manufacturing company to the choice of name for a product or project and the selection of a topic for research study. It is, therefore, not surprising that this approach is now being applied to the identification of potential hazards in an activity, situation, or complex system.

In order to understand the technique it will be helpful to discuss the various features under separate headings as follows:

Principle

A group of people is assembled and each is willing to come up with ideas, without any inhibitions regarding their practicality. A fixed time period and a target number of ideas are agreed in advance. There is usually a coordinator or promoter, whose role is to encourage everyone to contribute, while trying to ensure that the target is met within the agreed time.

Description

The first task is to assemble the group. Ideally it will consist of around 12 people with a range of experience, knowledge, outlook and attitude. Its first task is to appoint or elect a coordinator. Everyone should have been notified in advance about the objective of the exercise, but the coordinator should reiterate the key issues and urge everyone to contribute. Once the process starts, suggestions are called out at random and listed on a flipchart, whiteboard or a display screen using a laptop computer in conjunction with a multimedia projector so that everyone can see what ideas have already been suggested. No initial discussion is allowed but all effort is concentrated on reaching the target. Once the brainstorming session is over it is then possible to consider all the ideas, grouping some together and discarding those which may be too preposterous. The end product should be a comprehensive list of the most likely hazards associated with the activity, process, or system.

Merits

The main merits of the approach are:

•   A lot of hazards can be suggested in a short period, once participants have overcome their initial inhibitions about unusual or outrageous suggestions.

- Good use is made of the contributions from people with different backgrounds, experience and expertise.

- It is a flexible approach, which is applicable for examining either a complete system or its various sub-systems.

- The results obtained can be taken further by another technique such as "What If?", which looks at the effects of something going wrong.

Drawback

The main drawback of this approach is the need for participants to have the right skills and attitude before the session starts. This can be difficult for people with little experience of this open way of operating.

Application

This method is used in many types of situations relating to safety, as well as other non-safety situations, activities issues.

General comments

The success of the brainstorming approach depends on three factors.

Firstly, the selection of participants plays an important role. Sometimes they are all on the same wavelength and the session is both productive and enjoyable. At other times people cannot get going and it is extremely difficult to generate a list of more than the obvious hazards.

Secondly, the coordinator or promoter should be someone knowledgeable, who has the right personality for teasing out ideas from colleagues. Sometimes the promoter will also make suggestions to keep the momentum going, if he or she senses that a pause is unduly prolonged.

Thirdly, participants have to discard any inhibitions about making unusual suggestions in the confidence that they will not be ridiculed afterwards.

10.7 The HAZOP approach

HAZOP is short for HAZard OPerability. It will be useful to consider this approach under the headings of principle, description, merits, drawbacks and application. Further details can be found in Kletz (1992) and Lees (1980).

Principle

The principle of this approach is to identify hazards by using "guidewords" to study variations from the design objectives of a system and its components.

Description

To examine a complex system, in order to identify its potential hazards, a multi-disciplinary team is formed. This would probably include a designer, a safety specialist and a practical engineer. The complete system is divided into a number of smaller and more manageable sub-systems, that are examined using guidewords. The strategy involves seeking answers on the following four features:

- The *objective* of the sub-system in question.

- The *deviations* from the stated objective.

- The *causes* of these deviations.

- The *consequences* resulting from the deviations.

Guidewords are employed to generate ideas about a system. Typical words would be None, More, Less and Other. The word Other, for example, will persuade the team to consider what else could happen in addition to normal operation, and thereby to identify possible physical conditions that might lead to hazards.

Merits

The main merits of the approach are:

- It is more likely to provide information on the potential hazards to be encountered, because the questions used are "open-ended".

- The combined expertise of several experts is directed at the task through a team approach.

Drawbacks

The main drawbacks of the approach are:

- For success, it is necessary to create the right team with members who have relevant experience and a balanced attitude to safety.

- If the job is to be done properly the team needs to be involved in every phase of the project.

Application

HAZOP is a popular technique in the chemical processing and petroleum industries, where complex plants are used. Its application has been extended to activities in the marine and offshore industries as well.

General comments

This hazard identification technique is based on qualitative methods supported by the experience and expertise of those involved in the safety assessment. Success depends on three basic factors.

Firstly, the systematic approaches adopted should be understood and applied by all those involved. All assumptions made about the safety aspect of the project, at each stage, must be challenged and tested before the actual work begins.

Secondly, the team members must have not only expertise and experience, but also the proper attitude to safety. It is all too easy to identify every possible hazard for a project, but it is much more demanding to prioritise these correctly. In this connection, hazards should be considered in the context of the total project.

Thirdly, hazards are not confined to engineering aspects. It is important to remember that management, operational, commercial and political hazards are all equally relevant.

10.8 Types of hazard

So far we have been identifying hazards without differentiating them in terms of type. From a practical point of view, however, it can be useful to group hazards according to type. This has two main benefits. Firstly, grouping can help us to select the most appropriate identification techniques to use and the correct emphasis in each case, if the list of hazards lacks certain types. Secondly, grouping can be very useful when seeking methods for reducing the effects of hazards on the activity, project or system. From the definition of the term safety given in Chapter 1 it is possible to readily propose the following three groups:

Management hazards

These hazards are associated with management and organisational issues. Examples would include such items as policy, commitment of funds for training, the installation of specific equipment and schedules to be met.

Engineering hazards

These hazards are readily understood by those technically trained and are usually associated with the hardware of the system. Typical examples would include electrical and mechanical failure, valves not opening as required, pressure too high and a display screen giving erroneous readings. In general, the hazards in this group are influenced by design.

Operational hazards

These hazards are associated with the operation of the ship or system. Examples would include such features as misreading a dial, switching off an engine which is functioning normally instead of a faulty one or forgetting to close the bow door of a Ro-Ro ferry. It will be noted that these hazards are dominated by human factors.

Other main types of hazard include the following:

Commercial hazards

These arise from commercial considerations and are particularly associated with decisions on spending money. A typical example is the selection of a less expensive piece of equipment that just meets the minimum standard required instead of opting for a more expensive item with higher specification and a track record of high reliability. Sometimes a contract is accepted at a cost below the desired level, and savings have to be made in order to complete the work. This in turn may lead to potential hazards due to commercial factors.

Political hazards

These are possibly the most important hazards of all but they are extremely subtle which makes it very difficult to deal with them in practice. A typical example would be for a licence-awarding body to require a particular composition of crew for a ship, offshore installation or other operation, e.g. 20 per cent of members should come from the ship's home port region or the country in which the operation is taking place. This can be a hazard in the short term, if there is a shortage of competent applicants from the area specified.

Time hazards

Many projects have to be completed by an agreed date, e.g. the planned launching of a ship or the departure/arrival time of a ferry. Delays due to such factors as late delivery of materials, unforeseen production difficulties or failure to meet specification would affect ability to meet a deadline. Failure to meet deadlines can affect future contracts from clients and also disrupt schedules, with associated knock-on effects. These events can also be regarded as hazards or time hazards.

10.9 An illustrative example

In this section an illustrative example is used to show how hazard can be identified in an important maritime activity.

a)   Background

The activity is concerned with a lifeboat launching exercise from a Ro-Ro ferry. Lifeboats are installed on the ship for evacuating passengers from the open deck of the ferry to the sea in the event of an emergency. The conventional lifeboat has a full hull form and is located on the open deck and at both sides of the ship. The lifeboat is attached to a davit and, when it is not in use, rests on a cradle frame. Figure 10.3 (overleaf) shows a typical group of lifeboats installed on the port side of an open deck. The operation begins by rotating the davit so that the lifeboat is hanging outside the deck edge and passengers and crew then get on board when it is lowered to the deck level. A brake is released so that a controlled lowering of the lifeboat to the sea can be activated. Regular exercises are performed in simulated emergency conditions to check the workings of the procedure and the equipment.

Figure 10.3 A typical group of lifeboats on the port side of a ferry deck

b) *Hazard identification*

The objective of the lifeboat exercise can be stated as follows:

To ensure the lifeboat can be launched efficiently and safely within a target period.

A typical period may vary from 5 to 7 minutes. The hazards can be identified by examining the various stages of the launching process. These involve:

Stage 1: The lifeboat moves from the rest position to being level with the deck, can be bowsed in, and has its painter run forward

Stage 2: Boarding of passengers and crew into the lifeboat.

Stage 3: Lowering the lifeboat until it comes into contact with the sea.

Stage 4: Lifeboat is detached from the cables and floating on the sea.

A summary of a short list of hazards identified is given in the following table.

Ref. No.	Hazard	Undesired outcome in meeting the objective
H1.1	Launch motor breaks down	Lifeboat is stuck in the rest position
H1.2	Davit jams	Lifeboat cannot be launched
H2.1	Passenger trips on deck	Personal injury
H2.2	Crew slips in the lifeboat	Personal injury
H3.1	Lifeboat-hull impact	Damage to hull and lifeboat
H3.2	High wind condition	Lifeboat is difficult to control
H4.1	Lifeboat rocks violently	Passengers become ill
H4.2	Passenger falls overboard	Personal injury

It will be noted that the hazards can be identified by asking, at each stage, the question "what aspects can go wrong?"

10.10 Conclusions

(a)   Hazard identification plays an important role in the safety scheme and there are various methods of performing the task.

(b)   The best results can usually be obtained by doing the work in teams and working methodically and imaginatively.

(c)   It is helpful to check the results against team members' experience and, if there are significant variations, logical reasons should be sought.

Chapter 11

RISK ASSESSMENT — QUALITATIVE METHODS

11.1 Introduction

Once the hazards in a situation, activity or system have been identified it is important to establish their significance by doing what is known as a risk assessment. The second task in the Safety Scheme is illustrated in figure 11.1.

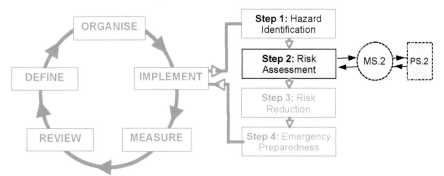

Figure 11.1 Risk assessment in the context of GMS for safety diagram

This chapter focuses on qualitative risk assessment and the aims are as follows:

(a)   To explain the term qualitative risk assessment.

(b)   To outline the basis of the approach.

(c)   To illustrate the method of application.

(d)   To give some interpretations of the results obtained.

11.2 What is qualitative risk assessment?

To place a hazard on a risk scale according to its significance, i.e. severity and probability of occurrence, there are two principal methods. They come under the names of qualitative and quantitative risk assessment. Care should be taken to differentiate between the two methods, as their spellings are so close. This chapter focuses on methods of doing qualitative risk assessment while Chapter 12 examines quantitative risk assessment.

Risk assessment is a process that places hazards on a risk scale which normally has the following three regions:

•   Intolerable risk region.

•   Tolerable risk region.

•   Negligible risk region.

An illustration of the process is given showing in figure 11.2 the lists of hazards being placed on the three regions.

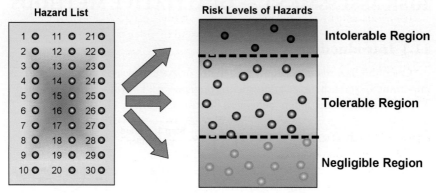

Figure 11.2 Pictorial representation of risk assessment

Qualitative risk assessment can be performed by the following techniques:

(a)   Past experience:

The combined experience of team members is used to determine how severe each hazard is and its likelihood of occurrence. The agreed value is then used to place the hazard in the appropriate location on the risk scale.

(b)   Risk matrix:

In this technique the consequence and probability of occurrence are divided into discrete units and a matrix is used to relate them. This technique is usually referred to as qualitative risk assessment with past experience incorporated and is examined in Sections 11.5 to 11.9 of this chapter.

It may be helpful to question the main purpose of doing a risk assessment. For practical reasons it is useful to know which hazards are the more significant ones, since it requires resources to reduce the risk levels of hazards. The risk assessment prioritises hazards based on the risk levels and allows resources to be used effectively by addressing the most significant ones. It is the effective use of resources that is the main reason for doing risk assessment.

11.3 Risk and its interpretations

In Chapter 5, it was shown that the popular relation for risk is as follows:

$$R = C \times P$$

where the terms are as follows:

R: Risk.

C: Consequence or severity of the hazard.

P: Probability of occurrence of the hazard.

It will be useful to consider a number of "extreme" situations and to provide an interpretation of them, based on the relationship of risk given in the last section. Using a scale running from 0 to 1.0 for illustrative purposes, four special situations will be considered, as follows:

Situation 1: Extremely High Consequence

This is a situation in which the severity of consequence is so high as to be unacceptable. It will definitely involve loss of life and danger to property, and possibly the environment. In this case the consequence (C) is equal to unit, or C ➜ 1, and so the risk relation becomes:

$$R = C \times P = 1 \times P \rightarrow P$$

The risk is equal to the probability of occurrence. For example, if the engines of an aircraft fail in flight, there is only one consequence — the aircraft will have to come down to the ground. The risk is calculated entirely on the value of the probability of occurrence and this is a special case which is often confused with the general expression.

Situation 2: Extremely Low Consequence

In this situation the severity of the consequence is regarded as very low, i.e. C ➜ 0, and the relationship becomes:

$$R = C \times P = 0 \times P \rightarrow 0$$

An example of this situation would be the spilling of some clear water on a tablecloth, which will leave no stain and will dry out quickly. This is an extreme value because there are very few situations in which the risk is actually zero.

Situation 3: Extremely High Probability

In this situation the probability of occurrence is equal to unity and the risk relationship becomes:

$$R = C \times P = C \times 1 = C$$

An example of this situation would be the fact that a book will fall to the ground when dropped.

Situation 4: Extremely Low Probability

In this situation there is no likelihood of occurrence, so the probability tends to zero and the risk relationship becomes:

$$R = C \times P = C \times 0 \rightarrow 0$$

An example would be our planet colliding with Mars or Venus.

Other situations

For all other situations the risk relationship will yield a value of the risk level, which can then be used to provide a judgment on its tolerability while taking into account other features such as experience. Two examples will be used to provide general illustrations to show how the problem can be tackled.

Example 11.1: High Consequence and Low Probability

The consequences of a supertanker colliding with an offshore structure in the northern North Sea would be extremely serious. The offshore structure would be damaged, fire might break out, and the environment would suffer damage from oil spillage, etc. Using available techniques it is therefore reasonable to predict a high consequence factor. For the purposes of illustration, we shall assign a value of 0.8 to this event, i.e. C = 0.8. The probability of occurrence of such an event can be estimated from known statistics of supertanker operation, the locations of offshore installations, the routes taken by the vessels, the safety management system of the operating company, etc. Again, for the purposes of illustration, we assume that results are available for a study done on a particular installation, and it is reasonable to assign a value of 1/10,000 to the probability, or $P = 10^{-4}$.

The numerical value of Risk (R) is found to be:

$$R = C \times P = 0.8 \times 10^{-4} = 8 \times 10^{-5}$$

Further studies need to be done to establish whether such a value is tolerable. If not, possible methods of reducing the risk level include restricting tankers to specified routes, improving information on the location of offshore installations and improved training on collision avoidance for ships' officers.

Example 11.2: Low Consequence and High Probability

The consequences of dropping nuts and bolts during the installation of a piece of equipment on a rig would be of limited significance, although they could include possible injury to those below, together with some pollution of the environment, loss of materials and delay in completing the job on time. In this case it may be reasonable to assign a value of 0.1 to consequence, i.e. C = 0.1. Assessment of the probability of occurrence is based on observation, inventories, etc. and these lead to a probability of three in 100, i.e. P = 0.03.

The numerical value of Risk (R) is found to be:

$$R = C \times P = 0.1 \times 0.03 = 3 \times 10^{-3}$$

When other relevant information and operational practice are incorporated, this level of risk may not be acceptable and, if so, action can be taken to reduce the risk level to a value such as $R = 10^{-4}$. Typical examples include: installing protective nets to "catch" falling objects, introducing safer working procedures, etc.

It will be helpful to provide some interpretations of the term risk and they come under the following headings:

(a)   Scientific

Risk is a function of the consequence (C) and the probability of occurrence (P), i.e.

   R = f (C, P)

and the popular relation is R = C x P

In practice both C and P are taken together when risk is considered. For example, if an oil tanker hits an offshore installation the consequence would tend to be catastrophic but the probability of occurrence would tend to be very unlikely and risk would tend to be tolerable.

(b)   Probability only

In this case, the risk relation becomes

   $R_{PO} = P$

In practice, risk is only thought of as the probability of occurrence. For example, if aircraft engines failed during a flight the consequences would tend to be catastrophic and uncontrollable so P represents risk. Depending on the value of P, a judgment would be made as to the tolerability.

(c)   Consequence only

In this case, the risk relation becomes $R_{CO} = C$ where risk is only thought of in the context of the consequence. Take, for example, when a youngster learns to ride a bicycle. Because it is bound to happen, the probability of occurrence of falling off would be a constant and very high. Risk would be judged on the various types of injuries sustained by falling off the bicycle. Thus the judgment of tolerability would be based solely on the consequence. It should be noted that the risk can be reduced by adding stabilisers to the rear wheel.

(d)   Lay persons

In this case, the risk relation becomes $R_{LP} = U_{LP}$ f(C,P) where R_{LP} = risk interpreted by the lay persons and U_{LP} is a safety factor given by lay persons — for example, when deciding whether to accept a sailing trip involving crossing a busy channel. The consequence of an accident is visualised and the likelihood estimated, but a safety factor is added and the value is greater than unity. This leads to a result with a risk value more severe than when the popular risk relation is used.

11.4 Risk levels

Risk assessment techniques would use the relation R = C x P to locate the hazards on a risk scale which conventionally has three risk regions. For a 3-region risk presentation, see figure 11.3.

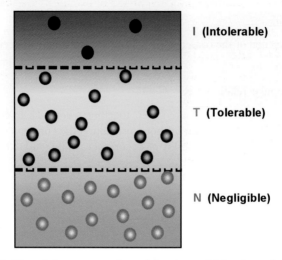

Figure 11.3 Pictorial representation of the three risk levels and the regions

Definitions of the three risk levels are as follows:

- *Intolerable Risk Level*: The presence of the hazard in the system or situation cannot be justified and this is the intolerable region.

- *Tolerable Risk Level*: The hazards in the system or situation may lead to accidents. If it is possible to reduce their risk levels cost-effectively then an effort should be made to do so. However, if the effort required far outweighs the benefits, these risk levels should not be reduced and the hazards remain in the tolerable risk region.

- *Negligible Risk Level*: Certain hazards will exist in the system or situation but are most unlikely to lead to accidents and no effort should be expended on reducing their risk levels. These hazards are in the negligible risk region.

As can be seen, some hazards are in the region of the negligible risk level, a certain number are in the region of the tolerable risk level and some in the region of the intolerable risk region. The ideal solution would be to shift all hazards into the region of negligible risk level, but this would be impracticable in a complex system such as a ship or offshore installation . Instead the target must be to shift all the hazards within the intolerable risk region to the tolerable region.

There are some difficulties which require brief mention. In the conventional 3-region risk presentation (see figure 11.3), the boundary between the intolerable and tolerable region is a line. Bearing in mind the accuracy obtainable in risk assessment, we can come to a very sensitive decision regarding where a hazard will be located around the boundary between the intolerable and tolerable risk regions. It has been suggested that an extra risk region should be introduced between intolerable and tolerable risk regions and be given the name "uncertain risk region". The 4-region risk presentation will be examined in Chapter 13 on risk reduction.

11.5 Basis of the qualitative approach

In this approach the team would follow a number of steps and these are:

Step 1: Understand the background

The starting point is to understand the background of the situation, activity or system and in particular its functions, design philosophy and operational mode, using the past experience of the team members.

It is useful to mention that the team doing the qualitative risk assessment should have a variety of experience so that the situation, activity or system can be examined from different angles. In addition, like all successful teams, there needs to be a leader and a working method should be aimed at achieving efficiency and effectiveness.

Once the team has been formed, it will be important to decide on how the problem should be tackled and which responsibilities and duties given to team members.

Step 2: Classify the consequence (C)

The consequence is divided into discrete units using words to describe the effects and further consideration is given in section 11.6.

Step 3: Classify the probability of occurrence (P)

The probability of occurrence is also divided into discrete units using words to describe the likelihood. Further consideration is given in section 11.7.

Step 4: Construct risk matrix

Using the results of Steps 2 and 3, a risk matrix is constructed and the team has to adopt the risk relationship, R = C x P. Further discussion is given in section 11.8.

Step 5: Apply the risk matrix

Team would decide on the boundaries between the three intolerable, tolerable and negligible risk regions. The method of applying a risk matrix is given in section 11.9.

11.6 Classify the consequences

The consequences would be divided into several categories with descriptions and indices and this process is done collectively by the team members. Once this is understood and agreed, they would be used for reference throughout the qualitative risk assessment process.

As an example, the severity of operational failures can be divided into the following four categories:

Description	Index	Severity
Catastrophic effect	Z	One or more deaths
Hazardous effect	Y	Loss of limb
Major effect	X	Broken limb
Minor effect	W	Cuts/bruises

The choices given in the example would be for the team doing the qualitative risk assessment, and different teams could come up with alternative categories. In practice, a set of severity indices can be obtained to give agreed standards.

Certain types of failure can be grouped on the basis of "similar consequence", e.g. similar consequences can be expected from a leakage of gas, whether the source is a ship, a ruptured pipe or a storage tank. It should be noted, however, that the impact of the leakage will depend on parameters such as its geographical location "How close is it to a populated area?" and the speed and direction of the wind "How far will the gas be carried?", etc.

11.7 Classify the probability of occurrence

Similarly to the consequence classification, the same process can be applied to classify the probability of occurrence into various categories. To estimate the probability of occurrence in reality of a potential hazard, it is important to draw on the personal experience and expertise of those involved, and also to use some systematic representation of the causes leading to the realisation of the hazard. On the basis of peoples' experience and expertise it is possible to define a scale of probability of types of occurrence, incorporating summarised descriptions, as shown below.

Description	Scale	Range
Frequent	5	10^{-0} to 10^{-3}
Reasonably probable	4	10^{-3} to 10^{-5}
Remote	3	10^{-5} to 10^{-7}
Extremely remote	2	10^{-7} to 10^{-9}
Extremely improbable	1	Below 10^{-9}

Such a scale may be devised by an appropriate organisation and people can be trained to use it to provide a first approximation of the probability of occurrence. The important thing to remember is the need to be consistent in the use of such a scale, i.e. everyone should interpret the different levels in the same way. Since the range does not give the precise occurrence, it is not unusual for teams to adopt an approach similar to the one given below:

Description	Scale	Occurrence
Frequent	5	Once a week
Less frequent	4	Once a month
Remote	3	Once a year
Very remote	2	Once every ten years
Extremely improbable	1	Once in a lifetime

11.8 Construct a risk matrix

The classifications given in Sections 11.6 and 11.7 can be used to construct a risk matrix, with the severity of consequence forming the columns and the probability of occurrence forming the rows. The results in the risk matrix are given in figure 11.4.

C	Z						
	Y						
	X						
	W						
		1	2	3	4	5	P

Figure 11.4 A typical risk matrix framework

It will be noted that the scales selected for both severity of consequence and probability of occurrence are discrete values, e.g. 2 or 3. No intermediate values are used, such as 2.4 or 2.5. For this reason, the resulting location of the hazard or risk level can only be approximate. However, this matrix does have its usefulness and provides a ready indication of the importance of specific hazards before more detailed quantitative methods are applied.

11.9 Main features of the risk matrix

Before the risk matrix can be applied to perform a risk assessment of the hazard the team need to decide where blocks are to be distributed in the three intolerable, tolerable and negligible risk regions. One approximate way of doing this is to replace consequence severity indices of W, X, Y and Z by 1, 2, 3 and 4. Taken in conjunction with probability of occurrence, using the relation $R = C \times P$, the risk matrix from Section 11.8 takes the form given in figure 11.5.

	4	4	8	12	16	20	
C	3	3	6	9	12	15	
	2	2	4	6	8	10	
	1	1	2	3	4	5	
		1	2	3	4	5	P

Figure 11.5 Numerical elements for the risk matrix

The team can then decide the risk regions using the numbers, e.g.

Risk above 15 — Intolerable risk region

Risk below 15 and above 6 — Tolerable risk region

Risk below 6 — Negligible risk region

Figure 11.5 is presented in such a manner that it can be used to do qualitative risk assessment, see figure 11.6, with I = Intolerable, T = Tolerable and N = Negligible.

	Z	N	T	T	I	I	
C	Y	N	T	T	T	I	
	X	N	N	T	T	T	
	W	N	N	N	N	N	
		1	2	3	4	5	P

Figure 11.6 Risk matrix and the risk regions

Take the example of the helicopter engine failure during cargo transfer. Using the risk matrix given in figure 11.6, Consequence = X and Probability = 4 are obtained and the risk level for the hazard is tolerable.

It is important to remember that C and P are complex functions involving variables such as management, operation, engineering, timing and human factors. The answer can only be an approximation.

It will be noted that the scales of consequence and probability can be divided into finer steps, e.g. expanded from 4 to 20 letters in the consequence description and from 5 to 50 intervals in the probability of occurrence. It would then be possible to construct a more detailed risk matrix, similar to that given in figure 11.7 (overleaf).

C												
Z	N	T	T	T	T	T	I	I	I	I	I	I
Y	N	N	T	T	T	T	T	I	I	I	I	I
X	N	N	T	T	T	T	T	T	T	I	I	I
W	N	N	T	T	T	T	T	T	T	T	T	T
V	N	N	T	T	T	T	T	T	T	T	T	T
U	N	N	N	N	N	N	T	T	T	T	T	T
	1	2	3	4	5	6	7	8	9	10	11	12
P												

Figure 11.7 Risk matrix with finer divisions of C and P

It is also possible to replace the blocks on the two boundaries by two curves (see figure 11.8), and such a display of the risk regions is often seen in publications. It is important to recognise that the assumptions and approximations involved have not altered.

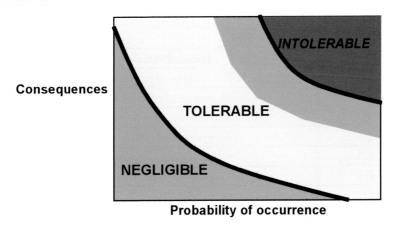

Figure 11.8 Risk matrix with curve boundaries for the regions

If C and P are on a logarithmic scale, the boundaries of the risk region would be a straight line instead of curves. This form of presentation can also be found in publications on safety.

11.10 An illustrative example

In this example, the risk matrix given in figure 11.6 is used to assess the risk levels of identified hazards associated with a transfer operation between ship and harbour launch. The various features are considered under the following headings:

(a)   Background

A medium–sized Ro-Ro passenger ferry operates cruises around a series of islands which do not always have port docking facilities suitable for the ship to disembark passengers to go on shore visits. However, launches are available to take groups of passengers from the anchored ship via a gangway at the side of the ship. Once the decision is made for the groups to go ashore, one end of the gangway — which has a small platform attached — is lowered to a position just above the water level. The launch would be secured to a support of the platform before passengers descend from the main deck for transferring to the launch. The process is reversed for the return journey. Since the environmental conditions will vary from site to site, the crew decide to perform a qualitative risk assessment on the personnel transfer operation.

(b)   Identifying the hazards

Using the various techniques given in Chapter 10 together with the practical experience of the team members, i.e. the officers on board the ship responsible for the personnel transfer operation, various hazards were identified and a shortened list is given here.

Reference	Hazard description
H1	Slippery gangway
H2	Freak gust of wind hits the gangway
H3	Waves wash over the platform
H4	Inexperienced officer on duty
H5	Excessive launch motion
H6	Large gap between platform and launch
H7	Launch engine cuts out
H8	Rope holding launch to platform breaks

It will be noted that all the hazards can lead to undesired outcomes, such as personal injury due to falls, shock from getting soaked and collision between the launch and the gangway or platform.

(c)   Qualitative risk assessment

The process of determining the risk level involves examining the consequences and probabilities of occurrence in turn before deriving the tolerability rating using the risk matrix given in figure 11.6. The actual steps are as follows:

Firstly, the hazard H1 has to be examined so as to decide on which category of consequence it belongs, i.e. catastrophic, hazardous, major and minor (see section 11.6 for further details). After discussion, team members agree that "major effect" would be the most appropriate. A value of Y is now given to the consequence part of risk for H1.

Secondly, the probability of occurrence of Hazard H1 has to be determined using the scale of frequent, less frequent, remote, very remote and extremely improbable (see section 11.7 for further details). After further discussion, team members selected "remote" and give a value of 3 for the probability of occurrence part of risk for H1.

Lastly, by using the agreed values of C and P for H1 along the vertical and horizontal axes respectively, the risk matrix readily shows the tolerability of H1 as "tolerable".

When the same process is repeated for all the hazards, the obtained results are given in the table below.

Ref.	Hazard description	Conq.	Prob.	Risk
H1	Slippery gangway	Y	3	T
H2	Freak gust of wind hits the gangway	Y	1	N
H3	Waves wash over the platform	X	4	T
H4	Inexperienced officer on duty	Y	3	T
H5	Excessive launch motion	Y	4	T
H6	Large gap between platform and launch	Z	2	T
H7	Launch engine cuts out	Y	2	T
H8	Rope holding launch to platform breaks	X	2	N

I: Intolerable risk, T: Tolerable risk; N: Negligible risk

The information about the risk level will enable the team to decide what risk reduction methods should be applied and how to deal with any accident which may occur.

11.11 Conclusions

(a)   Risk assessment using the qualitative method relies heavily on the experience of those involved in doing the assessment and the introduction of the concept of risk matrix has ensured that more consistent results can be obtained.

(b)   The qualitative risk assessment methods provide a quick assessment of a hazard's risk level and the result will be a useful guide to safety management.

(c)   The accuracy achievable should be checked and results carefully interpreted so as to reduce uncertainty.

Chapter 12

RISK ASSESSMENT - QUANTITATIVE METHODS

12.1 Introduction

The topic to be examined here is Step 2, or the second task of the Safety Scheme and the sketch is similar to the one given in figure 11.1, with the exception that it is quantitative methods that will be considered (see figure 12.1).

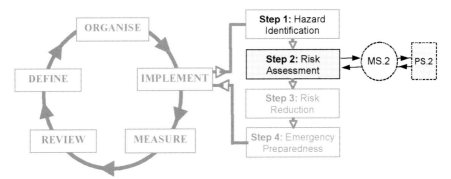

Figure 12.1 Risk assessment in the context of GMS for safety diagram

This chapter focuses on quantitative risk assessment and the aims are as follows:

(a)   To explain the term quantitative risk assessment.

(b)   To outline the basis of the approach.

(c)   To illustrate the method of application.

12.2 What is quantitative risk assessment?

Risk assessment has been explained in the first part of Section 11.2 and quantitative risk assessment can be defined as follows:

> *Quantitative risk assessment determines the risk level of hazards by modelling consequences, and analysing the probability of occurrence using accident statistics and relevant information.*

The actual tasks usually consist of the following:

a)   Modelling consequence

This task is concerned with acquiring a thorough understanding of how a situation, activity or system functions, in order to determine the consequence of any hazard. The information is in quantitative form or expressed in numerical values.

b)   Analyse probability of occurrence

The probability of occurrence is influenced by a number of factors and it is possible to use techniques such as Fault Tree Analysis (FTA) and Event Tree Analysis (ETA) to obtain numerical values for the probability.

The reasons for performing a quantitative risk assessment are the same as those for qualitative risk assessment as explained in section 11.2.

12.3 Basis of the quantitative approach

In this approach the team will follow a number of steps and these are:

Step 1:   Understand the background

This step involves a number of tasks and these include the following:

- Seek available information about the situation, activity or system from all sources, e.g. accident records of similar cases.

- Acquire a physical interpretation on how the situation, activity or system functions.

- Determine those parameters that have major influence on the consequences or the probability of occurrence.

- Discuss with team colleagues the key issues.

- Exchange experiences amongst team members.

Step 2:   Model the consequence (C)

The technique used will be influenced by the nature of the situation, activity or system. The modelling process is dependent on its function and the environment in which it is taking place. In general, it is useful to trace the event from the point of view of safety, i.e. to identify how far it is likely to cause loss of life, damage to property or harm to the environment. This analysis has to take into account all the relevant features that could have a bearing on the predicted failure. This is best illustrated by an example. The fracture of a gas pipe in a ship will lead to the escape of gases. The location of the fracture, the pressure of the gas, the speed and direction of the wind, and the closeness of the ship to areas where people live and work will govern the effects on the environment. The modelling will need to examine a range of fracture sizes, gas pressures, wind speeds and directions. The results can then be analysed to determine the consequence of the worst case.

Step 3:   Analyse the probability of occurrence (P)

A systematic method usually involves constructing a form of "tree diagram" which links possible causes of failure by a series of logical decision points. The contribution of each cause, also in probability terms, will have to be determined and the final value calculated by integrating the various values in stages. The techniques are well established, coming under such names as Fault Tree Analysis (FTA) and Event Tree Analysis (ETA). Further consideration is given in sections 12.5 and 12.6 and a number of textbooks provide more extensive details of these methods.

Step 4:   Make risk assessment

After determining C and P for the hazard or subset, the results are located on the risk scale.

12.4 Difference between qualitative and quantitative approaches

There are two main differences between the two approaches and these are as follows:

(a) Extent of the investigation

• Qualitative risk assessment relies on experience and uses a risk matrix to provide a location for the risk of individual hazards. This is quite straightforward.

• Quantitative risk assessment performs a more in-depth study, using available data in determining the risk value of a hazard before locating it on the risk scale.

(b) Focusing of effort

• Qualitative risk assessment is performed for all hazards which have been identified.

• Quantitative risk assessment is done only for a limited number of hazards with significant risk levels.

It is argued by safety personnel that quantitative methods give more accurate results. This can be true in certain practical cases but it has to be recognised that this is not always true. Knowledgeable experience in the operation of a system can often provide a valuable insight and make the risk assessment results more meaningful and reliable. There are many situations where the data needed for quantitative risk assessment are either not available or not relevant and, for this reason, quantitative results are less meaningful in spite of the impressive looking statistics and computer output in graphs!

12.5 Fault tree analysis method

This method is a popular technique used to analyse the probability of occurrence. It is, therefore, useful to highlight the key features of the method.

Principle

The principle involved in analysing a complex system is to link potential hazards in the activities, called events, in the form of a tree with a number of branches. Probability is then determined and assigned to each event. Boolean algebra is used to decide on the route to follow at the junctions of the branches. Thus at every junction of two or more branches, the following two options, known as logic gates, are offered.

The first option is satisfied if any one of the possible conditions or events is met. The second option is satisfied only when all the possible conditions or events are met.

Description

The operation of a system can be regarded as a series of events structured like a tree with its various branches. In a ship situation, for example, the top event (a major failure) is treated as being the result of a number of causes. In some cases several of these need to act together before a failure can occur, while in other cases a single cause can be responsible in itself for a failure. The tree and its branches are linked together by means of OR and AND logic gates at the junctions. The symbols used in each case are as follows:

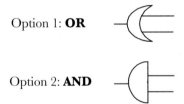

Option 1: **OR**

Option 2: **AND**

Figure 12.2 The "OR" and "AND" gates of the fault tree analysis method

It will be noted that the OR gate probabilities are summed to give the resultant value. The AND gate probabilities are obtained usually by multiplication to give the resultant value.

In practice, once the top failure has been selected it is possible to construct the tree diagram by identifying the causes as branches, before linking them with the two types of logic gate. The sub-branches of each main branch are then constructed in a similar way, until all the relevant causes are incorporated. A value must then be assigned to each cause to represent the probability of its occurrence. The final probability is determined from integration of the probabilities of all the causes. For complex systems, computers are employed to draw, display and work out the final probability.

Merits

The main merits of FTA are:

- In the case of a complex system the fault tree provides a good way of logically integrating various causes. Constructing the tree diagram and determining the probability values helps to provide a better understanding of the system.

- The fault tree can be used to do sensitivity analyses so that the relative importance of the various causes can be compared, i.e. the effect on the whole system if a change is made to the probability of one cause.

Drawbacks

The main drawbacks of this method are:

- Considerable experience and knowledge of the system are needed to construct a meaningful fault tree. Failure to incorporate a critical cause can readily provide an incorrect result.

- It can be difficult to select the most appropriate logic gates at the junctions and this could lead to widely varying probability values.

Example 12.1

The principles of fault tree analysis can be illustrated by this example in which a project engineer has to visit the country's capital city. Two factors to be taken into consideration are:

Trip opportunity: The main reasons for the trip are to take part in committee meetings, conferences, contract discussions and training courses.

Being able to go: This factor comprises the time available for the trip and the existence of funds allocated for travel.

The total number of trip opportunities to the capital is obtained by adding committee meetings, conferences, contract discussions and training courses, therefore an "OR" gate is used, i.e. 10+7+8+5 = 30 visit opportunities. The time available to go is 40% and funding available for the trips is 50%. Since an "AND" gate is selected, because one can only travel when there is time and funds, so the able to go probability becomes 0.4 x 0.5 = 0.20 or 20%. To determine the number of annual visits, account must be taken of both the opportunities to go and the ability to go at the same time, i.e. an AND gate. This leads to 30 x 0.2 = 6 or six trips per year.

The results are shown in figure 12.3 (overleaf). The result would be altered if more time or funds were available or additional assignments had to be carried out.

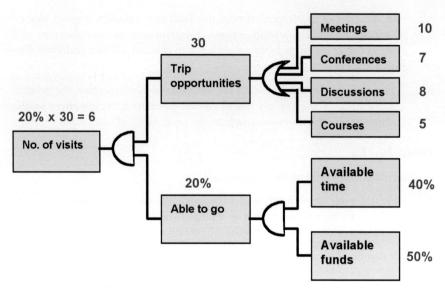

Figure 12.3 An example of a fault tree analysis

Application

This technique has been used extensively in industry, including the offshore and marine industries. It is particularly useful when applied in the early stages of a project, for example the concept, feasibility and detailed design phases. Properly applied it can help to reveal major causes of potential failure. Examples of marine applications can be found in Aldwinkle and Pomeroy (1983) and Spouge (1990).

12.6 Event tree analysis method

This method is also used to analyse the probability of occurrence but is less popular than the fault tree analysis method because binary logic is used in decision making.

Principle

A series of events or variables that can affect the safety of the situation, activity or system. Each are examined in turn using a binary logic and the process goes in one direction until the answer is obtained.

Description

The tree structure representation is made up of a number of columns for each of the events or variables. In each column there are a pair of horizontal lines which are used to give a "yes" or "no" answer for each event. Usually the yes horizontal line is then divided into two more horizontal lines while the no horizontal line is allowed to go straight to the end column. Using the available information and binary decision logic, the event is then taken forward to derive the outcome.

Merits

The main merits of the event tree are:

- It is very simple to construct and display. The skills needed to do the work can readily be acquired.

- The variables are taken one at a time and this, in turn, enables the problem to be examined step by step.

- A limited sensitivity analysis can also be performed to achieve a better understanding of the problem.

Drawbacks

The main drawbacks of this method are:

- It can only be used for relatively straightforward situations, activities or systems.

- The binary logic can be restrictive and inflexible for certain situations and more effort is needed than may be justified.

Application

It is used in situations when only a limited amount of data is available and, increasingly, the fault tree analysis method is being used for probability analysis.

Example 12.2

In this example, the same data used in the Fault Tree Analysis is used (see Section 12.4). The starting point would be the availability of time to go on the visit and this is followed by the availability of funds for making the trip. The results would be combined with the opportunity to go to the various functions to yield the number of trips made per year. Figure 12.4 illustrates the Event Tree diagram and it will be noted that in this straightforward problem the answers are the same for both methods.

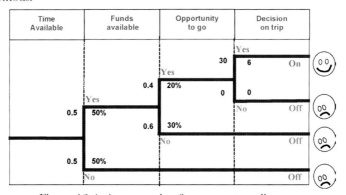

Figure 12.4 An example of an event tree diagram

12.7 An illustrative example

An example is now outlined, in order to illustrate how a quantitative risk assessment can be performed:

Step 1:   Background

The example is concerned with the risk of a supply ship and an offshore installation colliding during cargo transfer. This is a regular weekly operation, with the cranes on the offshore installation lifting containers from the supply ship's deck.

The problems that can lead to collision are the need for the supply ship to be relatively near the rig as the crane's reach is limited and the weather conditions can alter quickly, i.e. both magnitude and direction can change.

Information sought includes:

- Closeness of ship and rig.

- Position of the ship relative to the rig, e.g. stern-on position, side-on position.

- Weather e.g. strength and direction of wind, waves and current.

- Visibility, e.g. mist and fog.

- Ship performance characteristics, e.g. power available, response time.

- Crew experience, e.g. ship handling skills, number of trips made.

- Tightness of schedule, e.g. half a day, a few hours.

- Presence of other ships, e.g. delay in operation.

Step 2:   Consequence modelling

Key tasks include:

- Identifying the critical parameters.

- Selecting ship motion software.

- Simulating ship operating near the rig.

- Formulating a collision situation, e.g.

    Impact force = $f(M_s, A_s)$.

    f : function.

    M_s: ship's mass.

    A_s: ship's acceleration.

- Calculating collision force.

- Estimating damage scenarios.

Step 3:   Analyse the probability of occurrence

A Fault Tree can be constructed using the following data:

*   Poor weather   : 60 days/year (0.164 per year).

*   Engine failure   : 5 days loss per year (0.014 per year).

*   Bulk containers   : Twice a week (0.286 per year).

*   Senior crew   : Present 75% of time (during the transfer i.e. about 0.071 per year).

Use relation $P = (0.164 + 0.014) \times (0.286 \times 0.071) = 0.004$

It should be noted that the first two items relate to working near the rig and each can cause an accident. The latter two items are concerned with quick transfer when both items are active. All the items influence the likelihood of a ship-rig collision. The fault tree derived is given in figure 12.5.

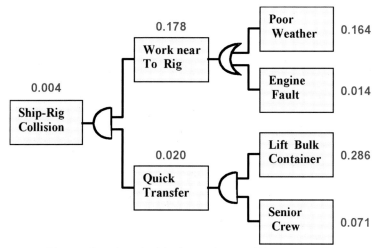

Figure 12.5 A typical fault tree for an offshore operation

The points to note are:

*   Check "local" probabilities and logic gates.

*   Do sensitivity tests by varying the values of local probabilities and changing the type of logic gates.

Step 4:   Do a risk assessment

The tasks of this step involve the following:

*   Obtain risk using the relationship $R = C \times P$.

*   Try to acquire a physical interpretation.

*   Place the hazard on the risk scale.

- Compare with results obtained from a qualitative risk assessment.

12.8 Acquiring relevant statistics

It can be seen from the foregoing section that in order to determine the risk level of a hazard, use has to be made of statistical information relating to the operation, activity or project. Unfortunately, relevant statistical information is a "rarity" for two reasons. Firstly, accident statistics were not gathered systematically in the past and there is, therefore, a lack of data. Secondly, the available information is often not gathered consistently and, as a result, its users cannot be sure whether a set of data is really applicable to the situation in question. In spite of these problems, information has to be used with the appropriate assumptions while bearing in mind its scope of applicability. As a general guide, the following sources of information should be given attention.

General accident statistics

Many publications, e.g. HSE (1992-1), Home Office (1990), provide data on the risk of a particular activity. Such data give general trends although they are not suitable for direct use in quantitative assessments. Typical examples would be "deaths per person per year" in an activity or "accidents per passenger kilometre".

Marine accident claims

Insurance companies compile statistics relating to accidents and claims. By far the most meaningful sets of statistics on marine accidents are presented in the publications of the UK P&I Club of Insurers (Protection and Indemnity). These include reports covering five-year periods, e.g. 1987-1992, 1988-1993, 1991-1996. A typical useful publication is Analysis of Major Claims 1996 (see P&I Club (1996). These analyses are very detailed and cover around 1,500 claims valued at over US$700 million. The reasons for them range from cargo damage and pollution to collision damage and injury to both crew and other personnel. A typical sample of the information provided is given in figure 12.6.

Accident location	Percentage of Total Accidents
Weather Deck	41%
Engine Room	14%
Hold	12%
Ashore	8%
Cabins	7%
Galley	5%
Tween Deck	4%
Other	6%

Figure 12.6 Percentages of accidents/injuries and locations of the occurrence

Accident statistics of special ships

Good records of accidents do exist for certain types of ship, e.g. high speed craft. The information has been specifically gathered because these ships are of a new type and the operating companies have made a concerted effort to record contributors. Generally speaking, the information tends to concentrate on certain areas where many of these ships are operating and its use may well need careful scrutiny. An example of the data obtained for high speed craft is summarised in figure 12.7. This information provides a basis for more detailed study.

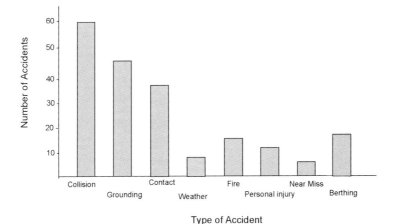

Figure 12.7 Typical accidents associated with high speed craft

Accident databases

Some organisations have focused on developing databases of accidents and incidents. The accident information is presented systematically and in some cases correlation is available as well. Typical examples include:

a) *Marine Information Systems*: Data on ship accidents and other information is available, and offered usually on a commercial basis, e.g. Lloyd's register offers such a service. Data sheets are provided following searches based on key words.

b) *Marine Accident Investigation Branch (MAIB) reports*: In the UK a percentage of accidents, usually involving fatalities, are investigated by MAIB which is a part of the government's responsibility for transport. Reports are available and databases are accessible on the web.

c) *Marine Accident Report System (MARS)*: Seafarers can give their experience on incidents and accidents confidentially to a designated individual who collects the information and presented in a form that can be readily accessed on the web. The reports do not use any standard format and represent the views of maritime personnel and the main aim is to provide lessons learnt for others. The service is provided by The Nautical Institute.

d) *Worldwide Offshore Accident Database (WOAD)*: This database of offshore accidents began collecting data in 1970 and has been published since 1983. Users of the data usually subscribe to the provider and the information is updated annually, see DNV (2004).

Presentation of practical data

It is also possible to present data gathered from practice graphically by plotting the F-N curve. F represents the frequency of N or more fatalities over a given period such as a year. It is normal practice to use the logarithmic scale on both the vertical and horizontal axes. This makes it possible to establish regions where the risk levels are intolerable, tolerable and negligible. For further discussion see HSE (1992-1).

12.9 A risk assessment strategy

Taking into account the contents of Chapters 11 and 12 it is now possible to adopt a strategy for doing risk assessment for any situation, activity or system. The sequence of actions is:

- Understand the background of the situation, activity or system.

- Perform a qualitative risk assessment so that the risks of hazard are placed in appropriate locations on the risk scale.

- Select the critical hazards with high risk levels and perform a quantitative risk assessment on them.

- Compare the risk values obtained by the two methods and note any items of interest.

- Draw general conclusions on the safety of the situation, activity or system.

12.10 Conclusions

(a) Quantitative risk assessment can provide more accurate locations on the risk scale but success relies on the availability of reliable and consistent input data.

(b) To do quantitative risk assessment requires more effort than qualitative risk assessment. It should be done only for critical hazards with high risk levels.

(c) To gain the full benefit from quantitative risk assessment, the results should be examined carefully while gaining a physical interpretation.

Chapter 13

RISK REDUCTION

13.1 Introduction

Risk reduction is the third element, or Step 3 of the Safety Scheme and is illustrated in figure 13.1.

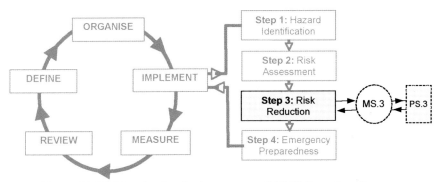

Figure 13.1 Risk reduction in the context of GMS for safety diagram

The aims of this chapter are as follows:

(a)   To give the main reasons for risk reduction.

(b)   To outline the basis of the approach and methods of risk reduction.

(c)   To consider the cost-effectiveness of risk reduction via the As Low As Reasonably Practicable (ALARP) principle.

(d)   To propose a new method of addressing the subject.

13.2 Why reduce risk?

Before examining the approaches and methods of reducing risk, it will be useful to clarify in our own minds what risk reduction is and why is there a need to reduce risk.

As explained earlier, the hazards of a situation, activity or system are distributed in a number of risk regions and the popular approach is to adopt a 3-region risk presentation, given the names of intolerable, tolerable and negligible regions. Risk reduction is a term used to describe the moving of a hazard from one location higher on the risk scale to a lower location. Figure 13.2 (overleaf) illustrates the process graphically.

There are a number of reasons and some are practical and can be regarded as logical, scientific or ethical. These are now given under the following headings:

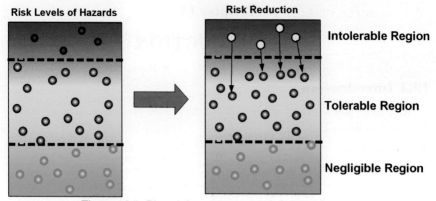

Figure 13.2 Pictorial representation of risk reduction

a)   Reducing the danger level

Safety is a non-absolute quality and different people have different perceptions, but in general risk level signals some form of danger. Because safety is multi-dimensional and involves interaction with humans, hazards with intolerable risk would be regarded as high danger, that could affect life, property and the environment. It could be argued that everyone has a stake in the situation, activity and system and it would be morally wrong to ignore or do nothing about hazards with high risk levels.

(b)   Uncertainty in risk determination

The techniques outlined in estimating the values of risk, by qualitative or quantitative methods, cannot expect to achieve high accuracy because of personal perception, the non-absoluteness of safety and problems associated with acquiring the relevant data on accidents and near misses. For this reason, we cannot be totally confident that a hazard with a tolerable risk level located near the intolerable region is indeed tolerable. In these circumstances it would be wise to make attempts at lowering the risk level away from the intolerable region.

(c)   Statutory requirements

In situations, activities and systems that involve many users, or accidents which could have a very high consequence, the government authority or its agency requires that the risk of hazards be assessed and reduced in the interest of the public. For example, the Health and Safety Executive (HSE) of the UK government has a statutory power to demand and verify that an offshore installation has the risk levels of selected hazards reduced to As Low As Reasonably Practicable (ALARP), i.e. apply the ALARP principle to reduce the risk for the installation.

(d)   Design for safety culture

By giving attention to risk reduction at the concept or design stage of a product's life-cycle, it will assist designers to propose ideas which would do the job effectively and are safer. In general, designers tend to use only engineering solutions to improve safety. Risk reduction will help in developing a "design for safety culture" that can lead to encouraging the use of a range of methods for achieving the target amount of risk reduction.

(e)   Risk reduction skills

Skills acquired in risk reduction can have uses beyond safety and should help in addressing non-safety related everyday issues. For example, the methods can be applied to decision making in activities such as purchasing a house, investing in a venture or borrowing money.

13.3 Basic approach

As a result of risk assessment it can be seen that hazards are distributed throughout the intolerable, tolerable and negligible risk regions. It is, of course, essential to reduce those in the intolerable region to the tolerable region, but it may not be cost-effective to move any from the tolerable to the negligible region. Bearing in mind that there are bound to be hazards in any system, activity or project, it would be useful to establish a number of fundamental guidelines for risk reduction.

Hazards in the intolerable region

Eliminate the hazards with intolerable risk levels. This should be done by using appropriate methods to reduce them. If, however, it is impossible to achieve risk reduction cost-effectively, serious consideration should be given to abandoning the project, activity or system for another option.

Hazards in the tolerable region

Consider whether it is worthwhile to reduce hazards in this region by asking two basic questions:

(a)   Is the hazard close to the intolerable region?

(b)   Can the reduction be done cost-effectively?

An affirmative answer in the first case might well involve risk reduction even if it proved expensive. In the latter case a positive answer would indicate that it is sensible to reduce that particular hazard because the process is cost-effective, regardless of its actual location in the tolerable region.

Hazards in the negligible region

It is recommended that these hazards should be left alone, as it would probably not be worthwhile trying to reduce their risk levels further. However, the risk levels of hazards in this region should be re-examined from time to time, to check whether they have moved up the risk level scale due to interaction with other hazards.

Risk reduction options

There are three basic options within the approach for risk reductions:

- Reduce the severity of consequence (C): This is usually possible in the early design stages of a project's life cycle.

- Reduce the probability of occurrence (P): This can usually be done at any stage of a project's life cycle.

- Reduce both C and P: This can offer greater flexibility.

Reduction can be achieved by means of management methods, engineering methods, operational methods or a combination of the three types. These methods will now be examined and illustrated by examples.

13.4 The management method

Solutions under this heading involve activities related to the management of the organisation. It should be noted that effective communication plays a key role in achieving success. The most important solution is connection with the development of a safety culture. The key features of this are people's attitude to safety, their behaviour in a safety context, and making it "normal practice" to carry out tasks in a safe manner. The other solution would be a willingness to put resources into the training of staff, specifically in safety matters, in order to enhance the safety competence of each individual.

Merits

The main merits of this method are:

- It can address the real problem involving human factors.

- It can provide positive leadership in the development of a safety culture in the organisation.

Drawbacks

The main drawbacks of this method are:

- Generating a safety culture can take a long time.

- It is difficult to measure the advances that have been made.

- It takes a lot of effort to achieve effective communication, in particular on board ships with multicultural and multilingual crews.

Application of this set of methods will now be illustrated by an example.

Example 13.1 The use of management solutions

Background

Concern has been expressed that when high speed craft, such as Stena Line's HSS 1500, are operating at speeds in excess of 40 knots in congested waters, the risk level of the collision hazard would become intolerable. The operator could therefore be asked to put forward management methods for reducing this risk level.

Solutions

Two possible management related methods are:

- The use of a simulator for training: To provide all intended masters and navigators of these high speed craft with simulator training before they are given control of a vessel. The main emphasis of this training should be becoming familiar with the bridge, gaining hands-on experience of the controls and the reactions of the craft and trying out emergency procedures.

- Crew resource management training: To give crew resource management training to all masters, navigators and engineers. This training is aimed at encouraging teamwork and using team members to derive important decisions, e.g. the master should consult the navigator on the various options before taking a critical decision.

13.5 The engineering method

Typical solutions arising from this method involve the design or construction of the ship. They can include modifying the structural design or arrangements and installing additional safety equipment. Those with technical training find the engineering method the easiest to accept and understand.

Merits

The key merits of the method are:

- The solutions are clearly visible, e.g. the introduction of double hulls in tankers in order to prevent oil pollution in the event of grounding.

- The solutions are particularly suitable for new designs when the risk reduction options are considered during the pre-contract phase.

Drawbacks

There are several drawbacks, of which the key ones are:

- A proposed solution may not readily be introduced into an existing ship or system.

- With possible exceptions in the case of a new design, engineering solutions are generally very expensive, particularly when modifications are required.

- The solutions may not address the real problem, e.g. the double hull requirement for oil tankers stems from an accident caused by failings of a navigator, a problem which will not be addressed in any way by the new design feature.

Example 13.2 The use of engineering solutions

Background

Contact between high speed craft and a pier or another fixed object is a frequent occurrence. Although no life is endangered, any damage to the craft does have to be repaired and this means that it has to be taken out of service for a certain amount of time, leading to loss of revenue. It is therefore desirable to have engineering methods for reducing the risk level of this hazard.

Solution

Two possible solutions are suggested here:

- Introducing Special Fenders: It is possible to reduce the amount of contact damage suffered by the craft by installing suitable fenders on piers that they are likely to use.

- Installing Intelligent Sensors: Position sensors, responding to the trim and heel of the craft, can be installed to provide early feedback to the navigator undertaking the docking procedure.

13.6 The operational method

Typical solutions used in the operational method of risk reduction involve devising appropriate procedures for doing safety-critical tasks and improving the competence of personnel in these tasks by regular practice. Operational solutions are particularly useful, as designers often do not appreciate precisely how a given design will be used in practice and hence its safety implications.

Merits

The key merits of this method are:

- It can address issues concerning human factors, such as the attitude towards doing a task in a safe manner.

- It can also ensure that common safety standards are adopted.

Drawbacks

There are several drawbacks and these include:

- Prescribed operational procedures may inhibit personal initiative, e.g. a procedure has to be followed although it is not fully effective in practice.

- There is a need for extensive training and practice before the required competence can be achieved in many areas of operation.

Application of this set of methods is now illustrated by an example.

Example 13.3 The use of operational solutions

Background

Possible grounding is a hazard, which is of concern to all ship operators. This is particularly true when the vessel has to be navigated in unfamiliar waters or where tidal conditions are subject to wide variations. It would therefore be useful to have operational methods for reducing the risk level of this hazard.

Solution

Two possible solutions are suggested here:

- Grounding Avoidance Procedure: An operational procedure should be introduced on board the vessel which requires route planning to be formally carried out by the navigators and their colleagues before each trip

- Supervised Approach: Introduce a procedure whereby a senior master is required to provide hand-holding guidance on the first two occasions to any navigator who has not used the port in question before.

13.7 The combined method

In the last three sections attention has been focused on the use of management, engineering and operational methods for risk reduction, but in practice it is usually necessary to employ a combination of the three. In a typical example, risk reduction can be achieved by introducing a modified piece of equipment into the ship or system, providing a new operational procedure for its use and devoting resources to training crew members, so that they reach the desired level of competence in using that equipment safely. In addition, it may be useful to educate the crew so that members develop a positive attitude to the use of the modified equipment.

Merits

The key merits of the combined method are:

- It addresses the real issues involved.

- A more complete solution can be achieved by this method than by any of the other three alone.

Drawbacks

The main drawbacks are:

- It can be quite difficult to achieve the correct balance of the three methods involved.

- It can also be time-consuming and expensive to achieve the required solution because of the amount of discussion required of management, engineering and operational methods.

Application of this method is illustrated by an example.

Example 13.4 The use of combined solutions

Background

In general the risk level of a hazard can be reduced by a combination of management, engineering and operational methods. Fire in the galley of a passenger ferry is used to illustrate the application of these various risk reduction methods to a single hazard.

Solution

Three possible solutions are suggested here:

- <u>Education on Fire Hazards</u>: Management should encourage every member of the crew to develop a positive attitude towards the prevention of fire, to recognise the importance of this, and to report likely causes to whoever is responsible for the galley.

- <u>Installing More Sensitive Fire Detectors</u>: Install fire detectors with higher sensitivity in locations where it has been identified that fires are more likely to occur.

- <u>Devising Procedures for Dealing with Fire</u>: Establish an operational procedure for fighting fire and preventing it from spreading, carrying out regular fire drills to enhance crew readiness.

13.8 The ALARP principle

In determining how much risk reduction should be done and whether possible solutions are cost–effective, use is made of the principle As Low As Reasonably Practicable (known as ALARP). The term was introduced by the UK Health and Safety Executive (HSE) and derived from a legal interpretation of a court judgement (see HSE 1992-1).

> *The methods of reducing the risk level of a hazard can be put in one scale and balanced against the effort needed in another. The effort may be represented by money, time, or a combination of the two. If it can be shown that there is a gross imbalance between the two, e.g. the reduction in risk level is insignificant compared with the cost of implementing the proposed solution, it would not be reasonably practicable to go ahead.*

The UK HSE has produced a general guideline in the form of a diagram as given in figure 13.3:

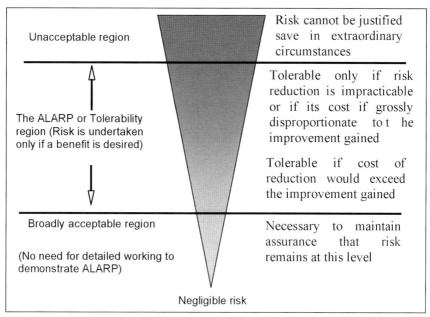

Figure 13.3 The UK HSE's risk diagram

The rationale behind the UK HSE presentation can be summarised as follows:

• The inverted triangle means that a high risk hazard should be pushed down towards the negligible risk region.

• The tolerable region would be the ALARP region, i.e. all the hazards in this region have to be examined to see if they could have their risk level reduced further.

This has been a UK legal requirement for the ALARP principle to be applied when the safety of a system or equipment that involves a large number of users is being considered.

The UK HSE presentation has several basic faults which can be stated as follows:

(a) The inverted triangle tends to suggest that in any situation, activity or system there are more hazards in the intolerable region than in the other two regions. In practice, very few hazards have intolerable risk and the majority have tolerable and negligible risk levels.

(b) By calling the intolerable risk region an "unacceptable" risk region it is confusing a proposal with a "ruling" or "decision". As discussed earlier in Section 5.6, it is important to differentiate between tolerability and acceptability. It will be noted that the risk regions are defined by a team involved in safety assessment, and it may use information from various sources to determine the tolerability for each of the regions. It is possible to accept a situation that has intolerable risk, e.g. the pressure of a job is intolerable but there are no comparable jobs available and there are also heavy financial commitments. The boundaries are not absolute and would change with time, e.g. what was accepted in the year 1920 by the crew on board ships would not be accepted in the year 2005. Hence, it has to be recognised that acceptance is a decision and tolerability is a proposal.

(c)   Since there are many hazards in the tolerable risk region, it is inefficient and unnecessary to apply the ALARP principle to all of them. It would be more sensible to focus resources on fewer and more "special" hazards.

A suggestion on how to overcome this weakness is given in section 13.9.

13.9 The 4 region risk presentation

The main criticism of the 3 region risk presentation is that the boundary between the intolerable and tolerable regions is a single line (see figure 13.3). This means, in practice, that the decision with regard to acceptable and unacceptable risk levels becomes much finer than the accuracy achievable in determining the value of risk. For example, if the boundary takes a value of 10^{-3}, it is not difficult to visualise a decision whereby a value of 0.999×10^{-3} would allow the risk to be in the tolerable (acceptable) region and a value of 1.001×10^{-3} would class it in the risk in the intolerable (unacceptable) region. To overcome the problem, a 4 region risk presentation is proposed. In this presentation a region called the 'uncertain region' is introduced between the intolerable and tolerable regions (see figure 13.4).

The merits of this presentation are:

(a)   It makes the boundary between intolerable and tolerable regions less sensitive to the estimated risk values.

(b)   The width of the uncertain region will indicate the degree of understanding of the situation, activity or system. For example, a large width would show there is little knowledge and a narrow width would show the opposite.

(c)   By applying the ALARP principle only to the risk inside the uncertain region, focused efforts would be devoted to reducing critical risks.

There remains the question of how the uncertain region is to be determined. A number of methods can be used to evaluate the spread of the risk region and the most useful would be based on fuzzy logic which is ideal for items with uncertain features.

13.10 The ALARP and Pareto principles

It is worthwhile taking a closer look at the ALARP principle. Since risk reduction involves both the effort needed and the risk level reduction achieved, the term implies that an attempt may be made to achieve a balance between the two. Effort can be measured by means of the cost involved or the time spent, or

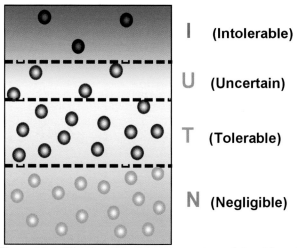

Figure 13.4 The 4 region risk presentation of the risk scale

a combination of the two. "Reasonably" demands that the appropriate effort is expended to achieve a given reduction of risk. "Practicable" really holds the key, in that – regardless of cost, time or effort – if a risk reduction method is not practical it will be unsuitable.

It can be argued that the ALARP principle is too vague and could be interpreted in many ways. In practice, however, different kinds of ships and systems are operated by different methods and ALARP is no more than a principle to be adapted to individual situations.

It is possible to consider the ALARP principle in another way, by plotting risk reduction of effort against the risk level reduction achieved (see figure 13.5, overleaf) for a typical curve giving the general trend. It can be seen that, at the start, significant risk reduction can be achieved with a relatively small amount of effort. The effort increases rapidly when further risk reduction is required and the effect is to make the curve very steep as it approaches the ideal.

It should be noted in figure 13.5 that the risk reduced axis is divided into three zones: "Cost-effective", "Rising cost", "Extreme cost", and the ALARP principle is really applicable only in the cost-effective zone. In practical terms, not all the hazards will follow the curve precisely but the shape does provide a useful trend for general application.

It will be noted that the curve looks similar to the curve which shows the Pareto principle. This principle is due to Pareto, an 18th century Italian economist, who noted that 80% of Italy's worth was in the hands of 20% of the people. When this was applied to other instances, situations and events, the same trend also applied. In a general context, the principle can be stated as follows:

20% of the effort applied will achieve 80% of the goal while the remaining 80% of effort will be needed to meet the remaining 20% of the goal.

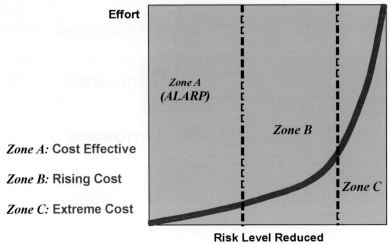

Figure 13.5 The proposed effort versus risk level reduced diagram

The principle is also known as the "80-20 rule" and has a universal applicability.

As an example, a high speed craft with a top speed of 50 knots is proposed and someone suggests exploring the possibility of increasing the speed by 10% to 55 knots. The cost would now be in zone C of figure 13.5. An experienced ship designer suggests that the cost increase would be at least 100% because the craft would be at the top end of our knowledge, a new power plant would be needed, research would have to be done and tests performed.

Applying the Pareto principle to the curve given in figure 13.5, it is possible to make the following comments:

- Zone A: The first 40% of risk can be reduced with 10% of the effort.

- Zone B: The second 40% of risk can be reduced with 30% of the effort.

- Zone C: The final 20% of risk reduced will require 50% of the effort.

It is, therefore, not surprising that only Zone A would be regarded as the risk reduction which satisfies the ALARP condition.

13.11 Cost-benefit analysis methods

The cost benefit analysis or CBA methods have been applied in many subject areas to assist in decision making. The basic concept is to put costs and benefits on a common basis, usually in monetary terms, so that a comparison can be made between various possible options. In this way, the decisions made can be regarded as objective rather than subjective. In the context of safety, the methodology is used to relate the costs of various risk reduction options achieving some desired benefits and thereby enabling broad comparisons to be made in a consistent manner.

The idea can be readily understood and its usage seems logical. It is therefore not surprising that a statutory requirement has been made by the prescribing authority for a cost benefit analysis to be performed when the safety of major projects is examined. The purpose is to determine whether the risk levels regarded as "tolerable" can be further reduced cost-effectively.

However, the practical application of the CBA methods is far less straight forward for various reasons and the key ones are as follows:

• Since safety is dependent on personal perception the benefits would to a certain extent be difficult to determine precisely and there is therefore a need to make assumptions. However, they can influence significantly the results. Thus using valid assumptions that represent what actually happens in practice would yield valuable results. Incorrect assumptions, on the other hand, can give misleading results.

• There is no direct correlation between costs and benefits, i.e. the costs relating to safety matters are not constant over time with usually a high initial cost followed by lower yearly maintenance or recurring costs. Thus it is necessary to work out average costs and average benefits.

• The costs and benefits generally arise in different time periods. It is the usual trend to spend money up front or early to implement a risk reduction measure, whereas benefits can occur every year. In order to cater for this feature it is necessary to apply discounting before making the comparison. It is the common practice to select an appraisal period e.g. 10 years, and discount all the costs and benefits arising each year to the first year of the appraisal period.

• The results of a CBA can depend on the persons carrying out the study and the organization they represent. For example a government department representing the public interest might require a CBA to take into account the full cost of a pollution incident as part of a safety assessment. A shipping company which operates a fleet of crude oil carriers, might take into account the compensation available through the civil liability convention which provides one type of industrial insurance.

It is useful to illustrate how various items have to be evaluated in performing a cost benefit analysis under the main headings of costs and benefits.

Costs

There are three principal costs areas and they are concerned with personal injuries, property damages and impacts on the environment.

(a) Human costs: For this item it is necessary to assign monetary values for averting a fatality or what is called "cost per statistical fatality averted". This can be expressed in whatever is the preferred currency, e.g. UK pounds, Euros or US dollars.

This approach is attractive because the concept can be readily understood, but its practical implementation requires a number of "value judgments" involving components such as the valuation of life, see Fleshman and Hogh (1989) for further discussion on this point. Two popular approaches to the valuation of life are "human capital" and "willingness to pay", and it would be useful to discuss briefly the bases of these treatments.

- *Human Capital*: This approach assumes that individuals may be regarded as a special type of equipment whose potential output would be lost as a result of premature demise. Life is therefore equated to the value of a person's potential earnings plus a notional sum for the "pain, grief and suffering" experienced by those affected by his or her death. This valuation was given in 1989 as £2 x 10^{-5} per statistical fatality averted, and the figure was derived from studies done on radiological protection and road accidents in the UK see Radiation Board (1980). In more recent years, the figure is £3 million per statistical fatality averted, see HSE (2004).

- *Willingness to Pay*: This approach was devised to overcome recognised deficiencies in the previous approach, such as failure to consider the preferences of those at risk. The calculation is based on peoples "willingness to pay" for either risk reduction or compensation to those involved in activities with a higher level of risk. Dawson (1967) showed that the approximate value of life is counted in millions of pounds sterling.

(b   <u>Property costs</u>: The calculations would be based on the estimated replacement or repair costs for the damages caused to the ship plus revenue lost if the ship is out of service and unable to trade i.e the lost opportunity costs when the vessel is being repaired. The costs are time dependent but can be more readily defined.

(c)   <u>Environmental costs</u>: The costs involved are made up of two parts. Firstly, when the environment is polluted, e.g. oil spillage, there would be a cost for clean up. The actual amount of money can vary considerably depending on where this occurred and the responsibility of the parties involved. Secondly, compensation has to be paid to those affected by the spillage such as loss of earnings or the inability to perform normal business activities. Disputes can arise when deciding on the amount of compensation.

Benefits

In the context of safety the main benefits would be for reducing the risk level by a specific amount in association with the three items considered in previous sections. In the case of humans, the most important benefit would be to reduce the risk of serious personal injuries. Likewise the benefits for the latter two would be to reduce the risks or avert property damage and pollution of the environment.

However, it has to be recognised that it is always possible to put forward arguments for devoting more effort and money to reducing risk. The role of CBA methods is to examine the various options in order to derive the most cost-effective solution or be able to offer solutions which are value for money. The latter is the thinking behind the ALARP (As Low As Reasonably Practicable) concept and its usage for decision making. Bearing in mind that safety is not something absolute, there is no guarantee that investing a certain amount of money would yield the desired amount of benefits. This statement seems to contradict the case for doing cost benefit analyses but it has to be realised that it is the thinking behind applying the CBA methods which is most valuable. Once a habit is developed so that all solutions are examined from a CBA prospective, it is then that the results for specific situations can become more meaningful and informative for decision making.

13.12 Conclusions

(a)   The risk levels of hazards should be reduced by addressing both their consequences and the probability of occurrence using a combination of management, engineering and operation based methods.

(b)   The idea that risk should be reduced to As Low As Reasonably Practicable (ALARP) is sound but there has to be a more usable method of implementing it in practice.

(c)   It would be helpful to divide risk into four regions — intolerable, uncertain, tolerable and negligible so that the ALARP principle is applied only to hazards with risks in the uncertain region.

(d)   Cost benefit analysis methods are useful in assisting decision making in the selection of risk reduction options, but it is important to ensure that the assumptions used provide a realistic representation of the practical situation.

Chapter 14

EMERGENCY PREPAREDNESS

14.1 Introduction

This chapter is concerned with the fourth element of the safety case scheme, namely emergency preparedness. Its position in the context of the concept is shown in figure 14.1.

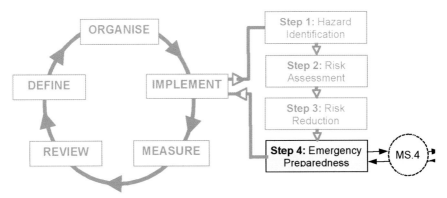

Figure 14.1 Emergency preparedness in the context of GMS for safety diagram

The aims of this chapter are, therefore, as follows:

(a)   To explain why emergency preparedness is needed in safety management.

(b)   To outline the principal activities involved in preparing for an emergency.

(c)   To examine the key issues relating to treating an emergency.

(d)   To illustrate the implementation with an example.

14.2 What is emergency preparedness?

It has to be recognised that no matter how carefully the previous three elements of the safety case scheme are implemented, the chance of an accident occurring is still there, mainly because of human involvement. The role of emergency preparedness is that of being completely ready to take action when an unexpected event or accident occurs, or an incident threatens to become serious, in order to minimise injury to personnel, damage to or loss of property, or pollution of the environment. See figure 14.2 for an illustration of emergency preparedness. The goal of emergency preparedness can be stated as follows:

> *To be prepared to take the most appropriate actions and to respond rapidly in the event that a significant hazard becomes a reality in order to minimise its effects.*

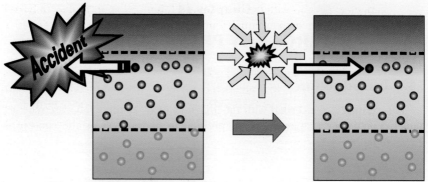

Figure 14.2 Pictorial representation of emergency preparedness

Emergency preparedness can be defined as:

The thinking and planning anticipating the possible event of an accident occurring, together with the steps needed to be taken to ensure people can be moved from a location with hazard(s) having high risk level to one with lower risk levels.

This definition can be explained with the aid of an example. If a fire breaks out on board a ship, the first step would be to investigate its seriousness followed by taking appropriate decisions, informing key parties, attending to the injured and containing the spread. Evacuation would only take place if it could be ascertained that the seriousness of the fire is more threatening than the current sea-state, i.e. if the likelihood of being burnt is stronger than the dangers of exposure to the sea environment.

It should be noted that time limits have been set up for the total series of activities, e.g. 30 minutes to evacuate a passenger ferry, and critical path methods need to be used to ensure that such targets can be met.

14.3 The need for emergency preparedness

There are several reasons why it is essential to prepare for emergencies and the main ones are:

(a) <u>Safety is not absolute</u>

It has been explained earlier that safety is not absolute, i.e. there is no fixed standard to be met and everyone has his or her perception as to what is safe and what is not safe. Thus in any situation, activity or system we need to give thought in advance to the possibility that a significant hazard may become a reality.

(b) <u>Humans can make mistakes</u>

Human error is a well recognised problem and its occurrences can cause accidents. For example, a momentary loss of concentration while following a well-established and familiar routine has led to major accidents. This can happen to persons with the best training. It is therefore important to be well prepared for such an eventuality in advance.

(c)   Developing good practice

For products such as ships and offshore installations it is good practice for designers, operators and other stakeholders to think and plan ahead. This will lead to better products and efficient operations. In the long term it will help to generate a positive safety culture.

(d)   Statutory requirements

For equipment which is used by people or for rigs that have people working on them, e.g. a floating offshore installation, it is a statutory requirement that a plan for treating emergencies should be submitted and given approval before it is formally allowed to operate.

14.4 Approaches to preparing for emergency

When an emergency occurs, such as a fire outbreak on board a passenger ship, the following actions would take place and some of them in parallel:

•   Moving people to assembly points from cabins, lounges, dining rooms, theatres and other locations used by passengers.

•   Containing the fire so as to prevent it from spreading.

•   Abandoning the ship using lifeboats, life raft and marine escape systems.

•   Rescuing people from the boats and craft from the sea.

In general, a number of approaches can be adopted to treat emergency preparedness and they tend to place emphasis on either design or operation. Each will now be briefly reviewed.

Approach 1: Assess design for evacuation
Background

After a ship is designed and built, for various reasons — mainly regulatory ones — studies are made to determine how long it will take to move people to assembly points, and then the time taken to evacuate in lifeboats and craft. Computer simulation techniques could be used, with selected passenger/crew populations located at various parts of the ship. Actual exercises, with people taking part, are performed and timed so as to provide data for correlation with computer simulation. Results obtained would be compared with benchmarks for similar types of ship.

Merits

The main merits are:

•   The designs are studied scientifically to derive information for indicating how long it would need to evacuate people from one location to another.

- Information obtained can improve future designs.

- Greater appreciation can be gained by those operating the ships.

- It can identify where bottlenecks are and allow ways to be found for releasing them.

Drawbacks

The main ones are:

- After the ship is built, there is only limited scope for changes without involving high costs and disrupting operations.

- The computer simulation may not provide data on what actually happens in practice.

Application

This approach is increasingly being used as a part of emergency preparedness because of the requirements of various authorities, e.g. The UK Health and Safety Executive require this type of information in the safety cases for offshore installations. The International Maritime Organization (IMO) asks for similar studies for passenger vessels.

Comments

This is a positive step forward but because the analyses are done after the ship is built, the approach tends to be reactive rather than proactive.

Approach 2: Design for ease of evacuation

Background

When a ship is designed, there are many factors to be satisfied within a series of constraints. This is even more challenging for passenger ships, where there could be a very large number of passengers and crew. In this approach, the design goal is not confined to achieving the highest performance specification but includes a "design for ease of evacuation" component. Computer simulation would be used to compare alternative layouts so as to enhance evacuation times.

Merits

The main merits are:

- This is a proactive approach that allows alternatives to be considered before a decision is made.

- It makes good use of advances in computer technology and software developments.

- It encourages designers to give adequate attention to issues relating to emergency preparedness.

Drawbacks

The only drawback relates to the need to educate designers and operators in this thinking and approach. It can also take time to achieve the desired standard.

Application

This approach is being introduced into the design of new passenger and cruise ships where there are thousands of passengers and crew on board.

Comments

Design for ease of evacuation is the best way to link design with emergency preparedness and should be adopted into the thinking of all maritime stakeholders.

Approach 3: Gathering of full scale data

Background

There is a belief that practical data are needed to prepare for the emergency evacuation of passengers from ships. Two methods have been used to gather full scale data. Firstly, information from volunteers is gathered on board. They are moved from various locations and timed, with video recordings of movements being made. The information gained is analysed to assist operations on board ships. Secondly, strictly conducted exercises can be performed on mock-ups of a section of the ship, e.g. moving people along a sloping passenger way or stair. The data from these sources can then be used to improve the understanding of evacuation.

Merits

The main merits are:

- Valuable real data are gathered and video recordings provide useful insights into potential problems.
- Data can be used to interface with and verify computer simulation.

Drawbacks

The drawbacks are:

- It is extremely difficult to reproduce real emergency scenarios, e.g. volunteers tend to be able bodied persons, generally young and are not a true representative sample.
- Data provide trends rather than specific results.

- It is very costly to acquire the facilities and do the exercises.

Application

This approach is used to acquire data for research purpose in order to assist the development of more representative computer simulation programs.

Comments

These exercises are valuable for developing effective computer simulation solutions and the data obtained, together with assumptions, should be made generally available to assist other researchers.

Approach 4: Operational computer simulation

Background

In this approach, computer simulation techniques are used to model all aspects of evacuation, such as ship's layout and dimensions, people's characteristics and their likely behavioural trends, door locations and dimensions and obstacles. The simulation provides displays so that a visual view is available on how groups of people move in a given environment.

Merits

The main merits are:

- A total evacuation can be studied.
- A tool is available to assist ship operators.
- Visual pictures of evacuation are displayed and will be valuable in the training of the crew for effective management of people movement.

Drawbacks

The main drawbacks are:

- There is no real check on the simulation model unless full scale data are gathered.
- It is costly to develop appropriate computer programs and they are generally difficult to use.

Application

This approach will be a very valuable in the development of very large passenger and cruise ships.

Comments

This is a useful way forward and care should be exercised to ensure that the capability of advanced computer technology does not blur the goal of evacuation.

14.5 The emergency plan

The term "emergency preparedness" implies that there is a plan and a number of responses have to be ready for implementation should an unexpected accident occur. The plan involves having policies for dealing with emergencies. Typical examples include assigning responsibility to crew members for helping passengers to reach the assembly points quickly and safely and, if required, assisting in the evacuation process using lifeboats and marine escape systems (MES). For ships there are general guidelines, e.g. IMO's International Code for High Speed Craft, IMO (1995), which addresses all the relevant issues.

In practical terms there are eight tasks or activities which must be given advanced consideration for hazards which have a significant risk level. These tasks are grouped under separate headings as follows:

• Investigating an incident.

• Deciding what to do about it.

• Communicating internally and externally to key people.

• Attending to the injured personnel.

• Containing the causes in order to minimise effects.

• Escaping from more endangered areas to assembly points.

• Evacuating personnel from the ship.

• Rescuing those evacuated from the sea.

These eight activities will generally follow the sequence indicated above, but the length of time involved for each one will vary and some could take place in parallel. For example, attending the injured and communicating can take place at the same time. The decision made at each stage, together with the outcome of each activity, will have a strong influence on those which follow. Furthermore, each activity has a specific objective that needs to be understood and implemented. The sections that follow will examine each activity in turn.

14.6 Implementing the plan

The main objective when implementing the plan is to ensure all the actions are performed as rapidly as reasonably practicable and time is the essence. The eight activities of the plan are now examined.

(a)   Investigating an incident

The process begins with an incident being reported to the captain or commander of the ship. Typical examples of such incidents would range from the failure of a piece of machinery or a pressure gauge giving no reading, to an outbreak of fire in the engine room or a member of the crew falling overboard. The logical reaction would be to order an investigation into the incident. The objective of this is to establish the seriousness of the incident and its status. Establishing the cause(s) of an incident may not always be possible, in the time available, but it is very important to ascertain its likely effect. For this reason all relevant information should be sought. The investigation may be done by the person who was at the site of the incident and made the report, but other people are often involved as well. This may be because the master had sent them to the site, or they were working nearby and became aware of the incident. The information should be compiled in a concise and accurate form that will enable the most appropriate decision to be made. This is a demanding task when carried out under stress. Prior training and experience is therefore to be recommended. Some accidents, like man overboard, demand an immediate response by the officer of the watch and well prepared drills for recovery.

(b) *Making a decision*

Once feedback about the incident has been obtained it is necessary to analyse the information to determine how serious the incident is and to explore the options available. The objective of this activity is to decide what to do next. It is recognised that the master of a ship would normally ensure that the shore base is informed of the occurrence, the seriousness of the incident and what actions are planned. The staff at the base are expected to inform all the appropriate offices and services. A number of decisions may need to be taken, depending on the nature of the incident and examples of possibilities include:

•   Evacuating personnel from the ship as quickly as possible.

•   Containing the cause of the incident.

•   Moving people to the assembly points ready for evacuation.

•   Combining incident containment with moving personnel to assembly points.

As a typical example, fire in the galley of a passenger ferry would involve the following decisions:

•   Providing immediate fire fighting response.

•   Containing the fire to prevent its spread.

•   Moving passengers away from the restaurant area.

•   Informing the shore base.

•   Prepare for evacuation.

Depending on the seriousness of the fire, options such as escaping and evacuating should also be considered. Because the initial decision can have a major influence on subsequent actions it is essential to be decisive, yet flexible as the incident develops. It should, however, be recognised that there may be very little time available for analysing information and reaching a decision.

(c) Communicate internally and externally

Following the decision made it is necessary to keep key people informed. The communication has to be made both internally to every one on board of the ship and externally to the key persons and parties. Internal communication is essential so that every one is aware of the status of the incident and be prepared to follow the instructions concerning what to do. External communication tends to involve the shore office and other ships in the vicinity. It is recognised that the captain of a ship would normally ensure that the shore base is informed of the occurrence, the seriousness of the incident and what actions are planned. The shore office would in turn pass on information to the relevant parties. Alerting rescue co-ordination centres and other ships when a serious incident has occurred on the ship is part of maritime custom, i.e. sending out "May Day" distress messages.

(d) Attending to the injured

The occurrence of an accident may cause no personal injuries but in general there will be injuries although the magnitude can vary widely ranging from cuts to fatalities. This activity is concerned with giving attention to the injured and would be performed by designated members of the crew with special first aid training. It can also be expected that the work would be done in parallel with deciding on what to do and communicating internally and externally. There can also be some iteration between the activities. Depending on the seriousness of injuries to personnel, the decision to communicate could be affected. For example, some one badly injured due to explosion in the machinery space would need to be air- lifted to hospital on shore for medical treatment.

(e) Containing the incident

The objective of these activities is to minimise the extension of an incident by taking preventive measures to contain its effect. It should be recognised that, in certain circumstances, there will be very few options available. For example, on a Ro-Ro ferry operating in the North Sea, if a lorry falls on its side as a result of the vessel's large rolling motions in adverse weather conditions, prevention would involve keeping watch on the lorry to prevent ignition of any leaking flammable liquid. Righting the lorry has to wait until the ship docks. However, if as a result of the ship's motion the fallen lorry starts to slide on the deck floor, either from side to side or backwards and forwards, action would need to be taken to protect the vessel structure and other vehicles on that deck from damage.

(f) Escape

Escape is the term used for the removal of people, e.g. passengers on a ferry, away from a critical area to designated assembly points. It is best if the procedure is led by well trained crew members. This is particularly important when smoke is present or the lighting system has failed and the escape has to be made in the dark. Depending on the shipping company's policy, it is highly desirable to assign responsibility for different areas of the ship to specific groups of crew members. This should ensure that the escape is made in an orderly way from both public rooms and cabins. It should be noted that this activity can begin as soon as the decision is made and can be carried out in parallel with containment and prevention activity. The objective of escape is to move personnel from places where the hazards have high risk values to an area where they have lower risk values. The problems of crew and passenger behaviour have been examined by Kuo et al (1993-2).

Courtesy of Ship Stability Research Centre

Figure 14.3 Simulation sequence of an evacuation on board a passenger ship

As outlined in section 13.4, Approach 4 uses computer simulation techniques to study the movement of passengers and crew from one location of the ship to another and this approach is now more popular due to advances in computer technology and better understanding of the issues involved. A practical tool based computer simulation is the Evi (see Vassalos et al 2004), which is being used to study the movement of people for various ship design concepts and operations. The computer program can assist in identifying bottlenecks and improve the flow of crowds. It is also possible to estimate the time needed to move people on the ship in an emergency. As an example of the application a series of pictures is given in figure 14.3 to show various stages of a study into the escape process for a passenger ship. The ship is first shown and this is followed by a view of water entering the car deck. People then start to go to the assembly point via the corridors and passages before boarding the lifeboat. The last view shows the lifeboat ready to be lowered into the sea.

The same technique can also be used to examine the movements of a large number of people on an installation such as a complex vessel like a FPSO (Floating Production Storage Offloading) system. The idea here is also to identify possible bottlenecks and to check that the time taken to move everyone off the installation is reasonable. Figure 14.4 gives an illustration of the application.

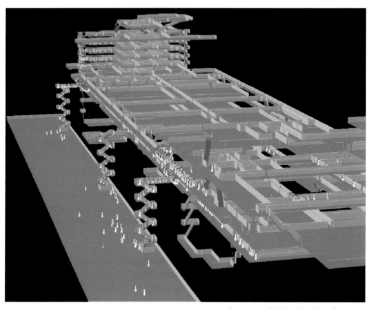

Courtesy of Ship Stability Research Centre

Figure 14.4 Simulation of an evacuation from an FPSO during construction

e)   Evacuation

Following on from escape, passengers should be waiting at designated assembly points for the next decision. The objective of evacuation is to transfer passengers and crew, efficiently and without danger to those involved, from the ship to life rafts or lifeboats. It should be noted that evacuation from the vessel does not necessarily have to follow on from escape. If the incident is contained, this would be a step towards safety. If, however, between the risk levels of evacuation to the surface of the sea prove to be higher than those of remaining on board, then the latter option is likely to be selected. Once, however, the decision is made to abandon ship, evacuation can be done by any one of the following methods:

i)   Conventional lifeboats: Passengers and crew get into the lifeboats and these are lowered using wires attached to a davit hanging over the side of the ship, see figure 14.5.

Courtesy of Lady of Mann

Figure 14.5 A conventional lifeboat

ii)   Marine escape system: This is a pressurised chute by which passengers and crew descend to a floating platform on the surface of the sea. Life rafts are launched independently into the water and the crew pull them alongside the platform, so that those on it can be transferred to the life rafts. They are then pulled clear by rescue craft, see figure 14.6. An escape tube can also be used and this system relies on friction to prevent people from descending too quickly leading to personal injuries.

Figure 14.6 Marine Escape System

iii)   Free-fall lifeboats: Passengers and crew are firmly strapped into seats inside a lifeboat which is allowed to drop into the water clear of a ship or an offshore installation, see figure 14.7.

Figure 14.7 Views of a free-fall lifeboat

iv)   Helicopter: Passengers are taken to land or to another ship from the open decks of the threatened one by a shuttle helicopter service, see figure 14.8. (Note: the range of helicopters is limited and this evacuation method can only be used near the coast where air rescue facilities are available).

Figure 14.8 Rescue mission using a helicopter

v)   Evacuation chutes: For offshore installations, where the distance between the deck and sea surface can be quite large, alternatives to ship evacuation methods have been introduced. One such a method is to have a spiral chute inside of a protective tube made of nets, and persons descend via the chute to a floating platform at the foot. Figure 14.9 illustrates such a set up.

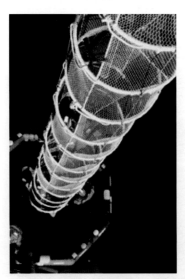

Figure 14.9 Evacuation chute system for offshore installations

For details of the merits and drawbacks of these methods, see DTp (1986), Hart and Pittilo (1996), de Jonge (1996), Paterson et al (1996), Spouge (1996) and Beech (1997).

(f)   Rescue

Once passengers and crew are safely on the water in lifeboats, life rafts or freefall lifeboats, they need to be rescued. This can be done by taking them aboard other ships which are operating in the vicinity. The actual task of rescuing can be quite straightforward in calm seas, but it becomes increasingly challenging as weather conditions become more adverse.

It can be difficult to rescue anyone who falls into the water, even from a rescue boat, because of the relative heave motions of the vessel and the person in the water. For this reason it is important to compare the risk levels of hazards associated with staying on board the ship with those associated with taking to the lifeboats and life rafts. The objective of rescue is to move people efficiently from the surface of the sea to locations where the hazards have much lower risk levels. Figure 14.10 shows a typical rescue craft in action.

Figure 14.10 A typical rescue craft in action

14.6 An illustrative example

The example is concerned with a fire outbreak on a passenger ship with 400 passengers and crew. Evacuation will be limited to using lifeboats. Preparation involves collecting data about the ship, numbers of passengers and crew and potential fire outbreak locations. The tasks include the following:

(a)   Investigate: the reported incident by examining the fire outbreak occurring in the galley and report the findings to the Captain.

(b)   Decide: what do based on feedback from investigation and compare the relative merits of the options.

(c)   Contain: in parallel with the previous task, actions would be taken to contain the effects of the incident and to overcome the effect, e.g. use fire fighting facilities, and prevent the fire from spreading.

(d)   Communicate: with everyone on board the ship by giving the status. If the incident turned out to be a fire which got out of control and threatened the ship, consider communicating externally by sending a MAYDAY distress message.

(e)   Attend: to the injured if necessary using the teams which are specially trained to deal with these types of situations.

(f)   Escape: move people from areas near the fire outbreak and use experienced crew members to shepherd passengers to assembly points.

(g)   Evacuate: if a decision is made to abandon ship, passengers and crew wearing life jackets, would proceed to lifeboats before they are lowered into the water and taken away from the ship.

(h)   Rescue: the passengers and crew would be rescued from the sea by other shipping or local rescue services.

   The points to note include:

•   It is useful to divide the tasks into small segments as this will enable more accurate times to be assigned to each segment.

•   Preparing for emergencies can help to clarify thinking, allowing solutions to be found in advance and ensuring plans are more realistic.

•   Computer simulation can be used to give a mental picture of the process and a visual view of how people move in groups from various locations to the assembly points.

•   Use data from full scale exercises to work out times taken for the various actions.

14.8 Conclusions

(a)   Emergency preparedness is a key element of the safety case scheme and a combination of experience and advanced computer technology can assist in achieving effectiveness.

(b)   There are a number of methods for evacuating personnel from a ship to the sea surface and the choice is dependent on the type of ship or offshore installation.

(c)   Emergency preparedness involves eight components of investigate, decide, contain, communicate, attend, prevent, escape, evacuate and rescue and all of them are critical to success.

(d)   Emergency response requires practice training and regular drills. The operations are complex and critical but occur very infrequently. To be effective regular exercises are necessary.

Chapter 15

HUMAN FACTORS AND SAFETY

15.1 Introduction

It is important to recognise that products and systems are designed, constructed and operated with a significant input from humans. Humans use the products and systems, make decisions, take actions and follow, modify or ignore instructions. It is humans who cause accidents, but they can also prevent accidents. Humans do not operate in isolation but interact with other humans, both socially and in the working environment. To implement safety management, an appreciation of the key features of human factors is critical to success.

The aims of this chapter are, therefore, as follows:

(a)   To highlight the basic issues concerning human factors.

(b)   To provide some explanation of the term human factors.

(c)   To consider human errors and violations.

(d)   To examine possible ways forward.

15.2 Why consider human factors?

Investigations into accidents have identified many causes contributing to their occurrence. One common element in all these unplanned, unexpected and harmful events is the role of human factors. A classic example of a case in which human factors contributed significantly to an accident is that of British Midland's new Boeing 737 aircraft, which crashed near Kegworth on the M1 motorway. During a flight from London to Belfast, on 8 January 1989, a fire was reported in one of the two engines and the pilot shut off the working engine instead of the faulty one. This mistake was recognised too late for the restarted engine to provide the necessary power to prevent the plane crashing, just before it reached East Midlands airport (see DTp 1990).

The fact that human error contributes to accidents is generally accepted, but there is no consensus on the importance of this factor. Suggestions regarding the proportion of marine accidents caused by human errors vary from 50 percent to 90 percent of the total (see Kletz 1991). By far the most meaningful statistics on this are presented in publications by the UK P&I Club of Insurers entitled *Analysis of Major Claims* for a given year. The statistics relate to five year periods, e.g. 1987-91, 1988-92 to 1999-2003. For example, the report of the P&I Club for the year 1992 covers the following items of interest:

•   The claims for the five-year period 1987-1991.

•   Detailed analyses on 1,380 claims out of 1,440 with a gross claim value of US $724 million (out of a total of US$784 million).

- The fact that claims were mainly in respect of cargo, pollution, collision, property damage and injury to both crew and non-crew.

The most informative evidence is related to the main causes of accidents and this is given in figure 15.1 for a typical five year period.

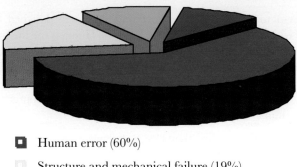

- ◻ Human error (60%)
- ◻ Structure and mechanical failure (19%)
- ◻ Equipment failure (11%)
- ◻ Other (10%)

Figure 15.1 Main causes of ship insurance for a typical 5-year period

The main conclusions to be drawn from this can be stated as follows:

Firstly, in 60 percent of the total number of claims recorded, human error was the *direct* cause and, in a further 30 percent, human error was an *indirect* contributory cause. In the latter case the accidents can be attributed, at least in part, to human decisions and human design solutions — hence the suggestion that 90 percent of marine accidents are caused by human error. Secondly, the 60 percent statistic is a global one.

Detailed analysis shows that certain types of accident are more likely to be caused by human error than others, e.g. 90 percent of the cases of a ship colliding with another ship or with port facilities are caused by human error. Thirdly, in view of the importance of human factors in marine and engineering activities, it is essential to acquire a thorough understanding of these factors and what causes human beings to make errors.

In addition to the data from the UK P&I Club, other information also shows similar trends. Typical sources from which data of accidents are gathered and analysed continuously include the Australian Transportation Safety Board (2003), the Canadian Transportation Safety Board (2003) and the UK Marine Accident Investigation Board (2004).

15.3 Understanding the term

The term "human factors" is increasingly used in many contexts associated with the performance of tasks, in particular when safety is involved. There are many definitions of the term in use, and it will be helpful to examine some of the currently adopted ones under the following three headings:

Human factors as an ergonomics discipline

The term "human factors" is used in the USA, but its study is understood and practised in Europe as a discipline under the title of ergonomics. Typical definitions are:

- *The science of the fit between jobs and persons, the study of the relationship between an individual's anatomy, physiology and psychology and the demands of particular forms of work*, Reben (1985).

- *The study of people at work and, in particular, their relationship with machines*, Statt (1990).

- *The study of the efficiency of persons in their working environment*, Gregory (1997).

Man-machine interface

With advances in the application of computers to many industrial functions, such as flexible manufacturing systems and the use of robots, there is a different emphasis. The term used here is Man-Machine Interface (MMI). The focus is generally on problems associated with information processing, decision making, perception and psycho-physics. Important features include equipment, the physical environment, the tasks to be done and the individuals who carry them out (see Reben 1985). Sometimes the term human engineering is used instead.

A popular definition by Chapanis was quoted by Sanders and McCormick (1987):

> *'Human factors' discovers and applies information about human behaviour, abilities, limitations and other characteristics for the design of tools, machines, systems, tasks, jobs and environments for productive, safe, comfortable and effective human use.*

It is recognised that such an understanding does move closer towards an application to practical situations, but the emphasis is strongly on information processing. This is understandable because it is treating the issue as something which can be measured and assessed.

The human element

It is useful to note that a broader conceptual term has been introduced by IMO called the human element to facilitate the introduction of human related aspects to rules and regulations. For example all new regulatory proposals now have to be scrutinised by the human element sub-committee to ensure that the measures introduced are compatible with the ability of humans to comply with them. In certain usages, the term may also embrace management information system, decision making, equipment integration and wider user interfaces.

Safety-related definitions

In the context of safety, the term human factors has been defined by the UK Health and Safety Executive as follows (see HSE 1989).

> *The perceptual, mental and physical capabilities of people and the interaction of individuals with job and working environments, the influence of equipment and system design on human performance and, above all, the organisational characteristics which influence safety related behaviour at work.*

This is a very comprehensive definition which covers the human being's capabilities, the jobs and the working environment and the effects of system design on performance, as well as organisational characteristics. However, the statement is unclear as to how the various features mentioned can be integrated into a general methodology and how it would be used to enhance safety.

15.4 A practical definition

Taking into account the definitions and explanations given above, it was thought useful to propose a definition which can incorporate the key features already indicated, while providing a positive direction towards their application. The wording for the proposed definition of the term by Kuo (1993-1) is as follows:

> *Human factors is concerned with the interfacing of a set of personal capabilities and characteristics with a combination of hardware, software, working environment and organisational culture in the effective performance of a task.*

Some of the words here require explanation.

- Interfacing: This implies matching a set of requirements with a set of responses to meet an objective, while taking into account the opportunities and constraints offered by elements of both sets.

- Task: This refers to any assignment or function which involves human beings in its performance. Typical examples include navigating a ship, flying an aircraft and designing a machine.

- Personal capabilities: These can be classified into two main groups, covering intellectual and physical capabilities. Intellectual capabilities cover competence, confidence and communication skills. Physical capabilities include health, fitness and human limitations.

- Personal characteristics: These include such factors as personality, response to stress, attitudes, leadership ability and teamwork qualities.

- Hardware: This term refers to equipment and its design features. Typical examples include a ship, an offshore installation or an aircraft and components of these, such as steering gear, generators or computer monitoring systems.

- Software: This term is usually associated with computer programs, but has in recent times come to be used in the context of procedures, instructions for doing a task and management related functions.

- <u>Working environment</u>: This term refers to the physical environment of the workplace and how a person matches up with the task to be carried out.

- <u>Organisational culture</u>: This term refers to how individuals have interpreted and put into practice the philosophy adopted by the organisation. This is reflected in its attitude to issues such as quality and safety.

- <u>Effective</u>: This implies that not only is the objective of the task met but it is done efficiently, comfortably, safely and to the satisfaction of the person concerned.

The attractiveness of this way of thinking can be summarised as follows:

Firstly, this definition treats human factors in the context of interfacing two distinct entities — people and their working environment. Each can be improved on its own and enhancement can also be achieved when they are interfaced.

Secondly, the components of personal capability can be assessed and, once a good understanding of the appropriate knowledge and skills has been acquired, it is possible to seek ways of making significant improvements in the performance of a task.

Thirdly, the components making up personal characteristics can also be recognised. However, radical changes can be very difficult to achieve and it may be more fruitful to incorporate them into the decision-making process when a task is first planned.

15.5 Further explanation of the key terms

It is helpful to give further explanation of the terms in the context of safety: personal capabilities, personal characteristics, hardware, software, working environment and organisational culture.

(a) Personal capabilities

The two main groups of capabilities deserving examination are intellectual and physical capabilities.

Intellectual capabilities

Three items can be considered, as follows:

Competence

The relevant abilities associated with competence are:

- Understanding fundamental principles.

- Acquiring and classifying information.

- Accessing and applying knowledge.

- Identifying and prioritising options.

- Solving problems and making decisions consistently and reliably.

- Completing a task.

Confidence

This term is less easy to define but in practice it can be represented by the following abilities:

- Selecting realistic goals.

- Winning peer respect.

- Effective organisation of activities.

Communication skill

Many issues regarding performance and safety depend on good communication between individuals and between individuals and hardware. In the present context communication skill will involve the following two abilities:

- Transmitting and receiving information: This is done orally, in written form, visually or physically, or by a combination of any of these forms

- Overcoming obstacles: The main types of barriers are leakage or interference in the transmission or receiving of media. It should be noted that these obstacles can be both mental, e.g. a closed mind, and physical, e.g. a high volume of noise.

It is important to note that success depends on achieving these three Cs at an optimal level and in balance at all times. Further details on this can be found in Kuo [1989].

Physical capabilities

These can be studied under the main headings of health, fitness and human limitations.

Health

The state of a person's health is a function of a number of factors, of which three examples are given here:

- Life style: Including factors such as taking exercise, smoking and the intake level of alcohol.

- Eating habits: Especially whether a balanced diet is adhered to or not.

- The capacity to relax: As illustrated by the ability to switch off from work.

Human limitations

The make-up of the human body determines the limits of its physical capability. Human beings, for example, cannot lift very heavy loads without assistance from some mechanical, electrical or hydraulic system. Other limatations are physical and mental fatigue.

(b)   Personal characteristics

A person's behaviour and performance in his or her job will depend on many factors, such as personality, experience, working environment, response to stress, motivation, commitment, attitudes, leadership and teamwork qualities. It will be useful to consider briefly some of these factors in the context of safety and performance.

Personality

Main personality characteristics can be described as follows:

* Proactive.

* Passive.

* Adaptable.

* Selfish.

* Generous.

In practice there are many combinations of these groupings and hence different types of personality. This, in turn, leads to various behavioural patterns on the job.

Response to stress

The term stress refers to pressures experienced by individuals which affect their job performance and daily activities, see for example, HSE (1987). These pressures can cause physical changes, such as increased pulse rate and blood pressure, raised levels of fat and sugar in the blood together with adverse psychological effects. Examples of the effects of stress include:

• Physical symptoms:	Headaches, cold sweats, shortness of breath
• Emotional symptoms:	Depression, irritability, anxiety
• Behavioural symptoms:	Poor performance at work, lack of concentration, increased consumption of alcohol, insomnia.

Attitude

The effective carrying out of a task depends to a large extent on the attitude of the person concerned. A positive attitude is demonstrated by a willingness to take responsibility for a particular course of action. This is usually done after careful examination of all the relevant factors and identification of the problems requiring to be solved. In the context of performance and safety, a positive attitude is shown by a willingness to reach for higher standards, even if that means altering present habits or demanding increased effort. This in turn encourages greater commitment.

Leadership and teamwork qualities

The subject of leadership is concerned with the roles of individuals at all levels within an organisation. The issues of importance include the style of leadership adopted; how to understand human needs at different stages of people's careers and how to motivate others by various means. Teamwork is the term used to describe what is required when a group of people work together to meet a common objective. The success of the team's work generally depends on a sense of common identity, the establishment of a good understanding between members and effective communication.

(c)　Hardware

Any piece of equipment is referred to as hardware and the term can refer to either the complete system or any of its components. In the present context this would include, for example, a ship or offshore installation, propulsion machinery, instruments, etc.

Human beings are involved in the conception, design, development, construction and operation of hardware. It is, therefore, essential to incorporate the needs of human users into any project at the earliest possible stage of design, when there is the greatest flexibility. Elements that should be given attention include:

* Reach.

* Comfort.

* Scope for viewing.

For further discussion, see Sanders and McCormick (1987).

(d)　Software

As used in the present context, software is concerned with management decisions and policies, guidelines, standards and procedures for performing a task. It is usually closely linked to hardware in that there is normally a recommended procedure or a set of instructions to be followed in order to get the best out of each piece of hardware. Safe operation and efficiency often depend on the quality of the software and it is highly desirable to integrate hardware with software, in order to meet these requirements.

(e)　The work environment

This term usually refers to the physical characteristics of the workplace. Elements of importance include the amount of space available and its arrangement, the illumination, the temperature, vibration and noise levels, atmospheric conditions and (in the case of floating structures) motions. The following examples illustrate the importance of this from the point of view of safety:

- In many cases failures attributed to "apparent" technical causes, have eventually been shown to be due to latent weaknesses embedded in the system, as a result of decisions taken by human beings at the design stage.

- The lack of clear markings and foolproof switches on the instrument panel of an offshore installation caused several accidents that could otherwise have been avoided.

(f)   Organisational culture

In addition to the features considered above, a most important factor is organisational culture. To a great extent it is the organisation that determines the behaviour and performance of its individual members. This is often referred to as the culture of the organisation. Every organisation has its own corporate objectives and, for a commercial one, the goal is to make a profit. There are good reasons for making a profit, the key one being to ensure that the organisation continues to be in business and is able to take up attractive opportunities. It is therefore not surprising that, while this goal is being pursued, other important issues such as safety may well be accorded a lower priority and good intentions are often not translated into action.

In the performance of any task, the right culture has to be adopted so that proper weightings are given to all the key parameters. From the point of view of safety, the following should be borne in mind:

- Individuals have to understand the safety goals of the organisation and work out how they should be implemented, in practice, in their daily activities.

- All personnel should feel free to express concerns about safety without fear of being seen as rocking the boat and receiving a reprimand.

- Appreciating that sound and safe practice is a contribution towards meeting the organisation's objectives.

Further consideration of the safety culture can be found in Chapter 16.

15.6 Human errors

Most people have some understanding of the term human error, or error generally. It is usually associated with a human action or omission, identified as that which prevented an event from meeting its intended objective or that led to an accident. This error is, not surprisingly, often associated with forgetfulness, neglect or even sheer stupidity. In reality, the situation is much more complex. This is best indicated by the number of textbooks on the subject by psychologists (see, for example, Reason 1990).

At a more practical level, there are many types of error, and the responsibility for a given event can lie either in the hands of the individual who caused the failure or accident, or in those of the one whose decisions put people in a situation in which that error or failure occurred. In the present context, discussion will focus on the main sources of human error, with the aim of providing a better understanding of it and of possible ways to minimise its occurrence.

(a) Types of human error

The classical method of treating human errors stems from the work of Rasmussen [1982] who defined the three levels of human performance which can readily be recognised by practicing engineers and maritime personnel. This in turn has been used to classify the human errors into the following three main types:

- Skill-based (SB) error: This is also referred to as the auto mode of performance. Essentially, the operator is highly skilled at doing the task but becomes so familiar with it that it becomes routine. The error occurs when the operator loses concentration. For example, many hit from the back car accidents are caused by highly skilled drivers, whose attention may be distracted by something on the side of the road and they may not notice that the car in front has stopped.

- Rule-based (RB) error: In this case the operator uses rules that are learnt for doing the tasks. It is also known as the semi-auto mode of performance. However, if there is a well established but cumbersome procedure for doing a task but, for various reasons, this is discarded, the operators, by taking a short cut and ignoring the rules, may cause an accident.

- Knowledge-based (KB) error: These types of error are due to a lack of knowledge of the task to be done and the operator must start from basics. This is called the conscious mode of performing a task. For example, repair work has to be done on a new piece of equipment. It is the first time for the operator, who has to use common sense, as much as knowledge. The method is usually based on a trial and error approach and, by its name, errors will be made though hopefully not serious ones.

There are other types of error and the two most common ones are:

- Active failure: The failure has an immediate impact on the safety of a situation, activity or system. For example, if an anchor is dropped in a wrong location, the effect would be known quickly.

- Latent failure: Potential errors are embedded in a situation, activity or system but they are dormant, until they interact with other factors or features, and this in turn may lead to significant failures. For example, a task is assigned a 20 minute schedule, but if this is changed suddenly and cut down to 10 minutes, pressure to finish more speedily may lead to mistakes in doing the task.

(b) Minimising human error

In view of the importance of human error, there have been many attempts at finding ways of addressing the problem. There are two principal methods:

•   <u>Reducing the occurrence of human error</u>: In this approach, methods are developed for predicting situations which can lead to human error and taking action to modify or design out the error prone situations. In addition, some extra barriers are introduced to prevent the occurrence.

•   <u>Containing the severity of human errors</u>: Once a human error has occurred, methods have to be used to contain or minimise its effect. Once again, the approach should also be considered at the design stage and allow extra redundancy to be incorporated in the system. An example of this approach includes the need to have more than one human error before a failure would occur.

It will be noted that the above suggestion is very similar to the risk reduction technique considered in Chapter 13, except that the emphasis is solely on human error. Some of the techniques used to address this problem will now briefly be examined.

(c) Improving awareness

One method of dealing with human error is to ensure greater awareness of the problem through various forms of education. The task involves explaining the causes and effects of human errors in language that can be understood by seafarers as well as managers. Good examples of this type of effort are the three monthly *ALERT* newsletters from The Nautical Institute (2005) and booklets from the UK P&I Club on human factors (2002).

(d) Error detection

Many studies are done to detect error prone situations. An example of this approach is to use computer simulation and modelling tools for the prediction of human error. A major project supported by the US National Aero Space Agency (NASA) used three human performance modelling architectures involving: i) Task network: Models human/system task sequence as the primary organisational structure. ii) Cognitive: Models simulate the mechanisms that underline and cause human behaviour. iii) Vision: Vision models focus specifically on the use of computational algorithms to simulate the human visual processing of an image. For further details, see Leiden et al (2001).

(e) Error prediction

Work has been done on predicting design-induced human errors and these methods are used on the flight decks of aircraft. In fact, many of the techniques developed for treating human errors have been applied to the airline industry, where considerable attention is given to human factors. A popular technique known as Systematic Human Error Reduction and Prediction Approach (SHERPA) is adopted to reduce the incidence of design-induced error on the flight deck. The method stems from the petrochemical and nuclear industries and validation studies have suggested it is amongst the best human error prediction tools available, see Harris et al (2005).

(f) Addressing human factors

Human error is not treated in isolation and relates closely to human factors. Put another way, improved team work and communication between people doing a specific job will help to reduce human error and enhance performance. In the civil airline industry, it is very popular to apply Cockpit Resources Management (CRM) for improving team work and communication, and minimising errors. A similar technique, called Bridge Resources Management (BRM), was introduced to the shipping industry in the early 1990s for training the crew of tankers and passenger cruise ships.

(g) Focusing on specific causal parameters

Since human factors and human error are very complex subjects, there is a tendency to focus attention on fewer parameters in the hope that the overall number of human errors can be reduced. For example, human fatigue and task omissions have been identified as being closely related to failures of situational awareness which is a major causal contributor of human error. Studies are being done, therefore, to find ways of minimising the likelihood of crew fatigue (see Baker and McCafferty 2005).

(h) Management system approach

Many human errors also stem from management failures. For example, a tight schedule to complete an assignment in a short time puts great pressure on individuals and this, in turn, leads to errors. Using the techniques given in Chapter 6 it is possible to use a management system approach to minimise human error. In applying the GMS for human error minimisation, the management system part would be the same as other GMS applications and the process scheme becomes a human error scheme. This scheme would have components such as i) identifying human errors, ii) assessing their risk levels and iii) reducing the risk of selected hazards by various techniques. Initial use of this application was given in a paper by Kuo and Craufurd (2000).

15.7 Human violation

Some people tend to confuse violation with error and it is useful to differentiate the two. Error can be caused involuntarily but violation is a deliberate decision and action. For example, driving at 90 kph in a 50 kph zone is not an error but a violation. The excuse that "the car took over when I was driving at 50 kph" would not have many takers. There are three types of violation deserving attention:

- Routine violation: This is an activity performed on a regular basis by deliberately ignoring best practice and/or ignoring known dangers. An example is the routine cutting of corners in doing a task, so that a habit is formed and applied to the task until something very serious occurs.

- <u>Necessary violation</u>: In this case the rules have to be disobeyed in order to get work done. It will be noted that those surviving the *Piper Alpha* disaster in the North Sea all jumped into the water from the deck. The evacuation regulations stated clearly that "on no account should anyone jump into the water from such a height as it would mean certain death". If the regulations had been followed, everyone would have burned to death due to the intense heat on the recommended route.

- <u>Self indulgence</u>: People violate safety regulations or safe practices for the thrill of doing it or for kicks — for example, two riders travelling on motor bikes at speed towards each other with the aim of turning away at the very last minute. This type of activity has a very high probability of failure but the kick is the thrill of just missing a collision!

It should be noted that in order to to minimise human violation, the most effective long term solution will be education. A short term reduction in routine violations can have some success using better procedures, punishment, incentives or a combination of all three. Developing a positive attitude to safety is more likely to be successful. Necessary violation is a special case, which requires a good understanding of the circumstances and sound judgment, so that a correct decision is made as to when this should, or should not, be applied. This, in turn, is related to practical experience and education. The self indulgence violation presents the greatest challenge and even the best thought out educational solution may not make much headway. The most effective method would most likely be to use respected role models to influence this type of behaviour.

15.8 Treating human factors

The subject of human factors is complex and there are no magic solutions to overcome the problems leading to failures due to human factors. Yet as far as safety management is concerned, a knowledge of human factors is essential because humans contribute around 60% directly and 30% indirectly to failure. Some suggestions will now be given to assist in dealing with this subject in a maritime context.

(a) Acquire an understanding of the subject

Human factors is a complex subject and sometimes made more difficult to understand by specialists. For example, some definitions are so long and complicated, it is not surprising that little progress is made from an application point of view. There is a case therefore to try to acquire a better understanding by examining issues relating to attitude, behaviour, errors and violations.

(b) Early attention to human factors

It is important to realise that humans are involved in the design, construction, operation and the use of a product such as a ship or an offshore installation. Hence, there are good reasons to integrate human factors into every phase of a product's life-cycle. For the operational design features of a product, it would be helpful to carry out a human factor task analysis. For example, there are many cases in which equipment cannot be readily maintained, due to lack of clearance spaces because the designers had not appreciated that maintenance would need to be done by humans or in the space available.

(c)   Human factors interfaces

Many failures can be attributed to poor interfaces between systems-to-systems, humans-to-systems and humans-to-humans. Examples of these three types include:

•   Poor interface between an existing ship and a refurbished part of that ship.

•   Human operator physically has to leave a work station in order to see the readings on a panel.

•   Two team members cannot get on with each other and, as a result, the project is poorly done.

To overcome the problem, interfaces should be given a high priority and encouragement given to the development of better interfaces.

(d)   The role of education and training

In many features and issues concerning human factors, education and training have significant roles to play. Education is to do with understanding the concepts, principles and methodology, while training is concerned with practical performance of the task. Sometimes they are referred to as theory and practice. For example, training will have little impact on violations while education can make more headway via reasoning. Likewise, education can improve the understanding of interfaces and training will encourage good practical interfaces being available for use. To summarise human factors, a mind-map is given in figure 15.2 (overleaf) to show the various relationships.

Figure 15.2 Human factors mind map

15.9 Conclusions

(a) Human factors play a critical role in safety and its effective management. The subject should be carefully studied in order to ensure that the best solutions can be achieved.

(b) It is important to give early attention to human factors and to do so at all phases of a product's life-cycle.

(c) Human error and violation should be clearly differentiated so as to ensure their effective treatment.

Chapter 16

SAFETY CULTURE

16.1 Introduction

Having an effective safety culture is increasingly being regarded as one way of achieving a desired safety standard because of its positive influence on human behaviour. It aims to seek ways of developing positive attitudes to safety, encouraging safe behaviour and minimising human errors and violations. It is a complex subject and some understanding is essential to safety management.

The main aims of this chapter are as follows:

(a)   To provide a brief background to the subject.

(b)   To explain what is meant by the term safety culture.

(c)   To show its link with safety management.

16.2 Background highlights

In analysing accidents, both marine and non-marine, it has been noted that humans play a key role. Sometimes they are responsible for causing the accident and sometimes their actions have prevented the incident escalating into a major disaster. While technology plays a part in contributing to accidents, the critical features are usually associated with how people behave before and during an accident and their attitude to their work. For example, in the analysis of a common type of accident such as collisions between cars in a city centre, almost everyone suggests that the critical features are attitude and a lack of concentration by the drivers, rather than faulty brakes or steering devices. Because humans play such a crucial role there is no simple answer for dealing with the situation, i.e. one direction or a recommended procedure is unlikely to solve all the problems. Bearing that in mind, each person is different and safety is a perceived quality, it is not too difficult to recognise the complexity of the subject. However, an improved understanding of what is involved in a safety culture will contribute to the way it can assist in overall safe performance.

The key features of safety culture can be considered under the following headings:

* Safety thinking: Safety culture is related to how people think about safety in the context of what they do in various activities and the decisions they take.

* Human behaviour: This is very much concerned with how a human would behave in various situations.

* Attitudes: This is influenced by the attitude held and this can vary from

a very responsible and positive attitude to an irresponsible and negative attitude.

It is useful to note that there is a belief in some quarters that a safety culture is the answer to all safety problems but, in practice, it is unlikely that any one factor can be expected to provide the complete answer.

16.3 Characteristics of safety culture

To gain an appreciation of safety culture it is useful to begin with an example:

In this case a marine task is running behind schedule and the project manager is very worried that the contract deadline is unlikely to be met. Efforts are being made to ensure that the target can be met. This, in turn, leads to short cuts being taken, e.g. the work is not checked as thoroughly as it should be and some safety aspects are compromised. These steps enable the task to be finished on time. The senior management then praise every one involved for meeting the target. The apparent safety culture projected can be summarised as follows:

- The deadline is crucial.

- Management is not really fully committed to safety.

This view will be held regardless of how often the management pronounces that "safety is given our organisation's top priority!" There are many definitions of a safety culture and they tend to put emphasis on specific issues. An example, see HSE (1992), is given here:

> The characteristic belief, values or philosophy held by organisations, groups and individuals and expressed within a safety and environmental management system. Evidence of a safety culture will be seen in the effort devoted to safety and environmental management and the quality of these outputs.

What therefore is a safety culture? It relates to people and the following features:

- Their attitudes to safety issues.

- How they deal with or treat safety in practice.

- Their perceptions of safety.

- Their expectations about safe operations.

There are many interpretations of the term with varying emphases and these can be grouped under the following main headings:

- Theoretical completeness: This interpretation would attempt to be theoretically correct and be as comprehensive as possible

- Focus on limited factors: This group accepts the difficulties associated with a comprehensive solution and selects a limited number of factors to be examined.

- <u>Practical application</u>: The methods in this group tend to put effort into applying the main features of the safety culture to practical situations while accepting the limitations.

It is not possible to cover the total spectrum of safety culture and instead one definition is used to highlight important issues, to explain the key terms and to demonstrate how it can be used to good effect.

Clearly there are a number of items such as values, belief, philosophy, the management system, evidence and efforts to be considered. At this stage, it would be helpful to focus on a limited number of them, i.e. the philosophy, and relating it to the issues examined earlier. Thus a practical definition of safety culture can now be given as:

> *The belief or philosophy on safety matters held by organisations, teams and individuals which is demonstrated in practice through their attitudes, actions and behaviour.*

16.4 The effect of underlining philosophies

There are several possible philosophies, which can influence a safety culture, and two extreme ones are examined here, under the following headings:

(a) *The blame philosophy*

The basic principle of this philosophy can be stated as:

> *When an accident occurs, a failure is noted or a target is missed, someone must be responsible and he/she should be identified and face the consequences.*

This philosophy is often seen in practice and has the following merits:

- Once the guilty party is identified, appropriate punishment can be handed out so that re-occurrence can be minimised.

- The failure will be investigated so that the cause can be established.

- It is a familiar concept to almost everyone, for example when a child does something that is wrong or against conventional wisdom, blame is dealt out by the parents or the teachers. The child grows up with the belief this is the behavioural norm.

There are also a number of drawbacks and these include:

- A defensive attitude is developed in order to avoid the possibility of being blamed.

- There is a tendency to try to put the blame on others.

- Taking the initiative is avoided, where possible, as failure will be laid firmly on the individual concerned.

- Pointing out that near misses and potential problems are also blamed as faults and so this valuable feedback is discouraged.

(b) The collaborative philosophy

The basic principle of this philosophy can be stated as follows:

Best solutions are usually derived via close collaboration between the prescribing authorities, users/providers and other stakeholders.

The merits of this philosophy include:

- The responsibility for an activity, situation or system is shared by all concerned.

- A broad range of issues are addressed and covered.

- It encourages initiatives and fresh ideas because it is in the interest of all the stakeholders.

- Positive attitudes are usually generated as a result of its application.

There are also some drawbacks and these include:

- A cosy relationship between prescribers, users and providers is not always a good thing, because complacency may develop.

- It may take a long time before the philosophy is fully implemented in practice and key people often change, take on different roles or move on.

16.5 Some key features

It is useful to discuss briefly some of the key features of a safety culture under the following headings:

(a) Positive attitudes

The factors associated with a positive attitude can be identified to include:

- A willingness to improve standards, or maintain the same standards with less effort, on safety matters.

- The actions taken reflect the importance attached to safety.

- An appreciation that improved safety standards is not a cost burden but will assist the organisation to achieve higher profits.

- A willingness to examine more than one option for dealing with safety issues.

Examples of positive attitudes include supporting higher safety standards and trying to solve a problem by examining a number of safety options. Typical negative attitudes can be represented by always claiming difficulties whenever some fresh safety features are considered or being critical of everything that is new.

(b) Responsible behaviour

The factors associated with responsible behaviour can be identified as including:

- Being responsible while doing every activity and in making decisions.

- Giving attention, in advance, to the outcome or impact of one's own decisions.

- Matching words with deeds.

Examples of responsible behaviour include keeping fit for demanding work and reacting quickly to changing circumstances such as adverse weather warnings. On the other hand, examples of irresponsible behaviour include drinking just before going out on watch at night on board ship and forgetting important duties.

(c) Safe action

The factors associated with this feature can be identified to include:

- Given a number of options for doing a task, the choice will always be the one which provides the safer approach.

- Accepting the need to have one's and colleagues' performances measured and checked.

- Setting a good example or being a role model for others to follow.

Examples of safe action include putting on a harness while working on the deck of a yacht even in good weather so as to develop the habit, or studying the procedures before embarking on a critical work task. On the other hand, examples of unsafe action include being poorly prepared before going on a trip and deliberately ignoring good practices.

(d) Just culture

It has been suggested that a positive safety culture is often associated with people having trust in the decisions or believing that the decisions are "just" and hence willing to give their full support. The concept of "just culture" has been examined by Reason-Hobbs [2003]. They argue that trust is the essential prerequisite for a reporting culture and an informed culture which is needed to develop a positive safety culture. It is useful to recognise that in situations where a punitive culture is operating, it is most unlikely that a person will confess to his or her errors and near misses. Nor can a blame-free culture be feasible because there will be a very small minority who will commit unsafe acts which can endanger the safety of the whole system. In these circumstances, these few individuals deserve severe sanctions and it they are not punished, the management would lose credibility. A just culture will assist in drawing a line between acceptable and unacceptable behaviour. In practice it is a challenge to determine this line.

16.6   Links to the safety management system

The key objective of safety management can be stated as follows:

(a)   To achieve a As High As Reasonably Practicable (AHARP) level of safety. This is important because safety is not absolute and different situations may require different standards. The requirement may not be the same for two situations when one is safety critical and the other is not.

(b)   To encourage every one in the organisation to develop a habit which adopts a positive safety attitude, behaves responsibly and acts in a safe manner.

A safety culture supports safety management in the following manner:

•   Providing a sound basis, via the selected philosophy, for safety thinking.

•   Helping to achieve operational goals safely.

•   Changing the way people behave.

•   Minimising the likelihood and consequences of accidents.

It is useful to remember that a safety culture is not a panacea for safety and it requires time to develop into something that comes naturally but it is critical for successful sustainable operations. It is suggested that a safety culture should be an integral part of safety management that starts with the application of the elements of the management system to the implementation of the safety scheme. This consists of the technological components of hazard identification, risk assessment, risk reduction and emergency preparedness. In this way, safety management does not become just a process that is done mechanistically, documented and forgotten once it is completed.

16.7 Conclusions

The main conclusions to be drawn are:

((a)   It is important to have a good understanding of the key features such as attitude, behaviour and action that underpin a positive safety culture.

(b)   The blaming philosophy is commonly used in practice and is well understood but it can be counter productive when adopted to achieve a high standard of safety.

(c)   By adopting the collaborative philosophy in safety culture, over time it will ensure an "as high as reasonably practicable level of safety" is achieved.

(d)   Effective safety management requires the presence of a positive safety culture to support all aspects ranging from applying the elements of the management system to implementing the components of the safety scheme.

Chapter 17

LEADERSHIP, TEAMWORK AND SAFETY MANAGEMENT

17.1 Introduction

Safety management, as explained in earlier chapters, is concerned with coordination of resources and activities to meet the safety objective. Resources cover human beings, materials, facilities and finance. Human resources, in turn, are dependent on the effectiveness of leadership and teamwork in order to obtain the best out of everyone concerned. The subject of leadership and teamwork is very broad but it is helpful in the context of safety management to have an appreciation of the key issues.

The main aims of the chapter are therefore:

(a)   To explain the importance of the subject and its usage.

(b)   To give the basic educational needs.

(c)   To outline the contribution of leadership.

(d)   To consider the role of teams and teamwork.

(e)   To examine the effects of changing society on safety management.

17.2 Why consider the subject?

Before considering the subject of leadership and teamwork, it is appropriate to ask the following question:

> *What is the usefulness of leadership and teamwork knowledge in relation to safety management?*

The main answer is that leadership and teamwork are directly related to a safety culture, which plays a critical role in safety management. The issues concerning safety culture have been covered earlier in Chapter 16. Leadership is responsible for generating, developing, implementing and maintaining a positive safety culture within an organisation. Teamwork is responsible for interpreting, putting into practice, measuring results and giving feedback on the level of safety culture in the organisation when tasks are performed to meet the objectives.

It is the resulting safety culture that will help to produce "safer" and more efficient seafarers and, in turn, lead to better performance. This fact is recognised by organisations such as The Nautical Institute and the UK's Maritime and Coastguard Agency (MCA). The former offers short courses on good leadership and these courses are formally accredited. The MCA has produced a booklet which gives practical guidance on ten aspects of leadership for safer performance.

These efforts and useful contributions can enhance the awareness of the role of leadership in attaining improved safety performance. However, it has to be recognised that both leadership and teamwork have to be considered together because a positive safety culture has to be "bought" in by everyone in the organisation. In a maritime context, the safety culture must be embraced by all from the onshore senior management of the shipping company through to the masters, chief engineers and crews on board ships.

A firm commitment from the top management is essential to ensure that everyone knows that the shipping company takes safety seriously. It is the teams that will put various aspects of a safety culture into practice in their daily activities via their attitudes, actions and behaviour. It is for these reasons that acquired knowledge in leadership and teamwork is so valuable. As mentioned earlier, both leadership and teamwork are associated with doing tasks in meeting an objective. The actual assignments can be quite different but the principles are the same, i.e. good leadership and effective teamwork will ensure the objectives are met efficiently with an acceptable level of safety.

17.3 Key educational attributes

For human resources to be of value in doing an activity, carrying out a task or tackling on a project, there is a need to have acquired a number of fundamental attributes or capabilities through education and training. These can be classified under the following headings:

- Competence.
- Confidence.
- Communication skills.

When combined they form the 3C educational philosophy which achieves success by ensuring that everyone has a balance of competence, confidence and communication skills. This achievement, at a high level, will assist them in gaining satisfaction and rewards from their daily work and in making useful contributions in whatever job they do. Further discussion of this approach can be found in Kuo [1992] and an illustration of the 3Cs is given in figure 17.1. Each of the 3Cs is now discussed briefly in turn.

(a)   Competence

The achievement of competence is probably the best understood and best developed part of our educational programme. A great deal of effort is expended in ensuring that learners or students are good at whatever is being taught. Abilities which make up competence can be summarised under the following sub-headings:

- Understanding the fundamentals: For every subject, it is essential to acquire a good understanding or appreciation of the basic features on which the

Figure 17.1 A representation of the 3C educational philosophy

subject is built, e.g. it would be very difficult to design ships without knowing the buoyancy principle.

- Acquiring and classifying information: In this age of the knowledge-based society there is a considerable amount of information and so it is essential to have the ability to select relevant information sources and group the essential bits so that their links can be identified and interfaced in the most effective manner.

- Accessing and applying knowledge: It is important to be able to access relevant knowledge at the right time and to use it to do the work in order to obtain the desired results.

- Generating and developing ideas: Technology will advance because users are always seeking better more cost-effective solutions. This, in turn, requires fresh ideas to be generated. This is only the first step, as an idea is not really of use until it can be developed into a feasible purpose.

- Identifying and prioritising options: In general there will always be choices and they should be identified and then prioritised so that the ones with the highest potential are examined first before considering other options.

- Analysing and making decisions: All situations must be analysed first and, if possible, compared with similar situations before a decision is made. This process can be done both informally or formally, depending on the situation in question.

- Formulating and solving problems: In all activities there will always be problems or difficulties, of varying magnitudes. To solve them it is helpful to formulate some methods of solution. These can be on an informal basis using past experience, or in a formal manner via procedures. This ability will enable problems to be solved more efficiently.

(b) Confidence

For many people, the acquisition of confidence can be an extremely slow and difficult process. Those who are naturally confident find it hard to understand why others should lack self-belief. There is no simple solution but the key abilities which make up confidence include the following:

- Selecting realistic goals: Lack of confidence often stems from individuals setting unrealistic goals. When these are not achieved one's confidence is undermined. It is therefore better to have an overall goal matched by an appropriate time scale and to have a series of less ambitious aims which can be reached in smaller steps. Completion of each will help in building up confidence.

- Managing time effectively: In general, there are always more tasks to be done than the time available and one often underestimates the time needed to complete an assignment. Ideally, one should have time for work, for recreation and for people. To achieve a balance there is a need to have self discipline combined with applying practical time management skills and gaining experience via regular application.

- Developing a positive attitude: It has been found that those who are very confident generally tend to take an optimistic approach towards everything they encounter, ranging from their work to their every day activities. By having positive attitudes it helps to derive and reach solutions which otherwise may not be found. The expression no problems was first adopted in the USA to signify self confidence and being positive.

- Winning peer respect: In many activities, respect is gained when good decisions are suggested or taken. This, in turn, increases their respect further and the individual's confidence. This ability is, therefore, a key feature for developing one's self confidence.

- Taking on responsibility: Closely linked to the previous ability is a willingness to take on responsibility and make progress in reaching the goal of a task or project. Achieving the task will assist in generating confidence.

- Gaining practical experience: Basic principles and theoretical knowledge acquired are often presented differently in practice and it needs experience to be able to apply them safely and appropriately. Young graduates would take time to adjust to their first jobs and good leadership would help to bridge the gap between theory and practice effectively. This is usually achieved by providing opportunities for individuals to gain operational experience. This, in turn, can greatly enhance the confidence of those involved.

(c)   Communication skills

In the present context, communication is considered as a two way interaction process, which involves transmitting and receiving information between two or more human beings. The principal forms of communication are:

*   <u>Oral form</u>: Talking, listening, etc.

*   <u>Written form</u>: Hand prepared, use of a keyboard and computer, etc.

*   <u>Visual form</u>: Pictures, sketches, video, animation, body language, etc.

*   <u>Physical form</u>: Contact via hand shaking, hugging, etc.

It will be noted that there are obstacles to effective communication and the transmission of information. The key ones include:

*   <u>Blockage</u>: Physical barriers such as walls and mental barriers such as negative attitudes and pre-conceived views.

*   <u>Interference</u>: Presence of noise from an external source is a physical example and mental ones are associated with concentration being distracted by other matters.

*   <u>Leakage</u>: Only part of the message is transmitted and some parts withheld intentionally or by accident.

It will be realised that the three Cs are an essential foundation for everyone who works in the maritime industry. More recently, there is an additional attribute deserving inclusion and this is associated with being innovative and a willingness to take on an assignment or a project with a less than an even chance of success. This attribute is called "entrepreneurial flair" and should be added to the 3C philosophy to show that, in the competitive world of 21st century, people have to pay attention to being innovative and creative in the things they do.

17.4 The basis and the role of leadership

To understand the term "leadership", it is helpful to gain an appreciation of what a leader is and what is expected of a leader. A leader is a person with authority in connection with a task or job. The position of authority is acquired through a variety of ways and some examples are given here:

*   By appointment: The person takes on the position as the head of an entity, e.g. master of a ship.

- By election: The person wins a popular vote during an election and this can be at various levels, ranging from a social club to the top post in a country, e.g. the prime minister or the president.

- By force: The person acquires the controlling position of an organisation by force, e.g. nationalisation of an asset held by private investors.

- By reputation: The person becomes a leader, often informally, via the belief or philosophy promoted and this is done through published books and articles, speeches made and transmitted via media such as television. In this case, it is the thinking which provides the appeal, e.g. publication of an economic theory to be used in a country.

Irrespective of the route taken to become a leader, continued success will depend on the leader's performance over a given period, regardless of previous track record. As regards to what is expected of a leader, this will be influenced by the goal to be achieved in the job. This is best illustrated by an example from the UK offshore industry.

Example 17.1

When viable oil fields were first discovered in the North Sea in the early 1970s the UK national energy policy had a goal which can be stated as follows: "Self sufficiency in oil by the end of the decade". The leaders of major oil companies and, in particular, the project leaders were "goal getters" who could be expected to achieve the targets by solutions that were well established and had worked in the past. Efficiency was a secondary problem. These project leaders ensured that the UK was self sufficient in oil by the year 1980. Once this was achieved, the goal was changed to produce offshore oil cost-effectively. This, in turn, required leaders who could examine alternative solutions to achieve the new goal. It was not very long before the project leaders who were successful in meeting the goals of the 1970s were replaced by a new breed of leader. These leaders thought more systematically, were ready to consider different options and used more scientific methods in decision making.

The example tends to confirm the applicability of the leadership theory that different leaders are needed for different situations, i.e. the leadership styles have to match the situations as illustrated below:

- Autocratic leadership: For emergency situations, such as responding to a fire outbreak when decisions must be made and followed without question.

- Democratic leadership: For sensitive situations, such as exploring a salary increase and negotiating a financial deal where flexibility is required and alternative choices must be examined.

- Free-rein leadership: For situations when a wide range of options should be examined. An example would be leading a research project, where novel ideas have to be generated using techniques such as brainstorming.

It is not surprising, therefore, that the leadership style adopted for ships tended to be autocratic because the decisions have to be obeyed and implemented. In the past it is well known that on the ships of certain flag States, the master acted like an "emperor", whose words were unchallengeable and who had to be obeyed immediately at all times. In the 21st century, this approach has become modified to cater for changes in society. Good leaders are expected to be "multi-tasking" and be able to respond to all situations, i.e. able to adopt different leadership styles to meet different requirements.

The subject of leadership has received deserved attention in the context of safety management by shipping companies and governmental agencies. The UK Maritime Coastguard Agency [2004] produced a booklet on the subject. In the booklet, it argues that to achieve effective safety leadership ten core qualities are needed and these can be put into four classifications as follows:

- Confidence and authority:

    (1)   Instil respect and command authority.

    (2)   Lead the team by example.

    (3)   Draw on knowledge and experience.

    (4)   Remain calm in a crisis.

- Empathy and understanding:

    (5)   Practise tough empathy.

    (6)   Be sensitive to different cultures.

    (7)   Recognise the crew's limitations.

- Motivation and commitment:

    (8)   Motivate and create a sense of community.

    (9)   Place the safety of crew and passengers above everything else.

- Openness and clarity:

    (10)   Communicate and listen clearly.

In the booklet it explains how to implement these ten qualities, by considering why they are important and using examples to illustrate things that tend to work and things that tend not to work. There are two points worth noting. Firstly, for leaders to understand and possess these qualities they need to have a balance of 3Cs relating to competence, confidence and communication skills. Without these, it can be difficult to implement ideas in practice. Secondly, leadership and teamwork go hand in hand and a leader will find it very difficult to achieve results without the support of good teamwork. The latter, in turn, also requires a balance of 3Cs at an acceptable level.

17.5 Teams and teamwork

The concept of people working in teams is well understood and appreciated by almost everyone from an early age when games are played in teams, e.g. football, basketball, netball and hockey. The word team usually refers to a group of individuals working together to meet an objective. The benefits to be obtained from teamwork are regularly promoted, with the key ones being as follows:

• Greater success can be achieved from the synergy of people with different expertise and experience.

• More fresh ideas can be derived from interaction between team members.

• Better performances can be achieved via a positive team spirit.

• Responsibility can be shared by team members.

Teamwork also suggests that all members are given equal status by a team leader, so that the line of communication is shorter and decisions are more transparent. In fact, the merits of the teamwork concept are so overwhelming that it is difficult to find any drawbacks. However, to achieve effective teamwork requires a number of factors to be satisfied. The key ones include the following:

(a)   The make up of the team

For a team to function effectively, attention must be given to the choice of the team members. Features needing to be taken into consideration include:

• A spread of expertise: Most teams require members with a range of expertise that could cover specialist technical skills to financial and organisational expertise.

• Availability of technical experience: Expertise should be backed up with appropriate experience so that the results obtained can be assessed from both a scientific and common sense point of view.

• Personalities of team members: Ideally the team should have someone who can have plenty of fresh ideas and has a strong personality. There should be others who are good at implementing ideas and at examining details. If the team has too many strong personalities it is likely that there will be constant clashes which can be destructive.

(b)   Methods of working

The efficiency of a team is dependent on how it goes about its work. Generally, most team members have experienced working in teams but with different style of leadership. Some teams are structured to work via committee meetings, others are assigned tasks to do — with members getting together on a regular basis to exchange progress information. The secret of success lies in choosing the most appropriate work methods that will obtain the best out of everybody while maintaining a strong team spirit.

(c)   Full participation by all

Team members will have varying educational qualifications and experience, derived from different cultural backgrounds. In some cases, the team's working language may not be the first language of some members. For example, a well established expression may be entirely new to some members and it can lead to misunderstanding. In certain situations, some members may be reluctant to give an opinion because this is not expected within their national culture or due to language difficulties. However, it is important for team members to be involved and achieve a high level of interaction and participation in all aspects of the team's activities.

(d)   Role of team spirit

Success is often associated with a happy team, or where there is a strong spirit and bond between team members through their partnership. This, in turn, is dependent to a large extent on the attitude and behaviour of team members and the effectiveness of the leadership. Strong spirit implies there is mutual trust within the team and a willingness to assist each other and to share responsibility and the sense of achievement. This state can only be achieved with effort from everyone.

17.6 The shipping community

To understand the contributions of effective leadership and teamwork to shipping it is useful to highlight some key features of the shipping community. In any effective organisation there will be clearly defined goals. To achieve these goals it needs people acting as leaders and as team members. This, in turn, involves interaction amongst themselves and with those outside the organisation. The shore based part of a shipping company is not very different from other land based organisations, except that it is a 24 hours and 365 days international business activity.

The on board part of a shipping company has its own characteristics, in that the community exists in a special environment. Shipboard personnel live and work together to meet the objective of ship operations and they interact primarily with each other. For example, a cargo ship can be at sea for several months with only a few brief stops to load and unload cargoes. During that period, the interaction would predominately be internal. This makes leadership and teamwork even more critical in the process of meeting the objective. Bearing in mind that the crew on board are often multi-cultural and multi-lingual, with varying qualifications and experience, this in turn can add an extra dimension to communal leadership and teamwork.

To reach and maintain a high standard of safety is very challenging because people on ships form a close community and they live and work together through a 24 hour cycle. To meet operational objectives there has to be harmony, with positive leadership and a strong team spirit. Thus, in addition to professional qualifications and operational experience, maritime personnel should have competence, confidence and communication skills so that the safety objectives can be met effectively.

17.7 Effects of the changing society

It is well recognised that people change with time and there will always be differences between successive generations. However, it is not always appreciated what effect changing society has on the prevailing culture. The impact of change can affect the effectiveness of leadership and teamwork and, in turn, safety management. For example, a leader who has had experience of leading several teams can often find that some teams are more readily managed to achieve the objectives, while others are the opposite.

What has caused the rapid changes in the attitudes, action and behaviour of people? There are many factors and it is believed that a key one concerns the availability of information. In the past, people were very ready to accept the suggestions and opinions of experts because it would require a considerable amount of effort to find, understand and use the information needed to question those experts. For example, the medical profession has enjoyed great respect from the public and acceptance of their recommendations. Today, with the availability of information often presented in a reader-friendly form, from websites, libraries and publications, it is now not uncommon for patients to discuss their suggested treatments and other alternatives on offer with their doctors. This state of affairs has changed the relationships between parties, e.g. the medical practitioner-patient relationship has changed from one that is like a parent-child to that of a mentor-student.

The impact of available information can be illustrated with some other examples:

- Individuals have higher aspirations and more demanding career objectives, e.g. accepting higher education as the norm

- Individuals have a greater awareness of their rights in given circumstances, e.g. they must be informed first before certain actions are taken.

- A majority of individuals is attracted to commercially promoted icons, with their life styles leading to greater value being placed on material things, e.g. the cost and appearance of a car is often more important than its transport role.

- Younger generations are much more competent at using the facilities offered by advances in computer technologies, e.g. computer applications, mobile telephones and music playing devices.

It should be realised from these examples that the knowledge acquired has enhanced the competence and confidence of individuals which, in turn, has altered their attitude, actions and behaviour. The latter three can have a significant impact on the effectiveness of safety management.

17.8 Conclusions

The main conclusions to be drawn are:

(a)   In the shipping environment of today, maritime personnel should have a balance of competence, confidence and communication skills.

(b)   It is helpful for maritime personnel to acquire an appreciation of the key features of leadership and teamwork which influence safe performance.

(c)   Leadership and teamwork acting together will help to generate, develop, implement and maintain a positive safety culture in support of high standards of performance in maritime activities.

(d)   To respond to the commercial challenges in competitive maritime industries, leaders need entrepreneurial flair to find innovative and creative solutions to problems and to exploit new opportunities in changing circumstances.

Chapter 18

IMPORTANT SAFETY ISSUES

18.1 Introduction

In addition to the various aspects of safety considered in the previous chapters there are a number of important safety issues that have effects on shipping and deserve brief examination.

The aims of this chapter are:

a)   To consider the safety and related challenges facing the industry.

b)   To examine the contribution of education and training.

c)   To discuss the issues concerning liability and insurance.

d)   To highlight the factors affecting maritime security.

e)   To outline the environmental issues.

f)   To present areas for future development.

18.2 The challenges

To improve safety standards in the maritime industry without increasing cost or efforts disproportionately, it is essential to overcome many hurdles and this, in turn, introduces a number of major challenges. In this section, the key ones are considered under the following headings.

(a)   Understanding the term safety

The term "safety" is used commonly by everybody and it can, therefore, be assumed that it is a word well understood by everyone in a consistent way. To test this assumption, it is usual for the author to ask questions such as:

•   "What do you understand by the term safety?"

•   "Would someone like to suggest a definition for the term?"

The audience is usually practising marine personnel and engineers participating in safety workshops and students attending classes on safety management modules. It is surprising that only about 10% of several thousand people over a fifteen year period can suggest something which would be accepted and understood by the others. The majority have accepted the term as "avoiding something that can cause harm" without question. Very few appreciated that safety is not absolute and is dependent on personal perception.

The main reason for this state of affairs is best explained by some participants in the workshops. In their work they are asked to perform tasks safely, often with structured guidelines or procedures, but there is "no time" to go into what safety is all about. They commented that this approach was very helpful in gaining an understanding of the basics of safety. It can be argued that for non-absolute items such as safety, to make the best progress requires an understanding of or, at least an appreciation of, the fundamental issues.

(b)   Not relying only on regulations

As explained in Chapter 4, the prescriptive regulatory approach is used by an authority such as a government to manage the risk level of hazards which exist in all activities, operations or products which can affect the wellbeing of the public. For routine activities or situations where considerable amounts of past experience are available and the behaviour characteristics are well understood and readily predicted, the prescriptive regulatory approach would be very useful and valuable. This makes the work of the ship designer and operator much more straightforward. For example, procedures can be devised for the safe operation of equipment and this will be valuable in achieving the required safety standard. Initial and refresher training can be provided to new and less experienced operators respectively.

However, it has to be recognised that such an approach would not be suitable for new activities, novel systems and changed uses of a ship, because little or no experience exists to enable the prescriptive regulatory approach to be applied. The designer and operator must, in these instances, start from fundamental considerations and devise appropriate solutions in order to meet the required safety standard. This, in turn, can appear to make life more difficult. For example, not long ago one company changed over from expecting its workforce to follow a prescribed set of safety procedures to asking them to derive their own best solution for meeting the required safety standard. It was not long before complaints were heard and the most interesting remark was: "We are paid to work and not to think as well!" Yet with developments in technologies, and when new equipment is introduced fresh safety solutions have to be devised to meet the safety standard. These solutions require learning and applying a method that is different to the prescriptive regulatory approach such as the General Management System (GMS) for safety. Since technically trained personnel may be less familiar with management systems and their applications, this can become a significant challenge.

(c)   Balancing various interests

The regulations and rules on maritime matters are determined at international, regional and national levels. It is in the former two levels when safety and the national interest are seen differently that solutions can be inconsistent and the decision making process becomes more complex. Some typical situations which can give rise to conflict between safety, politics and the national interest are illustrated as follows:

•   A good and practicable safety solution has been agreed by technical representatives for addressing a type of accident at international level.

However, the implementation of such a solution would put ships of some influential nations at a competitive disadvantage and so the initiative would be blocked by their national representatives on the grounds of its effects on their national interest.

• There is a tendency for nations that have not experienced a particular type of failure to resist any change until they themselves have been affected. This is particularly true for certain types of ships, such as short route passenger ferries, which are operated in relatively calm environmental conditions when compared with other ships exposed to hostile operational conditions.

• When a major accident such as oil pollution caused by the breaking up of an old tanker occurs in the territorial waters of a country, this situation can lead to a strong national outcry. The government would be expected to respond by demanding for more stringent regulations at regional level which may not be technically sound but would demonstrate that something has been done.

These examples illustrate how politics and the national interest interact in the context of safety. In practice, this type of situation will always occur. However, to make progress there is a need for a better understanding of the implications of alternative solutions coupled with goodwill from all concerned. This is a challenge that will require a change of attitude and will take time to achieve.

18.3 The contribution of education and training

Standards of safety can, to a large extent, be improved through education and training. While these terms are familiar to everyone, it may be difficult to know what is involved in each, because of their close inter-relation. Some believe that education is *theory* and training is *practice* while others regard education and training as teaching respectively the *why* and *how* of a task. It would therefore be useful to use a scenario to explain what they are.

This explanation occurred during a safety workshop in which some delegates had problems in differentiating education from training. One person even hinted that there was no real difference but it was a good academic debating issue! He then asked for a simple example to explain the two terms. This led to the following conversation:

Tutor: "Do you have any children?"

Delegate: "Yes. I have two school age daughters."

Tutor: "Imagine a scenario in which your daughters bring home a letter from school for the parents. In this letter, the head teacher informs the parents that the school was thinking about offering classes in sex education and sex training. The parents are given the choice as to which one they would like their children to take. Would your reply be that it does not matter?"

Delegate: "I now can understand what is meant by education and what is training, and I will remember this example as well!"

In practice there are similarities and differences between education and training. These will now be examined.

(a)   Similarities

Typical examples of two items which are similar:

- Objective: The basic objectives are the same and can be stated as follows:

  "To achieve or enhance the competence of individuals for doing a specific task". The term competence covers both intellectual and physical capabilities.

- Communication of information: Both involve the communication of information between parties. Sometimes one party will transfer information to others parties, and at other times that first party will receive feedback. It should be noted that information includes knowledge, facts, figures, records, ideas and views. A typical example would be the giving of instructions on how a skill can be acquired.

(b)   Differences

The significant differences include the following:

- Emphasis: The emphases of the two activities are quite different. In education the achievement of competence will also involve developing and changing the attitudes and behaviour of those concerned, whereas training concentrates on improving their efficiency in doing specific tasks. In a typical example relating to a group working on the bridge of a ship, training will ensure that all the members work efficiently, but education will underpin their ability to navigate by providing the knowledge and understanding of theoretical principles. Education can also be used to enhance team spirit and generate positive attitudes towards the carrying out of duties on the bridge.

- Results: The results of the two activities are achieved at different rates. In general, training tends to achieve results more quickly, i.e. short-term, while education tends to take much longer to achieve a more fundamental outcome. A typical example would be training somebody to drive a car. Normally the desired competence can be achieved within a few weeks. Educating a driver about driving theory and knowledge of how to apply the highway code may take longer.

- Scope: Training tends to focus more on specific forms of competence while education normally has a much wider scope. Training someone to operate a machine in a factory would, for example, concentrate on demonstrating, and then getting the trainee to practice, the method of loading and unloading items to be machined, the correct buttons or levers to use for different purposes, how to deal with malfunctions and so on. Education would involve the trainee learning about the overall process, how the machine functions and its performance features.

• <u>Understanding</u>: It is nearly always possible for someone to acquire the competence to do a given task, i.e. to follow the correct procedure, without understanding the reasons why certain steps have to follow others. In education it is generally necessary to provide an appreciation of the thinking and reasons why a specific approach is adopted. A typical example of the difference would be the number of people who have been trained to use a personal computer compared with the number of those who have been educated so as to understand the design and functioning of the equipment.

Having considered the similarities and differences between the two activities, it has to be stressed that the level of personal capability in general can be enhanced by both education and training. In the context of safety management, the contribution of education and training can best be highlighted with some examples as follows:

a)   Training

   • Practising the emergency evacuation of personnel from a ship.

   • Doing fire drill to increase efficiency and fire fighting to enhance effectiveness.

   • Using a simulator to improve familiarity and efficiency.

b)   Education

   • Giving safety sufficient attention in every activity.

   • Developing a positive safety culture.

   • Appreciating certain aspects of safety fundamentals.

It should be noted that safety-related skill deficiencies need to be overcome by a variety of methods, depending on the particular deficiency. This is illustrated by the following examples of possible problems and solutions in relation to a given task.

The person concerned:

• Problem: Has never done the task.

   Solution: Organise formal training sessions.

• Problem: Does the task only occasionally.

   Solution: Arrange for practice before the actual job begins.

• Problem: Has some experience of the task but is not good at doing it.

Solution: Explain the principles involved and ensure that he or she attends a refresher course.

The actual methods of delivering training can take a variety of forms that range from traditional teacher talking to the students to the use of computer based training (CBT) techniques. The latter is becoming more popular and effective due to the improved facilities offered by advances in computer hardware and software. It is not unusual to find interactive CDs incorporating informative graphics and sophisticated animation to explain complex concepts and to demonstrate special features. For example Stena Line uses an interactive multi-media technology for safety training on its high speed craft HSS1500 to ensure all recruits meet the basic safety standard, see Kuo-Smith-Cain(2001). In many CBT usages, the delivery is done via the individuals having access to copies of CDs as well as via the internet. In the safety training CBT, most of the course materials include some form of self-assessment in order to test the user's comprehension. Examples of commercially available safety CBT training materials include the CD's of Marlins which are being used by the shipping industry to teach maritime English.

At a more senior level, there is a need for educational programmes in the form of workshops where safety concepts are explained and discussed, group exercises are undertaken and results presented. In addition the freshly acquired knowledge can be underpinned by asking the participants to do a short personal assignment in order to verify their understanding.

18.4 Liability and insurance

In everyday activities, one often does not appreciate the importance of liability until an accident occurs. Examples to illustrate this statement can be readily found:

•   Running into the back of the car in front.

•   A burst water pipe in an upper floor apartment.

•   Injury to a tradesperson working in one's home.

In all the examples, one party is liable to the other party or parties and may well have to pay compensation for repairing the car, for recovering the damages caused to one's own and other people's apartment and for the injury sustained. The amount of money can vary and sometimes very large sums are involved. To overcome this unknown liability in advance, the concept of insurance was introduced. The normal approach is for individuals and organisations to pay a sum of money over a given period, e.g. 12 months, to an insurance company and in return it provides cover for any accident(s) over the period. The actual sum will be determined by how likely an accident may occur and the consequence when it does occur, i.e. an application of risk assessment. In practice, it is generally the people with good safety records who end up paying for those who have accidents! More effective risk assessment could lead to higher profits for the insurance companies.

In shipping the same concept applies but practical implementation can be more complex because more entities would be considered and more parties could be involved. In the early days, shipping companies such as Blue Funnel of Liverpool provided insurance cover for their own ships. There were several reasons for this decision and these included the high standard to which cargo ships were being operated and a reluctance to pay high premiums to insurance companies, which could be significantly reduced by paying damages from internal funds. However, no shipping company would now cover the liability of its own ships for insurance purpose. The main reasons include:

- There are many more ships in operation and the standards and experience of nations vary considerably. This in turn leads to the belief that some poorly operated ships can cause damage to well operated ships, e.g. collisions in congested sea areas.

- The magnitude of liability for an accident to ships can be so high as to make covering a company's own risk impracticable.

Marine insurance is a specialist and complicated subject requiring people with knowledge and experience. The basis of the approach for addressing the risk of maritime hazards is to divide insurance into three classes as follows:

- Hull and machinery insurance covers damages to the hull and the machinery of the ship and includes the costs of surveys and repairs. The insurance is usually placed through the Lloyds market to a number of insurance companies or syndicates.

- Ship owners' liabilities are covered by mutual insurance arrangements known as Protection and Indemnity Clubs, generally called the P&I Clubs. The main areas covered are contractual liabilities, personal injury, repatriation of stowaways, strikes and other third party liabilities including a quarter of the cost of collision damage.

- Cargoes are insured by the cargo owners whose contract with the ship owner takes into account that the ship is seaworthy and operated by a competent crew. Cargo damages caused by improper packing for example will be paid by the cargo insurers. If, however, the cause is water ingress and it is found that the ship's hatch covers were is poor conditions, then the cargo insurers would claim against the ship owner and this damage would be covered by the P & I Club.

Further information on the subject can be found in the works of Anderson [1999] and Anderson [2006].

18.5 Maritime security

The security of ships has been recognised ever since cargoes were transported from one location to another on the high seas. Traditional issues include the following:

- Piracy: In the past ships were raided by pirates who tended to use smaller and faster craft to do their raids. Once they were near the target ship, pirates would go on board and overwhelm the crew by force, take money and other valuables before making their get-away. More recently, in certain parts of the world, pirates are known to be active again (see *SEAWAYS*, January 2007).

- Stowaways: These are people who get onboard ship uninvited, often economic migrants who do not want to pay for their passage going from one country to another. They create difficulties for ship owners and crew. This has become a sensitive security issue.

- Smuggling: This includes contraband goods and people. This is classified as a security issue because it usually involves going from one country to another with all the associated legal implications.

More recently it is terrorist activity that has given rise to concern, e.g. explosive attacks on the warships *USS Cole* and *Linburg*. In addition, hijacking of passengers can also occur, e.g. the hijacking of *Achille Lauro*. Such security issues require international cooperation. They also raise the question about security responsibilities. To gain an insight into security issues, it is useful to understand what is meant by security. A proposed definition is as follows:

> *Security is a perceived quality which determines to what extent the management, engineering and operation of a situation can minimise the effects of malicious acts leading to harming of people, damage to properties and pollution of the environment.*

It should be noticed that security closely resembles safety and a similar methodology would apply to both. The key actions in dealing with maritime security are:

- A management system is needed to define the security goals and performance criteria, organise the resources and plan to ensure that the goals can be achieved. It is then necessary to implement a security scheme, measure the results and review the lessons learnt.

- The security scheme should identify the threats, assess their risk levels and aim to reduce those threats with an intolerable risk level. Not all threats can be anticipated and so it is necessary to preparing for emergencies if an attack occurs.

It will be noted that responsibility for maritime security belongs to all stakeholders, with leading roles being played by ship operators, governments and the International Maritime Organization (IMO). Contributing roles are provided by the crew and transporters of cargoes. IMO introduced changes to SOLAS regulations and formalised security via the International Ship and Port Security (ISPS) Code with contracting governments playing a significant part. The impetus for speedy implementation of the ISPS Code came from the US government after the 9-11 tragedy when the Twin Towers of the World Trade Center in New York were destroyed on the 11 of September 2001.

The main demands of the ISPS Code for each ship are:

•   Provide a ship specific security plan: It must meet the security level of the flag State, which will also approve the ship security plan.

•   Perform a ship security assessment: This involves identifying the threats, assessing their risk level and reducing the more serious ones.

•   Provide a shipping company security officer: Their job is to ensure ships in the fleet meet the international security standards and to provide shore backup in emergencies.

•   Appoint a ship security officer: Their job is to implement the ship security plan, maintain it, arrange for internal audits, review security measures and monitor the security threat. The person also has a coordination role on security matters.

Port security relates to access to port and to the ships, the control of the movement of personnel, the screening of cargoes and the ship shore security interface.

It can be seen that application of the ISPS Code involves additional duties for ship operators, flag States and the contracting governments. The task presents a great challenge to cruise ships and liners where there are many passengers, supported by cruise personnel and crew. There is no doubt that, by devising a ship security plan, ship operators and crews become educated concerning important aspects of security. By performing a risk assessment they become aware of the threats with intolerable risk levels and find methods of reducing them to as low as reasonably practicable. The ship security officer can become more effective by combining security awareness and knowledge with good management to ensure a positive security culture is generated within the ship. This, in turn, will assist in achieving all key aspects of the ship security plan. For further information see Jones [2006].

18.6 Environmental pollution issues

More and more people are becoming aware of the harmful effects of environmental pollution, which is referred to by terms such as greenhouse effects, global warming and atmospheric pollutants. In the maritime industry, the term marine pollution has been well recognised since the grounding of the *Torrey Canyon* in 1967 and the *Amoco Cadiz* in 1978. These incidents led to the international convention on the prevention and control of pollution from ships known as MARPOL (see IM 2006). The growth of shipping coupled with the competitive nature of the business in recent years and the threat of global warming has raised concerns with respect to the levels of ship engine emissions to the atmosphere. The main marine atmospheric pollutants contained in exhaust gases with harmful effects are:

- Sulphur oxide (SO_x).

- Nitrogen oxide (NO_x).

- Carbon oxide (CO_x).

- Under-combusted carbon particles.

It is useful to use sulphur oxide emissions to highlight the issue and the implications. Sulphur oxide emissions from a marine engine are of particular concern because present trends have shown that SO_x emissions from land-based sources have fallen by 65% during the period 1990 to 2000 and are expected to reach 76% reduction by the year 2010. In the same period, marine shipping has increased SO_x emissions by 30% and the trends show that, by the year 2010, the increase will reach to between 40% to 65%. Sulphur is present in all raw material such as crude oil, coal and ore. On combustion, SO_x gases are formed and the emissions of SO_x generate acidifying properties which can lead to serious undesirable consequences.

- Environment: e.g. sulphur dioxide combined with water precipitates as acid rain.

- Human health: e.g. airborne particles can lead to illnesses such as lung cancer.

With these harmful effects, one may well ask why not eliminate the use of sulphur in marine fuels for ship propulsion. The simple answer is cost. Essentially, the presence of sulphur improves engine performance and the use of fuel without sulphur or with low sulphur content would require new marine machinery or significant modification to existing machinery. There is, therefore, reluctance by ship operators to adopt these solutions. Regulations introduced by IMO under the 1997 protocol included Annex VI for addressing emission issues, under the title "Regulations for the Prevention of Air Pollution from Ships." The issue is not altogether straightforward, because it requires extra energy to 'crack' cleaner fuels and the residual sulphur still has to be disposed of from the oil processing plant.

The regulations cover many aspects of air pollution and the key ones include:

- Flag States have to issue international air pollution prevention certificates for their ships.

- The SO_x emission from ships must be limited to 4.5% on the sulphur content of marine fuel oil as from 19 May 2005.

The choices for ship operators to meet the regulations include the following options:

- Use low marine sulphur fuel in new machinery or new ships

- Remove SO_x after combustion.

- Adopt a combination of the above two options.

For further discussion of the options, see report by Tan [2005].

It can be seen from the above that the level of permissible emission is prescriptively defined by the regulations but operators can select the most appropriate solution for their ships. This is a typical example of a departure from the traditional prescriptive regulatory approach where both the standards and solutions are prescribed statutorily. The alternative approach is similar to the safety case approach outlined in this book.

18.7 Future developments

There are a number of areas which deserve attention in the future and these are considered under the following headings:

(a)   *Making fuller use of the GMS approach*

In the earlier chapters, the safety case concept has been implemented from a management system perspective instead of a technical one, i.e. a management system is used to derive a scheme leading to the generic management system approach. In the safety context the scheme becomes the safety scheme which involves identifying hazards, assessing their risk levels, reducing intolerable risk from selected hazards and preparing for an emergency if an accident occurred. The versatility and power of the GMS approach is quite remarkable. In fact, for anything which is not absolute or exhibits the characteristics of non-absoluteness, a GMS approach is likely to offer the most effective solution. By gaining a good understanding of the basis of the GMS approach, technically trained persons will have a new dimension added to their capability.

Future fruitful developments include the following:

- Applying the GMS approach to several levels. For example, the safety scheme at the top level involves tasks covering hazard identification, risk assessment, risk reduction and emergency preparedness. Each task can have its own GMS at one level down. This process can lead to other levels, as long as the results obtained or the level can be justified.

- Performing GMS on specific activities, systems or projects to provide illustrative examples that can be used for educating and training other potential users of the method.

(b)   *Integrating safety techniques within a safety culture*

Up to now, advances in safety management have tended to be on the technological side, e.g. refining hazard identification techniques or improving the modelling of the consequence of a hazard. Equally, advancements in human factors have focused on human attitude, behaviour and actions. These sometimes appear to be parallel developments with few links between them. However, to achieve a high standard of safety, it is essential to integrate safety technologies and safety culture. It may be that some of the difficulties are associated with a lack of a suitable methodology or there may be communication problems.

One possible method of integrating the two would be for them to share a common methodology. In the present case, the common methodology would be the GMS approach. It is possible to use the GMS approach to implement and maintain a positive safety culture and human factor schemes can be used to minimise human error. If the two aspects used the same methodology it makes it much easier to achieve interaction. This is an area suitable for future development.

18.7 Conclusions

(a)   There are many safety related areas which deserve attention and only a short list of the more important ones have been highlighted such as maritime security, effects of pollutions from ships and maritime liability.

(b)   Criticality in some areas depends on timing, e.g. maritime security, while other areas are ongoing, e.g. navigation.

(c)   To provide effective responses to safety issues, pollution prevention and ship security, requires appropriate levels of education backed up by specific training.

(d)   There are several areas deserving future development and these include making fuller us of the Generic Management System approach for safety to integrate safety techniques into a safety culture.

Chapter 19

CONCLUSION

SUMMARY OF KEY SAFETY ISSUES ADDRESSED

19.1 Introduction

Having covered the various aspects of safety management in the previous chapters it is useful to summarise the key safety issues examined and considered.

The main aims of this chapter are:

(a)   To highlight the key topic areas covering the nature of safety, assessment methods, safety techniques and human factors related to safety issues.

(b)   To place emphases on issues that deserve learning and remembering.

19.2 The nature of safety

The nature of safety is covered in Chapter 1 and key features worth remembering include:

• Personal perception has a dominant role in safety, since everyone has his or her view on whether a situation, activity or function is safe or not.

• The principal parameters influencing safety are human factors, management, engineering and operations.

• Safety is not something absolute, i.e. there are no fixed standards for all situations, activities or functions. It is for this reason that a management system is needed to ensure safety can be treated effectively.

19.3 Safety assessment methods

This section considers a number of items under the following main headings.

a) The methods

The key features to be remembered include:

• There are several suitable methods that can be used to assess the safety of a situation, activity or system, see Chapter 2. These range from informal safety assessment methods for activities involving only a few persons to the safety case approach for use in offshore installations associated with hydrocarbon production. They all have their usefulness, depending on the situation being examined.

• The most commonly adopted regime is the prescriptive approach. It is often applied in association with regulations so that it is called the prescriptive regulatory approach. The main factors are covered in Chapter 3. The maritime industry relies heavily on this approach and Chapter 4 highlighted the background and the application of the more important regulations.

- The safety case approach is increasingly applied when the safety of new and extensively modified ships or systems are being considered. Examples include larger high speed craft, naval ships and ships working in the UK offshore industry. Before examining this method the key terms used in safety management were outlined in Chapter 5 while the underlying principles of the safety case approach were given in Chapter 6.

- The importance of having a good appreciation of the terminology used in safety management should be emphasised because terms are often used in a confused manner, e.g. a lay person tends to employ the word risk to mean hazard and some practising engineers use the two terms interchangeably. It is useful to think of hazard in terms of something that can prevent the objective being met. Risk is made up of two parameters — the probability of occurrence and the severity of the consequence. It is also useful to recognise that the terms tolerability and acceptability have different meanings.

- The main difference between the prescriptive and safety case approaches concerns the method of delivery. The former has both the requirement and methods of solution prescribed but the latter does not have the method of solution prescribed. However, the user must make a case to demonstrate scientifically that the safety standard can be met, together with the justification for the choices and the decisions.

- It is possible to interface prescriptive elements in the application of the safety case approach, i.e. prescriptive features can be included in the safety case approach. Examples include specially prescribed procedures for doing a task.

b) *Management system and its role*

- As stated earlier, a management system is needed to treat safety because it is not absolute and Chapter 7 was used to demonstrate the basis of a management system.

- Most of us use a management system for doing various tasks and making decisions but do not recognise it until the steps or elements involved are formalised. There are five basic elements in a management system and, when they are located on the circumference of a revolving circuit, a process of iteration and continuous improvement can be incorporated.

- A generic management system (GMS) approach is proposed because it can offer flexibility and has greater usability. The basis of the GMS approach was given in Chapter 8. The relationship between the GMS for safety and the safety case approach were considered in Chapter 9. It should be noted that GMS for safety is a more flexible way of applying the safety case approach.

19.4 Techniques for assessing safety

The techniques for assessing safety can be grouped under the main heading of the safety scheme and can be regarded as the components of the safety scheme. The key features include:

- The main components of the safety scheme are hazard identification, risk assessment, risk reduction and emergency preparedness.

- Hazard identification, considered in Chapter 10, can be carried out using a number of methods. It should be noted that these methods are all based on the same principle, which involves having a group of people with different expertise to identify problems that might prevent the objective being met. However, the details of a specific technique will differ due to the needs of different applications.

- Risk assessment can be done by the qualitative method based on the use of the past experience of team members or with the aid of a risk matrix as outlined in Chapter 11. It is useful to note that there is a need to achieve consistency in the interpretation of the discrete parameters.

- Quantitative methods were examined in Chapter 12 and should only be used in special circumstances where the hazards have very significant risk levels. The process requires more effort and information. In general, the consequences of the hazard have to be modelled and the probability of occurrence estimated using methods such as event and fault trees.

- Risk should be considered as both the consequence and the probability of the occurrence of hazards. Risk reduction can be facilitated by using a combination of management, engineering and operational methods, see Chapter 13.

- Emergency preparedness is an essential part of the safety scheme because humans play a dominant role. One must always have contingency plans to deal with situations when an accident occurs. There are a number of steps that include notification of accidents to moving people from a location of high danger to one that is exposed to lower danger. The techniques were given in Chapter 14.

19.5 Human related safety topics

The key features covered include the following:

- Under this heading the topics covered include human factors, safety culture, leadership and teamwork and special safety issues. These were given in Chapters 15, 16, 17 and 18 respectively.

- Since humans play a dominant role in safety, it is helpful to have an appreciation of the human factors that can have serious consequences. It should be remembered that human error and human violations stem from different causes and must be addressed appropriately.

- Safety culture is a complex subject and experts have widely different views on how it should be addressed. It has an important influence on the effectiveness of safety management and the choice of the underpinning philosophy can play a critical role, the two extremes discussed were the blaming and collaborative philosophies. These, in turn, affect the attitudes, behaviours and actions of organisations, groups of people and individuals.

- The previous two topics involve leadership and teamwork. In the maritime industry, as in many other industries as well, these components have an important role in ensuring safety management achieves its results effectively. The contribution of education and training is significant.

- There are a number of major subjects which are influenced by safety and deserve to be considered, because they depend upon similar responses to ensure successful outcomes. These subjects included security, pollution prevention and risk assessment for insurance.

19.6   Examples of safety management

A number of examples are used to illustrate the role of management in safety and these include:

- *Appendix A*: Giving short examples provided from real life cases to show situations where management has major and minor roles.

- *Appendix B*: Highlighting a more comprehensive example on how a management system can be applied to manage the safety of a household.

- *Appendix C*: Outlining an illustrative example of the prescriptive regulatory approach.

- *Appendix D*: Summarising the application of the safety case approach using the Generic Management System methodology for a large high speed craft.

19.7   Conclusions

The main conclusions to be drawn are:

(a)   Acquiring an appreciation of the various items highlighted in this chapter will assist readers in addressing safety management with confidence and will help them locate where the various key features and issues can be found.

(b)   It is important to understand that because safety is not something absolute, a management system is needed. This management system can be interfaced with the key assessment techniques given in the safety scheme. Together they make up the core of the safety case approach.

Appendix A

THE ROLE OF MANAGEMENT IN SAFETY

A.1 Introduction

For many technically trained people the role of management in safety is not always appreciated or given the attention it deserves. This is not surprising because their education and training have been focused on technological issues seeking numerical solutions. Even when management is included in the course, it is usually treated as an "independent" topic and not integrated with other subjects.

The aims of this appendix are as follows:

a)   To give some examples of every day activities involving safety in which management has played a significant role.

b)   To outline some examples of every day activities involving safety in which management has a minor role.

c)   To use another example to show how the risk of the hazards can be reduced by management methods.

d)   To present the sample results of a questionnaire seeking the views of practising professionals on the factors influencing safety.

It should be noted that the examples have all been acquired from the submitted assignments of students on degree programmes and by participants on short professional development courses on safety management. The individuals concerned were pleased that their experience could be shared with other people and even be helpful for improving safety management.

A.2 Background to the accident examples

This part of the book is devoted to giving examples of the role of management in safety from the point of view of users and practitioners. In some cases, management played a significant role in causing accidents and in other examples, good management had an insignificant role in connection with the accidents. The material is taken from student assignments in courses given by the author on safety. The contributors of the material varied in age, gender and experience. Some of them were young students and others were experienced professional engineers. In general, they were not "experts" in safety management, but had to think about the subject after attending a course on safety management. There were two aspects to the assignment and the first aspect was worded as follows:

> *Outline an accident or incident from your personal experience in which failure was due significantly to management. Do not use either national or international disasters or incidents associated with your work for which you were not directly responsible.*

The second aspect is similarly worded, except this time the management had a minor role, in the cause of the accident. The students generally had difficulties in finding examples which met the requirements of the second part. The examples selected are only a very small sample of the available submissions.

The selected assignments describing incidents in which management played a significant role are associated with the following topics:

Accident 1:   Working on an offshore fish farm.

Accident 2:   A summer job working in a city park.

Accident 3:   Driving to see my brother.

These assignments are reproduced in A.2 with minimal editing.

The selected assignments describing incidents in which management played an insignificant role are associated with the following topics:

Accident 4:   A motorway collision

Accident 5:   Visiting our future new home

Accident 6:   Falling down during a hill walk

These assignments are given in A.3 and again with minor editing. In A.4 an assignment is given of an incident associated with painting the outside of a house. Suggestions are made as to how the likelihood of occurrence and the consequence of the incident can be reduced.

In A.5 some results from analyses of questionnaires given out at the beginning and at the end of safety management courses are outlined.

A.3   Accidents involving a significant management role

Accident 1:   Working on an offshore fish farm

Background:

Over the summer months and before I came to university in Glasgow, I worked on my father's fish farm on the Shetland Islands. The fish farm consists of floating structures which support a net to keep the salmon fish in captivity. The structure of the floating cage is very simple, basically a large 'pipe' formed in a circle with an inner circle to hold the net in place. The weather and sea conditions on site can become very rough as it did a number of years ago.

While I was working on the case — mending the nets, I fell off backwards into the sea. I had to swim back to the structure and climb back up by myself. The main points of the accident are as follows:

- The sea temperature was about 4°C.

- I was not wearing a life jacket.

- The structure had no ladder or means of climbing out.

- There was no guard rail.

- There was nobody else working nearby.

Management failure

Without prejudice against small family-run organisations, there were some key management failure issues which are given under the following headings:

(a)   Life jacket

With regard to the provision of life jackets or survival suits, the likes of which are readily available, I would have been perfectly safe against drowning or catching hypothermia. However, such safety items cost money – which may be unaffordable to small businesses- or not enough importance is placed on such items. This is a management issue because, had I been given a life jacket and survival suit, the consequence of falling into the sea would have been reduced.

(b)   Guard rails

I fell into the sea because there was no guard rail along the walkway of the structure. This is down to choosing the correct design, with due regard to 'safety' as well as profitability. The fact that the structure was installed and operated without a guard rail would have been rectified by a proper functioning Safety Management System.

(c)   Working practice

The fact that I was mending the net 'offshore' is probably bad safety practice, hence the repairs were badly timed, this is due to management. It must be highlighted that I was working alone which means the accident was not 'seen' by anybody. This prevented any claim being raised. The management should ensure such work is undertaken in groups.

(d)   Safety measures

An efficient management system would have assessed the risk of falling into the sea and taken precautions to reduce it. For example, a ladder (which is very cost-effective) would make climbing back to safety much easier. The management system would enable new hazards to be identified.

(e)   Cost-effectiveness

Although profit margins in fish farming are extremely low, I feel that there are many risk reduction methods which would have been extremely cost-effective. For example:

Life Jacket	£ 50.00
Survival Suit	£ 100.00
Ladder	£ 200.00
Total	£ 350.00

For £350, I believe, this sum would have reduced the risk of falling into the water to an acceptable level. The management should have done such calculations and taken action 'before' the accident occurred.

Accident 2:   A summer job working in a city park
Background:

A new employee for a gardening contractor's company is performing the task of cutting grass on a city park during the summer months. The employee is a student and has got the job during his summer vacation as a means of earning money to support him during term time. He was able to get the job as many of his colleagues were taking their holidays at that time and the company required people on short term contracts to cover any temporary staff shortage. The student lives at home with his parents in a city centre apartment which has no garden attached. He has NO experience of cutting grass nor operating a petrol engine driven mechanical lawnmower.

The company has a large workload, as this is their busiest time of the year. On his first day the student is given a 5 minute introduction to the lawnmower operation i.e. how to fill with fuel, how to start and stop the machine and how to empty grass from the machine. The introduction only lasts 5 minutes as the instructor is in a rush to get started. The instructor has been operating the machinery for over 10 years, as a result he has become complacent about safe operation and fails to point out many of the hazards that are obvious to him but not so obvious to the new employee.

The employee begins the task of cutting the grass in straight lines, backwards and forwards. The lawnmower has been used heavily recently due to the increased workload. It is not a new machine and is starting to show its age, due to the heavy workload. Maintenance of the machine has been neglected and the lawnmower is not performing to the best of its ability.

After a while the student notices that the lawnmower is not picking up all of the grass he is cutting into the grass bag or basket. The employee stops to see if the bag is full, but has NOT switched off the machine. The bag is NOT full, the student is puzzled, and without thinking puts his hand into the machine to try and clear a grass blockage. An accident occurs – the boy's finger is struck by the moving blade and is very badly injured. He goes to hospital where his finger is operated on and saved. However, he cannot work again for the rest of the summer.

Management failure

This incident can be attributed to management failure because:

(a) A safety culture had not been developed among the team of workers. They had been doing the same tasks for so long without incident that they had become complacent to matters of safety. It was 'normal practice' to perform tasks in a "safe" manner.

(b) The management had not allocated resources to the training of new recruits. The new employee was expected to start work within 5 minutes of being on the job. They did not ascertain whether he had any previous experience, and he wasn't shown all of the safety features of the machine or warned of the potential hazards. He was also unaware of the correct procedures for safety critical tasks, i.e. unblocking the machine.

(c) The management was also to blame for investing in unreliable equipment, to save costs. They were using old lawnmowers that were no longer up to the task. The management has also allowed the maintenance regime to slip due to the heavy workload. Time should have been allocated to ensure all equipment was running properly, a maintenance routine with every Monday morning used for repair and maintenance should be implemented.

I think this example shows how management failings can contribute to an avoidable accident. Management is a parameter that greatly affects safety.

Accident 3: Driving to see my brother
Background

I am the owner of a second hand car which was bought when I started to learn to drive. After passing my driving test I was very keen to drive the car on my own. It was a bright and sunny winter Saturday and I decided, late in the afternoon, to drive to see my brother who lives at the centre of a forest not too far away. As I entered the forest the car came to a stop, I discovered the following:

• I had no idea of the cause of the failure as I am not too familiar with the finer features of a car.

• I had no mobile phone or cash with me to contact my brother about the incident.

• I had not brought any coat with me and the weather was becoming cold rapidly as the sun went down.

• It was getting dark and the road was quiet.

Luckily, I was able to stop a passing car and the person kindly took me to my brother's house.

Management failure

The first thing to be recognised is that I am the "manager" of my personal safety. As a woman driving on her own, I have failed to take the basic precautions. To be an effective personal safety manager, I should have acquired a basic understanding of the common failures of a car and what can and cannot be done. I need also to plan and organise my trip before driving a car and this includes for example:

- Take a mobile phone

- Put some loose change in the car for emergency telephoning

- Bring some warm clothing and fluids

If appropriate I should phone the destination before departure. I should also identify hazards and assess their risk levels before taking steps to reduce the critical ones. This should be followed as a habit until I gain more experience.

A.4   Accidents with minor management role

Accident 4: A motorway collision

Background:

I was involved in an accident while driving to see my parents over a weekend. I was travelling at the national speed limit along the motorway, keeping sufficient spacing between myself and the traffic ahead when an incident further down the road required the motorway traffic to stop. At this point I began to brake and simultaneously activated my hazard warning lights to warn following traffic. Unfortunately the car following in the same lane failed to notice the incident ahead and consequently failed to brake in time leading to a collision with the back of my car. Fortunately the impact speed was relatively low and only caused minor damages to both cars.

Minor management role

A number of measures were taken before the commencement of my journey to check that the car was in a safe and adequate condition to drive. I checked the oil level, brake fluid level, water level, lights, tyres pressures and tread thickness. The car had recently been serviced and obtained its Ministry of Transport (MOT) certificate to show that the car met the standards required on that day. I was in a fit state to drive because I have had 8 hours of sleep, with no alcohol being consumed within the last 48 hours. I set off with the confidence that the car and its driver were in road worthy condition.

Upon detection of the traffic ahead slowing down to a halt, I appropriately applied the brakes and hazard warning lights while maintaining a safe distance from the car immediately in front of my car. I believe I gave following traffic sufficient warning of an accident occurring ahead and that I was braking. Possible causes of the collision included:

- My car's hazard warning lights failed to work or were not visible.

- My car's brake lights were not visible.

- An error on the part of the other car driver.

Following the accident checks showed that my hazard warning and brake lights were still working. As far I was concerned, I could not have done any more that would changed the outcome. I feel my safety management was adequate and it had a minor role in this accident.

Accident 5: Visiting our future new home
Background

A number of years ago we decided to buy a house in a new housing estate and the design we selected would take around a year to build. The family was keen to see the progress at regular intervals and to take photographs of the various stages of construction. The builder was aware of this demand from their clients and made a good effort to arrange these visits.

Safety was treated seriously. On our visits, we received a safety briefing and the key hazards were drawn to our attention. All of us have to wear hard hats and there were always plenty of hats available. We were guided by the sales lady who was on duty and she also had her hard hat. The routes were well marked and signposted and there were safety reminders. Before entering our house, careful inspections were made and we were allowed into the building when conditions were appropriate.

On one of the visits, the weather was changeable and there was a shower followed by strong sunshine. For some unknown reason, our sales lady decided to take a short cut below some scaffold and she also took off her hard hat as there was limited clearance. Unfortunately, she slipped on the mud and hit one of the vertical supports during the fall. This, in turn, jerked the bricklayer to drop a brick which hit her on her shoulder and narrowly missing her head. Fortunately, the injury was not too serious but she was shaken with the shock.

Minor management role

In this accident, the management played an insignificant role because all the safety cautions were in place. It is assumed that the staff had good safety training. The safety briefing, the hard hats, positive culture and guided tours were effective from visitors' point of view. Due to human factors, management can really have limited control over individual staff behaviour. It was unclear why our sales lady took the hard hat off or decided to take a short cut. Possible reasons include humid conditions made wearing of hard hats uncomfortable. She was unaware of the muddy conditions or she was behind schedule. To avoid similar accidents, the management will have to instil a positive safety culture more vigorously.

Accident 6: Falling down during a hill walk
Background

I was a member of a walking club which organised a walk each week for its members. The walks were of different grades, ranging from the easiest (grade C) which would typically be a six mile flat walk to the hardest (grade A) which would be a mountain over 3000 feet. At the start of each year a programme of walks was compiled, with leaders being identified for each walk, and this programme was reviewed and endorsed by the walking club committee. Club members could then choose walks they wanted to take part in, depending on their ability.

One Saturday in autumn it was my turn to lead a party of 15 people up Ben Venue in the Scottish highlands. The mountain only had a difficulty grading of B despite its 2800 feet stature. This was due to it being not a particularly steep climb with a good path all the way to the top. The weather conditions were good that day with only occasional minor drizzle. We set out at 11 am, I was leading and the second leader was at the back of the group as 'back-marker'. After approximately 1.5 hrs into the walk, and about 500 feet from the top, one of the party took a tumble and fell almost 100 feet down the mountain. Fortunately the fall wasn't vertical (i.e. over a cliff edge) in which case she wouldn't have had a chance but instead she tumbled head first bounding on boulders as she fell down the mountain's gradual slopes.

I scrambled down the mountain to where she lay and could see she was unconscious shortly after I arrived. She appeared to be lucid and had no broken bones but I made the decision not to move her due to her age (over 50 years), the fact that she'd been unconscious and the distance she had fallen. I took the survival kit from my rucksack and made her comfortable whilst I went to the nearest telephone to call Mountain Rescue (this was the days before mobile phones). Two people stayed with her whilst the second leader (back-marker) led the remainder of the party off the mountain. I took the mountain rescue team to her and she was carried to safety and onto the nearest hospital. She had an overnight stay to ensure there was no head trauma or internal bleeding.

The cause of the incident was due to her turning round to talk to the person behind her. She wasn't looking where she was going, stumbled and fell head first down the mountainside.

Minor management role

In order that I can justify how good management did not affect the outcome and how management played a minor role I have first detailed the steps of my management system (define, organise, implement, measure and review), as shown below.

Define

Goal: To lead a party of 15 people to the top of the mountain and back down again safely.

Criteria: There should be no major injury or death to any of the walkers and care should be taken to minimise damage to property (deer fences, gates etc) or the environment (e.g. litter). Major injury is defined to be any injury that would require hospital treatment or incapacitate a walker to the extent that assistance would be required to get them off the mountain.

Organise

- Two experienced leaders accompanied the walk, as per walking club rules. The level of experience was endorsed by the walking club committee and included first aid skills, map reading skills and a significant number of 'walking hours' under their belt.

- I led the walk whilst the 2nd leader back-marked. The back-marker was responsible for ensuring no one got left behind and helped regulate the pace by advising the leader if the group become too spread out.

- The two leaders had to do the same walk no more than two weeks ahead of the actual walk. This was to identify any key hazards (e.g. fences or rivers to be crossed), to check that the walk was correctly graded for difficulty, to identify how long it would take and to identify the nearest communication points in case of emergency.

- On the day of the walk the leaders would assess the experience of the walkers to ensure they were fit and suitably attired and would discourage or prevent someone joining the walk if they felt they were a danger to themselves or others.

- The duration of the walk was estimated to be 4-5 hours, allowing for 30 minutes for lunch at the top and a few 5 minute breaks on the way up.

- An alternative easier walk was on stand-by in case the weather was too bad to do Ben Venue.

- The leaders were responsible for checking they had first aid and survival equipment in their rucksacks.

Implement

Hazards Identification:

As mentioned above the leaders did the walk two weeks earlier and discovered only one significant hazard. There were no fences or rivers to cross, there was a good tourist path to the top of the mountain, the top was flat and about 20 feet square. The duration of the walk was 4-5 hours which could easily be done after nightfall. The weather on the day of the incident was fair. The only identified hazard was possible injury to the walkers if they slipped or fell.

Risk assessment and Reduction:

Only one significant hazard was identified and that was injury to personnel due to slipping or falling. This risk would be considered intolerable, however it was reduced to ALARP (As Low As Reasonably Practicable) because of the 7 steps identified in the 'organise' section above, the steps taken for emergency preparedness and there was a good quality path up the mountain.

Emergency Preparedness:

Both leaders had first aid and survival equipment on them and we were aware of the nearest communication points for calling for help. If the weather had been bad the Ben Venue walk would have been cancelled in favour of the back-up one.

Measure

- Were there any fatalities or did any of the walkers require hospital treatment or were Mountain Rescue required?

- Were any unforeseen hazards identified on the day of the walk (fences erected, swollen rivers, etc)?

- Were we prepared for emergencies?

- Feedback from the walkers — for example, was it enjoyable or properly graded?

Review

- Experience gained from the walk.

- Scope for improvement.

Summary of the Justifications

- The weather conditions were fair and not responsible for the accident.

- The woman was an experienced walker, fit and suitably attired.

- The path was good quality and obvious.

- The walking club rules had all been adhered to i.e. there were two experienced leaders, one at the front and one at the rear, the pace was monitored and kept moderate, visibility was good, breaks were allowed on the way up the mountain to avoid exhaustion, the party were all properly attired, the leaders had first aid and survival kit with them

- Once the victim had fallen I was able to reach her, assess the damage and take appropriate action. The 2nd leader was able to lead the remainder of the party safely off the mountain

- The key hazard of personnel injury had been identified and reduced to ALARP.

As shown in the management systems steps above (define, organise, etc) everything possible had been done that day to ensure the walk was safe and enjoyable. Only one key hazard, possible injury to personnel, had been identified and measures had been put in place to ensure the risk was ALARP. She fell because of her own mistake, human error. No additional management steps could have prevented what happened other than her not doing the walk at all.

However, as the bullet points above indicate, good management prevented things becoming much worse. If I hadn't first aid knowledge I may have moved her and exacerbated her injury. If I hadn't map reading experience I may not have been able to direct mountain rescue to her. If we hadn't two leaders we would have put the remainder of the party at risk by either leaving them on the mountain getting cold or letting them find their own way down. If we hadn't the proper survival kit she could have gone into shock or mild hypothermia.

A.5   Management approach for reducing an accident

In this example, the accident was due to a failure of management and a method of overcoming this was later adopted. The background to the accident as related by the individual is now given.

Background

The objective of the activity was to position cans of paint on a pre-fabricated scaffold platform via a ladder before painting the external walls of my house. Several minutes were spent stirring the cans of paint in preparation for transfer from the ground to the platform. Before making the paint transfer, I double checked my hazard list i.e. what can go wrong and examined the security of the ladder to the platform and the scaffold to the building. I then began transferring open cans of paint from the ground to the platform.

While transferring a can of paint from the ground to the platform via the secure ladder, I lost my balance when a freak gust of wind came strongly from the south. This loss of balance caused me to lose my grip on the can resulting in the contents of the can being spilled in a random fashion onto my face, chest and legs. Naturally a great deal of paint also landed on the ground which pleased the dog immensely. Attracted by the smell of the paint, the dog walked through the paint and ran into the house to the "delight" of the wife!

The situation is summarised in an illustration, see figure A.1.

Management failure

There was little real attention given to safety management and therefore it is not surprising that such an accident occurred. There is need to give attention to possible failures at an early stage and certainly before the work starts.

In the light of the experience an alternative approach, with management playing a role, is introduced. The objective and performance criteria would be

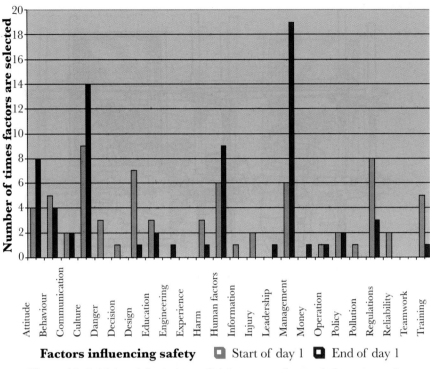

Factors influencing safety   ▢ Start of day 1   ▢ End of day 1

Figure A3: Initial and final views of delegates on factors influencing safety

The 24 factors are given along the horizontal axis and the number of times a given factor is selected is given in the vertical axis. There are two pillars for each factor but if no one has selected a factor, the appropriate column would be blank. The left hand and right hand columns represent the selections made at the start and at the end of the course respectively.

It is interesting to note that the most significant increase is the factor "management" and it is followed by "culture" and "attitude". The main reason for this is that most technically trained persons think technological issues are most important and do not realise the importance of management until it is demonstrated to them. The most significant decreases are generally associated with "regulations," "design" and "training". Although there will be variations between the groups of delegates on any given course, the general trend has been the same over the past 15 years.

A.7 Conclusions

From the experience of the accidents described, the following conclusions can be drawn:

(a)   Most of the accidents outlined tend to include a significant management failure and they can be reduced by giving some early thinking to safety and applying some forms of a management system.

(b)   Participants and students tend to find difficulties in identifying accidents in which management played an insignificant role and lots of the examples are related to car accidents because they came most ready to mind resulting from an undesired personal experience.

(c)   The safety questionnaire, which was given to the participants before and the end of each short course, provides a general measure of how the role of management on safety became to be appreciated.

Appendix B

HIGHLIGHT OF A SAFETY MANAGEMENT EXAMPLE

B.1 Introduction

The methodology for the safety management of a ship, its equipment and activity or a system, has been outlined in the previous chapters, and it is useful to consolidate by performing a safety management approach to an everyday situation. In this example it is concerned with a family living in a house in a European city. The situation is treated from fundamental principles as no special expertise or knowledge is required to perform the tasks of safety management.

The main aims of this appendix are:

a)   To show how a safety case can be prepared for an every day living situation without the individuals having to have specialised knowledge.

b)   To give an appreciation of the roles of the various stages of the safety case used in safety management.

B.2 Background of the situation

The background of the situation would be examined under the following headings:

(a)   Description of the house

The home of the family is a detached house standing on its own land. The house is built of bricks in the middle of the 1980s and has two floors. The ground floor consists of an open lounge with a separate dining area, a large kitchen with enough room for the family to eat their meals there. In addition, there is a utility room and a cloakroom. On the first floor there are four bedrooms, one bathroom and the main bedroom has en suite facilities attached to it. All the rooms are equipped with typical furniture, e.g. a sofa in the lounge, beds in the bedrooms. Gas is used for cooking and heating. The central heating boiler is located in the kitchen. Electricity is used for lighting and household appliances.

(b)   Lifestyle of the family

The house is occupied by a young family of four. The parents are in their forties, the son is 14 years old and the daughter is 12 years old. They use three of the bedrooms while the spare one is reserved for the elderly grandparents who come for periods of around one week. The parents are non-smokers. The parents regularly entertain visitors and friends of the children who also come and sometimes stay overnight. The father is a keen do-it-yourself person and does the interior decoration himself. The mother enjoys cooking and keep fit activities. The safety management is confined to the inside of the house.

B.3 Applying GMS for safety

In applying the GMS for safety to the apartment the three stages would now be considered.

Stage 1: The need

The safety requirement can be stated as follows:

> *The family want to enjoy a high quality of life living in the house while achieving and maintaining an acceptable level of safety.*

The term "acceptable" implies that the identified hazards would have tolerable and negligible risk levels.

Stage 2: The supporting information

Based on the background given in Section B.2 it is now possible to outline the application of the GMS for safety as two parts of the GMS unit, i.e. management system (MS) and safety scheme (SS).

(a)   The MS of the GMS for safety

The five basic elements will now be examined in turn.

MS Element 1: **DEFINE**

The safety goal can be stated as follows:

> *No one in the house should be involved in accidents requiring hospital treatment, there should be no damage to the property needing emergency services and causing concern to the surrounding environment.*

The performance criteria include:

E1.1   No accident requiring external attention or help.

E1.2   Limit annual minor personal-accidents within the house to four.

E1.3   Ensure near misses to be less than two per year.

MS Element 2: **ORGANISE**

There are a range of tasks to be done in order to satisfy the safety goal and these include the following:

E2.1   Installing or upgrading the fire detectors in the house.

E2.2   Providing safety guidelines on the safe use of electric devices.

E2.3   Giving safety briefings on the locations of key controls such as taps for the main supply of water into the house.

E2.4   Acquiring essential safety equipment such as fire extinguishers.

E2.5   Meetings to discuss matters concerning safety arrangements.

E2.6   Scheduling the maintenance of appliances such as boiler servicing.

E2.7   Inspecting areas or items in the house which can cause accidents to the occupants and visitors in the house.

MS Element 3: **IMPLEMENT**

This involves implementing the safety scheme which is given in (b) below.

MS Element 4: **MEASURE**

The results would be measured against the performance criteria defined earlier and this involves the following tasks:

E4.1   Examine the records to check the number of accidents requiring hospital attention or emergency services. Compare the period in question with similar periods in previous years.

E4.2   Study the record of minor accidents and check if there are more than four instances per year

E4.3   Use sensors located at critical parts of the house so as to measure selected near misses.

MS Element 5: **REVIEW**

The tasks involved here include the following:

E5.1   Document all the lessons learnt for a given period and explore scope for improvements.

E5.2   Compare the results obtained, e.g. the frequency of occurrences of accidents, and the consequences with other known information for houses located in the same or similar areas.

E5.3   Decide on what improvements can be introduced and incorporated in the future safety management.

(b)   Safety scheme of the GMS for safety

The components making up the safety scheme will now be examined:

Component 1: **Hazard identification**

A number of techniques such as brainstorming can be used to identify the hazards relating to safety. A number of strategies can be adopted to perform the identification, as for example:

- Identify the hazards systematically in each room or area.

- Identify the most frequently perceived hazards followed by less common and rare hazards.

The former strategy will be used in this example. Typical hazards were identified for the kitchen, dining room, lounge, utility room, bathrooms and bedrooms, see figures B.1a to B.1c.

Ref	Objective of activity	Undesired outcome	Hazard
K1	Prepare a meal	Finger bleeding due to cut	Using sharp knife carelessly
K2	Prepare a meal	Food burnt	Unsupervised cooking
K3	Prepare a meal	Pan fire in kitchen	Distracted during oil frying
K4	Prepare a meal	Explosion/banging noises	Metal utensil in microwave oven
K5	Prepare a meal	Lack of lighting, food burnt	Power cut
K6	Toasting bread	Smoke from burnt toast	Wrong time setting for toaster
K7	Switch on boiler	Smell of gas	Gas leak
K8	Making a cup of tea	Hand scalded	Boiling water spills
K9	Transferring plates	Plate breaks on floor	Carrying plates with oily hand
K10	Move about in kitchen	Injury to leg and shoulder	Slip on wet floor
U1	Washing cloth	Electric shock	Wet hand touches switch
U2	Washing cloth	Water flood floor	Water leak from pipe
U3	Washing cloth	Machine vibration	Uneven loading of machine
U4	Washing cloth	Soap suds on the floor	Put in too much soap powder

Figure B.1a: Hazards in the kitchen and utility room

Ref	Objective of activity	Undesired outcome	Hazard
D1	Eating meals	Burnt hand, damage table	Handling very hot plates
D2	Eating meals	Soil floor and table	Spill hot soup
D3	Eating meals	Soil table, floor, break glass	Spill drinks
D4	Eating meals	Experience choking	Eating too quickly
L1	Entering/leaving room	Personal injury	Trip over obstacles
L2	Moving furniture	Injury back	Incorrect work posture
L3	Relaxing	Injury back	Chair breaks
L4	Relaxing	Damage carpets and items	Water leak from ceiling

Figure B.1b: Hazards in the dining room and the lounge

Ref	Objective of activity	Undesired outcome	Hazard
W1	Using the bathroom	Person injuries due to fall	Slip in bath
W2	Using the bathroom	Person injuries due to fall	Slip on wet floor
W3	Using the bathroom	Water flood floor	Left taps running
W4	Using the bathroom	Water flood floor	Pipes leaking
B1	Breakfasting in bed	Scald hand and soil beddings	Take hot drink half asleep
B2	Arising from bed	Twist ankle	Slip off bed
B3	Tidying up	Personal injury	Grandma trips over item
B4	Cleaning window	Fall and personal injury	Over stretching

Figure B.1c: Hazards in the both room and the bedrooms

Component 2: **Risk assessment**

The identified hazards are assessed to determine their risk levels using the qualitative method, see Chapter 12 before examining a selected number of them with the aid of quantitative methods, see Chapter 13. Using the risk matrix, the risk level of each hazard can be determined using the following relationship:

$$R = C \times P$$

Where C (consequence) is divided into four segments as follows:

Z: Serious (e.g. injury requiring a stay in a hospital)

Y: Major (e.g. injury requiring out patient treatment)

X: Medium (e.g. injury can be treated at home)

W: Minor (e.g. cuts and bruises)

And P (probability of occurrence) is divided into five segments as follows:

5:     Very frequent (e.g. once a month)

4:     Frequent (e.g. once a year)

3:     Occasional (e.g. once every 5 years)

2:     Rare (e.g. once every 20 years)

1:     Very rare (e.g. once in a life time)

	Z	N	T	U	I	I	
	Y	N	T	T	U	I	
C	X	N	N	T	T	U	
	W	N	N	N	N	N	
		1	2	3	4	5	P

Where **I** : Intolerable risk region

U : Uncertain risk region

T : Tolerable risk region

N : Negligible risk region

Ref	Hazard	C	P	R
K1	Using a sharp knife carelessly	Y	4	U
K2	Unsupervised cooking	Y	2	T
K3	Distracted during frying with oil	Z	3	U
K4	Metal utensil in microwave	W	3	N
K5	Power cut	W	3	N
K6	Long time setting for toaster	X	4	T
K7	Gas leak	Z	2	T
K8	Boiling water spill	X	3	T
K9	Carrying plates with oily hand	Y	3	T
K10	Slipping on wet floor	Z	2	T
U1	Wet hand touching switch	Y	2	T
U2	Water leaking from pipe	W	2	N
U3	Uneven loading of the machine	X	4	T
U4	Putting in too much soap powder	W	3	N
D1	Handling very hot plates	Y	3	T
D2	Spilling hot soup	X	3	T
D3	Spilling drinks	X	3	T
D4	Eating too quickly	Y	2	T
L1	Tripping over obstacles on the floor	Y	3	T
L2	Incorrect work posture	Y	3	T
L3	Chair breaks	X	1	N
L4	Water leaking from ceiling	Y	1	N
W1	Slipping in the bath	Y	3	T
W2	Slipping on a wet floor	Y	3	T
W3	Leaving taps running	Y	2	T
W4	Pipe leaking	Y	2	T
S1	Spilling hot drinks in bed	X	3	T
S2	Slipping off the bed	Y	2	T
S3	Grandma tripping over garments on the floor	Y	4	U
S4	Over-stretching	Z	4	

Figure B.2: Risk of the hazards in the various rooms

Component 3: **Risk reduction**

An examination of Figure (B.2) suggests that there is one hazard with intolerable risk level and three hazards in the uncertain risk region. It is important to reduce the risks of these hazards so that they are in the tolerable risk region. These risk levels will now be reduced in turn.

S4: Over reaching

The hazard is concerned with "over reaching" while cleaning the bedroom windows from the inside of the house. The risk can be reduced by addressing both the probability of occurrence and consequence using the following methods:

(i)   Probability of occurrence: By using the management method, this would involve a decision not to clean the outside of the window from the inside as certain parts of the window could not be reached without stretching leading to over-reaching. Using the engineering and operational methods would suggest that the windows should be cleaned from the outside with the cleaning device at the end of a long extension pole.

(ii) Consequence: The risk level can be reduced by fitting a special harness to the shoulders of the person performing the cleaning and if a fall is likely to occur, the harness would prevent full realisation.

K1: Using a sharp knife carelessly

The most effective method would be to develop a positive safety culture that shows the correct attitude to safety and takes serious care when performing tasks with a high risk level. Methods of risk reduction involve the following:

(i)   Probability of occurrence: This can be reduced by devising a cutting procedure or technique which ensures the sharp edge is always directed away from the hand which holds the items to be cut. In addition, full concentration must be given while performing the activity.

(ii) Consequence: Reduce the consequence by using less sharp knives so that if the edge comes into contact with the finger, it would reduce the depth of penetration.

K3: Distraction during frying with oil

Cooking with a pan of hot oil is a cooking activity which should be conducted with the greatest care and requires full concentration. A number of methods can be effective in reducing the risk level.

(i)   Probability of occurrence: This can be reduced by careful preparation and the introduction of a management system. This will require an operational procedure for cooking with hot oil to be devised from safety considerations. Preferably these should be supported by some one with cooking experience. All attention should be focused on doing the single task.

(ii)   Consequence: The seriousness of any fire can be reduced by using specially designed cooking pan which can cut off air supply quickly and by having fire fighting equipment ready at hand.

S3: Grandma trips over garment on floor

Many bedrooms are scattered with garments by the bedroom users, and grandma may try to do some tidying up and would readily trip over these items leading to personal injuries. The more serious ones include heads hitting the furniture. Risk reduction methods are mainly based on reducing the probability of occurrence.

(i)   Probability of occurrence: The best method is to apply a positive safety culture by recognising the risk level of a hazard and minimising its effects by systematically removing any garment lying on the floor so the way is cleared of obstacles.

(ii)   Consequence: This can be reduced by using furniture in bedrooms with non-sharp edges or corners or even padding the likely contact points. However, these projections may well make the furniture unattractive.

Component 4: **Emergency preparedness**

To achieve a good safety standard it is important to have contingency plans for various types of responses. At one extreme, preparation should be made to treat hazards with minor consequences. For example, first aid items should be available for treating minor accidents such as cuts, bruises and twisted ankles. Typical items should include antiseptic solution, bandages and plasters.

At the other extreme, there are accidents which can occur even though all reasonable cautions have been taken. The main causes are associated with aspects of human factors – attitude, behaviour, errors and violation. In these circumstances it would be helpful to follow the tasks given in Chapter 12 on emergency preparedness. In this example, an outbreak of fire in a bedroom is used to illustrate the various tasks to be implemented and these are:

Task 1: *Investigate*: Prepare a procedure for dealing with an outbreak of an accident, in this case a fire. Ensure it is communicated to every member of the household. The first task should always be to make an investigation of the circumstance of the accident and the duration must be very brief.

Task 2: *Decide*: What actions should be taken and this includes informing everyone and seeking external help.

Task 3: *Communicate*: internally so that every one in the house is aware of the fire and externally to call for help from the fire brigade and letting neighbours know of the incident. If there is injury to personnel, calls may have to be made to the emergency services.

Task 4: *Attend*: To any one who is injured using first-aid kit while waiting for the arrival of emergency services.

Task 5: *Contain*: Train everyone so that they know the locations of the fire extinguishers and have some experience in handling fire fighting equipment. The containment and preventing fire from spreading will depend on circumstances, intensity of the fire and the scope for action.

Task 6: *Escape*: Follow the effective "escape" routes from where they are at the time to the most appropriate exit(s).

Task 7: *Evacuate*: Everyone inside should leave the house and go to a safer area outside. Generally, in land based emergencies this is the most direct solution.

Task 8: *Rescue*: This task may not be necessary unless some one has to be rescued from the house via a window.

It will be noted that emergency preparedness is more straightforward on land than that for ships or offshore situations.

Stage 3: Status

Having performed the safety assessment it is useful to document the safety standard or status at a given date. This will be helpful to the occupants of the house to be aware of the aspects of safety relating to living in the house. It may even assist in persuading insurance companies to reduce the insurance premium they charge the house owners and occupants!

B.4   Suggestions for enhancing safety

There are a number of suggestions which can be made under the following headings:

(a)   *Greater safety awareness*

In general, the safety standard in a household depends to a large extent on safety awareness. For example, the parents have experienced accidents in the past and know the likelihood of occurrence and the consequence, so they are more likely to promote better safety in the household. To achieve greater safety awareness, it would be helpful for the whole family to discuss the issues. Use examples of experience gained to illustrate what can go wrong. It is helpful to acquire published literature on accident prevention, e.g. how to deal with an outbreak of fire in the house, and this type of booklet is very popular in many countries. For the younger members of the family, they may have attended accident prevention classes at school and these sessions will enhance safety awareness.

(b)   *Developing a positive safety culture*

Following from greater safety awareness, it is important to develop a positive safety culture within the household. This means there should be a correct attitude, treating safety seriously and responsibly. Thinking about safety implications before undertaking more dangerous activities will lead to safer behaviour and better decisions. This in turn can reduce errors and minimise violation acts. It can be argued that such an approach would be too much for young members of the household. However, a positive safety culture has to be developed at an early age.

(c)   *Start with basic safety considerations*

In this example the safety scheme provided only a sample of hazards but it does give an indication of the types of hazards which can be found in a household. In risk assessment, only the qualitative technique was used with the aid of a risk matrix and a limited number of risk reduction methods were suggested. In spite of the simplification it is better to devise an overall safety management appreciation for the household rather than seeking improvement concerning just one or two hazards.

B.5   Conclusions

The main conclusions to be drawn from this example are:

(a)   The GMS for safety can be readily applied to many situations and it is particularly suitable for every day living where there are no formal prescriptive regulations to be met.

(b)   It is useful to adopt a systemic approach for applying the 'GMS for safety' approach and this, it turn, assists in identifying the main hazards, by assessing their risks before reducing selected hazards with intolerable and uncertain risks to tolerable levels using appropriate methods.

Appendix C

AN EXAMPLE OF THE USE OF THE PRESCRIPTIVE REGULATORY APPROACH

C.1 Introduction

It has been stated in the main text of the book that the maritime industry uses the prescriptive regulatory approach to treat safety and it has a very significant role. Many regulations exist and are used to address various safety issues, ranging from ship design to ship operation.

The main aims of this appendix are:

a)   To outline the basic steps involved in using prescriptive regulations in a maritime activity.

b)   To demonstrate the application of the prescriptive regulatory approach via an example.

c)   To consider the features relating to the prescribed requirements and prescribed solutions.

C.2 Stages in using the prescriptive regulations

The principle of the prescriptive regulatory approach is quite straightforward, i.e. the authority prescribes both the requirements and method of solution via various instructions. The practical application is less straightforward, because the provider of products and services has to be aware of the relevant regulations and correctly interpret the requirements before implementing the instructions. It is, therefore, useful to consider the implementation of prescriptive regulations as made up of various stages

Stage 1: Seeking information on the regulations

The starting point in applying a prescriptive regulation on safety is to find the relevant regulations applicable to the situation. The sources of regulations have been considered in Chapter 4 and the user has to bear in mind that there are international, regional and national regulations. The international regulations are generated by the International Maritime Organization (IMO). In addition, the regulations associated with the International Labour Organisation (ILO) may need to be consulted as well. Regional regulations are produced by the region in which a country is grouped, e.g. the UK is in the region of the European Community and its shipping has to meet these regulations, which have special features that differ from the international ones. The national or flag State regulations will vary depending on the country in question. Using the UK as an example, users have to be familiar with some of the following:

- The Merchant Shipping regulations: These are produced from time to time to address specific issues and the year these regulations come into operation is given.

- M Notices: There are three types of Marine Notices called respectively Merchant Shipping Notices, Marine Guidance Notices and Marine Information Notices. Only the first provides mandatory information.

- Statutory instruments: These are documents which give actual prescriptive requirements and instructions or methods for meeting the requirements.

With the availability of internet facilities and the world wide web it is now possible to find, electronically, a considerable amount of information on the required maritime regulations.

Stage 2: Interpretation of the regulations

Once the relevant information has been found, users must interpret the written requirements and instructions clearly. Regulations are usually prepared or checked by people with legal training and experience is needed to make a correct interpretation. This problem is recognised and, to overcome the difficulty, user aids are available. For example, a book called *The Shipmaster's Business Companion*, written by Malcolm Maclachlan, was published by The Nautical Institute. It gives interpretations of the shipping regulations in a systematic manner. Once again, experience is needed to perform this stage effectively.

A special feature of the prescriptive regulations is concerned with cross-referencing, whereby the user has to keep tabs on a number of regulations at the same time in order to arrive at an answer. What this means is that one set of regulations may ask the user to go to other sets of regulations in order to get more details or to meet other requirements in parallel. There is also the tendency to update regulations via the use of amendments which contain relatively short outlines of changes instead of revising the complete regulations. Thus it may be necessary for the user to be good at following a paper trail!

Stage 3: Implementing the instructions

The next stage will be to follow the instructions while bearing in mind the previous stage so as to benefit from correct interpretations. The benefits include improved efficiency, more cost-effectiveness and minimisation of the need for extra work.

C.3 Choosing a sample example

There are many prescriptive regulations and they vary in their form, length and detail. It is possible to choose an example which is very comprehensive but it would be too long and may not show the principles involved. However, to select a brief one can also present a problem as it may not illustrate fully the form of these regulations. Having considered several regulations, it was decided to choose an example which is fairly concise, yet can show the key features, i.e. the requirements and solutions are both prescribed clearly. The regulations are taken from Statutory Instruments 1988 No. 1638 issued by the UK Maritime and Coastguard Agency. It is concerned with entry into dangerous spaces. It will be noted that even in this example there is a tendency to cross reference to other regulations and sources of information. This example was selected for the following key reasons:

•   It is short and applicable to an important area from a safety point of view, i.e. entry into dangerous spaces.

•   There are only a few cross-references to other regulations.

C.4 Entry into dangerous spaces regulations

The contents of this section are taken from Maclachlan's *Shipmaster's Business Companion* [2003] and are concerned with the regulations about entry into dangerous spaces. There are six sections in this example. Sections (1) and (2) give the prescribed requirements and Sections (3) to (6) outline the prescribed methods of meeting the requirements. The form of the regulations is described using the relevant headings as follows:

(1)   The heading of the regulations

Entry into dangerous spaces Regulations

*   The Merchant Shipping Act (entry into dangerous spaces) regulations 1988(SI1988/1638)

  -     **apply**, except regulation 11, to UK ships (regulations 3(1)(a)).

  -     **apply**, except regulations 6 and 10, to non-UK ships in a UK port(regulations 3(1)(b)).

  -     **do not apply** to fishing vessels, pleasure craft, offshore installations on or within 500 metres of their working stations, or ships on which there is no master or crew or watchman for the time being (regulations 3(2)).

  -     **do not** provide for the granting of **exemptions**.

  -     provide in regulation 10 for the **inspection** of any UK ship by the MCA and for **detention** of the ship if found not to be complying with the regulations.

This section is equivalent to a requirement which is prescribed in various other regulations which are cross-referenced.

(2)   The definitions

Definitions

*   A dangerous space means any enclosed or confined space in which it is

foreseeable that the atmosphere may at some stage contain toxic or flammable gases or vapours, or be deficient in oxygen, to the extent that it may endanger the life or health of any person entering that space.

This section provides clarification of the requirement.

(3)   Master's duties

Master's duties

The master **must**

- except when necessary for entry, ensure that all **entrance to unattended dangerous spaces** are either kept closed or otherwise secured against entry (regulation 4).

- ensure that all **procedures** for ensuring safe entry and working in dangerous spaces are observed on board (regulation 5 (1)(ii)).

- **take full account** of the principles and guidance contained in the Code of Safe Working Practices relating to entry into dangerous spaces (regulation 5(3)).

- ensure that in any tanker of 500gt or over, and in any other ship of 1000gt and over, **drills simulating the rescue of a crew member** from a dangerous space are held at the intervals not exceeding 2 months, and that a record of such drills is entered in the Official Log Book (regulation 6)

- ensure that the oxygen meter and any other testing device required by regulation 7 is maintained in good working order and, where applicable, regularly serviced and calibrated to the maker's recommendations (regulations 7).

This section represents the instructions on how the requirements are to be satisfied by the master of the ship.

(4)   The employer's duties

Employer's duties

The master's employer **must**

- ensure that **procedures** for ensuring safe entry and working in dangerous spaces clearly laid down (regulation 5(1)(ii)).

- ensure that each ship where entry into a dangerous space may be necessary carries or has available an **oxygen meter** and such **other testing devices as appropriate to the hazard** likely to be encountered in any dangerous space (regulation 7).

This section provides instructions to the employer in meeting the requirement.

(5) *Duties of any person*

Duties of any person

*   any person entering a dangerous space must **take full account** of the principles and guidance in the Code of Safe Working Practices (regulation 5(3)).

This section has the same role as the two previous sections and is another cross-reference.

(6) *Prohibitions on any person*

Prohibitions on any person

*   No person may enter or be in a dangerous space except in accordance with the procedures laid down by the employer under regulations 5(1) (regulation 5(2)).

This section gives an instruction on meeting the requirement of the regulation.

C.5 Some general observations

Based on a review of prescriptive regulations and other examples, a number of observations can be made.

Firstly, there are many regulations in existence, as discussed in Chapter 4. To appreciate which regulations are in force can be a very challenging task when part of the requirement depends upon other sources. For those new to the application of regulations, finding out the current requirements can be very time consuming, especially when they refer to other regulations or amendments.

Secondly, since the regulations have generally been based on accidents or past experience, they are written in a precise way. For the prescribed requirement, if it contains special terms or expressions, these are always defined in order to avoid any misinterpretation. Likewise the instructions or the methods of solution are also clearly given and can readily be followed.

Thirdly, the methods of solution are given for users to follow and this, in turn, means that the user does not have to think about alternative solutions. When a new situation arises, it is not surprising that fresh regulations need to be devised, which can take considerable time.

C.6 Conclusions

From the contents of this appendix and the illustrative example, the following conclusions can be drawn:

a) Both the requirement and the instructions for the solutions of a prescriptive regulation tend to be clearly worded but attention should be devoted to making sure that they are correctly interpreted before implementation.

b) Prescriptive regulations tend to rely on other prescriptive regulations and amendments and the cross-referencing can make the application of specific regulations a very demanding task until some practical experience is acquired.

Appendix D

GMS FOR SAFETY FOR HIGH SPEED CRAFT HSS1500

D.1 Introduction

This appendix demonstrates how the generic management system for safety approach is used to establish a safety standard for a high speed craft.   It provides a similar answer to the safety case approach as indicated earlier in Chapter 9.   In view of the details involved in achieving the solution, only the key features and sample results will be given here.   However, it is intended that the steps involved in doing the safety assessment would be clearly illustrated.   The example selected is on the safety of the Stena Line's high speed catamaran called HSS1500.   The first HSS1500 came into operation as the largest passenger ferry with a speed of 40 knots and there was no operational experience.   A safety case was prepared in 1996 and updated in 2001, and the information has enabled the methodology of GMS for safety to be highlighted in the present example.

The aims of the appendix are as follows:

a)   To provide the background information on the Stena Line's HSS1500 catamaran Ro Ro ferry.

b)   To summarise the key steps in preparing the safety case using the GMS` for safety approach.

D.2 Background to HSS 1500

HSS1500, built in 1995, was the world's largest high speed passenger ferry with a service speed of 40 knots. The HSS1500 satisfies the regulations of IMO's International Code of Safety for High Speed Craft (see IMO (1996)) and is regarded as a Category B craft. However, there was no operational experience available for large craft travelling at such a high speed, so Stena Line decided to use the goal setting approach by producing a safety case for the first HSS1500 called Stena Explorer. This safety case was prepared for the vessel's operational phase and route was across the Irish Sea between Holyhead, England and Dun Laoghaire, Ireland. The vessel has a designed operational significant wave height limit of 5m though, in practice, a value of 4m significant wave height is used because it has not been possible to demonstrate the vessel's capability in heavy weather because such extreme weather conditions are rare on the Irish sea route. For loading and unloading arrangements in port, use is made of a four-line link span. For further details on the safety case, see Kuo et al (1997).

In 2001, the safety case was updated, referred to as "The Safety Case 2001 for Stena Line's HSS1500s" and it covered all the following three vessels:

- *Stena Explorer* - Holyhead, England to Dun Laoghaire, Ireland in service in 1996

- *Stena Voyager* - Stranraer, Scotland to Belfast, Northern Ireland in service in 1997

- *Stena Discovery* - Harwich, England to Hook of Holland, The Netherlands in service in 1999

The safety standard of HSS01500 was established based on the conventional safety case concept approach and not the generic management system approach (see Chapter 8 for the discussion on the differences between the two approaches). Since the GMS approach is the more versatile of the two approaches, this chapter uses the data from the Safety Case 2001 but adopting the GMS for safety approach.

Brief description of HSS1500

The principal features of HSS1500 are:

Length overall:	126.40 m
Length between perpendiculars:	107.81 m
Breadth moulded:	40.00 m
Draught:	4.80 m
Vehicle deck above keel:	12.50 m
Light ship:	5,892 tonnes
Displacement:	19,638 tonnes
Main Engines:	2 x LM2500 Gas Turbines providing 20 MW each
	2 x LM1600 Gas Turbines providing 13 MW each
Passengers:	1500
Cars:	375
Service Speed:	40 knots

The HS1500 is propelled by water jets generated by four turbines and there are two bow thrusters. An integrated bridge system is installed for navigating and manoeuvring using five monitor screens. A picture of the craft is given in figure D.1.

D.3   The stages of the GMS for safety

There are three stages to the GMS for safety which will now be considered.

Figure D.1 *Stena Discovery*, Stena Line

photo courtesy: Jesper T Andersen / jtashipphoto.dk

Stage 1: The need

Stena Line has adopted the following overall goal for the ferries which incorporates safety:

> *To be competitive in meeting the clients' specification with a ship that operates cost-effectively at an acceptable level of safety.*

The clients seek fast sea transport with the comfort of a modern passenger liner and the versatility of a Roll-on Roll-off ferry. To be cost-effective in its operation, the developed design has to offer sufficient load capacity and the ability to provide an all year round service so as to compete with other forms of transport. Recognising the public's concern regarding Ro-Ro ferry safety, the company has paid special attention to achieving an acceptable level of safety, i.e. As High As Reasonably Practicable or AHARP level. In practice, this includes the prescriptive requirements from the appropriate maritime authority that demands that all the identified hazards must have tolerable and negligible risk levels. Any hazard with an intolerable risk level must be reduced and there must be effective solutions in place to deal with an emergency. The suitable methods used to meet the requirements can be selected by the operator and this is the basis of the safety case approach, i.e. the safety standards to be satisfied are prescribed and the methods of achieving the solution are NOT prescribed.

Stage 2: The information for safety management

Using the background data given in the previous section, this stage applies the GMS for safety which is treated as two parts of the GMS unit, i.e. the Management System (MS) and the Safety Scheme (SS). These are now considered in turn.

(a)　The management system of the GMS for safety

The five basic elements are now examined.

MS Element 1: **Define**

There are two basic items to be defined and one is the safety goal and the other is the performance criteria for safety. The safety goal can be stated as follows:

> *To minimise accident injuries to passengers and crew on board HSS1500 requiring onshore hospital treatment, damage to the ship needing the help of the emergency service or pollution of the environment leading to public concern.*

The performance criteria for safety include:

E1.1　Any injuries should be confined to the categories of serious, moderate and minor with infrequent to very remote probability of occurrence and the ratios of personal injury to passengers transported should be similar for all three HSS1500s.

E1.2　The trends of all three personal injury types to passengers transported should be downward with time.

MS Element 2: **Organise**

There are various tasks to be done in association with the organisation of resources and the activities to ensure the safety goal can be achieved. These are in addition to those needed for normal ship operation. A shortened list is given here:

E2.1　Acquire weather data: Check the weather conditions on the routes, since HSS1500 has an operational limit of significant wave height of 4 metres.

E2.2　Onboard management: Ensure there is at least a minimum number of crew to passengers available for each journey, e.g. from 26 crew for 230 passengers to 46 crew for 1,500 passengers.

E2.3　Unruly passengers: Study all trips in advance, especially when the trips involve large groups of passengers where crowd control techniques must be given attention, e.g. football fans crossing for an important match.

E2.4　Safety briefing: Verify that appropriate safety briefing messages for the passengers have been prepared and tested for their clarity and comprehension.

E2.5　Safety equipment: Test the emergency equipment on a planned basis to ensure it is in good working order, e.g. fire fighting equipment.

E2.6　Safety training of on board personnel: Conduct safety training for everyone who works on board with special attention given to temporary staff, using dedicated safety training CDs.

E2.7　Docking manoeuvres: Take special care and provide refresher training for docking the vessel in adverse weather conditions.

E2.8　Evacuation facilities: Ensure all the facilities are in good order and crew are trained in their application.

MS Element 3: **Implement**

This involves implementing the safety scheme which is given in Part (b).

MS Element 4: **Measure**

The results obtained from the safety scheme would be measured against the performance criteria defined in MS Element 1 and examples of tasks involved include:

E4.1　Plot graphs of the ratios of personal injury type to passengers transported against time for all three HSS1500s, examine the results and seek an explanation for any significant deviations.

E4.2　Verify that the trend for the ratio of passenger injury type to passengers transported is downward.

MS Element 5: **Review**

The tasks involved here include:

E5.1　Documentation: Document all incidents and accidents so that lessons learnt for a certain period will readily be available. The information would be used to explore ways of improving operational performance.

E5.2　Benchmarking: Compare the results obtained for all three HSS1500s and benchmark them against other ferry operations using conventional Ro-Ro ferries. Compare both the frequency of occurrence of incidents and accidents and their severity.

E5.3　Improvements: Decide on what improvements can be incorporated into refinements to the safety management of the vessel.

E5.4　Feedback: From the experience gained, feed back the lessons learnt and refinements to MS Element 1 (Define), so that the next iteration can commence.

(b)　*Safety scheme of the GMS for safety*

Using the information acquired in the define and organise elements of the MS, it is now possible to process the four components of the safety scheme, i.e. hazard identification, risk assessment, risk reduction and emergency preparedness. These are examined in turn.

Component 1: **Hazard identification**

A combination of brainstorming techniques and systematic strategy are used to perform the hazard identification and, for further details, see Chapter 10. The sample hazards selected are classified by type under the following headings:

- Propulsion related hazards, see figure D.3a.

- Human factors related hazards, see figure D.3b.

- External operations related hazards, see figure D.3c.

- On board activities related hazards, see figure D.3d.

- Security related hazards, see figure D.3e.

- Onboard facilities and equipment related hazards, see figure D.3f.

The reference number is made up of three parts. The first letter, H, refers to hazard, the second letter indicates hazard type and the third is the number of the hazard identified, e.g. HB03.

Component 2: **Risk assessment**

The identified hazards are assessed to determine their risk levels, using qualitative risk assessment methods (see Chapter 10), before examining a selected number of hazards with high risk values. The latter methods can be found in Chapter 11.

Using a risk matrix, the risk level (R) of each hazard can be determined using the following relationship:

$$R = C \times P$$

Where C is the consequence and P is the probability of occurrence. In the present case, C is divided into four segments as follows:

Z (4):	Serious	e.g. one or more deaths.
Y (3):	Major	e.g. injuries leading to incapacity.
X (2):	Moderate	e.g. broken limbs.
W (1):	Minor	e.g. cuts and bruises.

P is divided into five segments as follows:

5:	Very frequent	e.g. 1 in 100 trips.
4:	Probable	e.g. 1 in 500 trips.
3:	Remote	e.g. 1 in 2,500 trips.
2:	Rare	e.g. 1 in 12,500 trips.
1:	Very rare	e.g. 1 in 100,000 trips.

This leads to the risk matrix shown in figure D.2:

	Z (4)	N	T	U	I	I	
	Y (3)	N	T	T	U	I	
C	X (2)	N	N	T	T	U	
	W(1)	N	N	N	N	N	
		1	2	3	4	5	**P**

Figure D.2 Risk matrix

The risk level is divided into four regions as follows:

I: Intolerable risk region ($15 \leq R$).

U: Uncertain risk region ($10 \leq R < 15$).

T: Tolerable risk region ($6 \leq R < 10$).

N: Negligible risk region ($R < 6$).

The application of this risk matrix leads to the results given in figure D.3.

The headings are Reference No (Ref), Hazard Description, C, P, R, Risk reduction suggestions and a rating of reduction cost-effectiveness (E). E is rated as H (High), M (Medium) or L (Low).

Ref	Hazard Description	C	P	R	Risk Reduction Suggestions	Rating
HA.01	Debris in water jet	X	2	N	-	
HA.02	Waterjet steering faulty	X	3	T	Early detection and repair	H
HA.03	Severe waterjet vibration	Y	4	U	Reverse flow, use divers	M
HA.04	Waterjet blockage	Y	3	T	Reverse flow, use divers	M
HA.05	Waterjet failures	X	4	T	Planned maintenance	H
HA.06	Fender damage to waterjet	X	4	T	Monitoring, education	H
Etc.	-	-	-	-	-	-

Cost-effectiveness rating: H (High), M (Medium), L (Low)

Figure D.3a Propulsion related hazards

Ref	Hazard Description	C	P	R	Risk Reduction Suggestions	Rating
HB.01	Crew fatigue	X	3	T	Improve work schedule	H
HB.02	Food poisoning	Y	2	T	Generate food hygiene culture	J
HB.03	Unruly passengers at sea	Z	3	U	Training in crowd control	M
HB.04	Bridge crew falling ill	X	1	N	-	-
HB.05	Passenger overboard	Z	1	T	Crew alertness, preventative action	M
HB.06	Motion induced slip/fall	X	3	T	Educate and provide information	M
Etc.	-	-	-	-	-	

Cost-effectiveness rating: H (High), M (Medium), L (Low)

Figure D.3b Human factors related hazards

Ref	Hazard Description	C	P	R	Risk Reduction Suggestions	Rating
HC.01	Wake wash	Z	4	I	Educate, follow speed chart	H
HC.02	Grounding	Z	2	T	Check soundings	M
HC.03	Collision with another vessel	Z	2	T	Route planning, lookouts	H
HC.04	Slamming damage	Y	2	T	Reduce speed or change heading	H
HC.05	Unexpected extreme weather	Z	3	U	Better data and reduce speed	H
HC.06	Contact with submerged object	W	1	N	-	-
Etc.	-	-	-	-	-	-

Cost-effectiveness rating: H (High), M (Medium), L (Low)

Figure D.3c External operations related hazards

Ref	Hazard Description	C	P	R	Risk Reduction Suggestions	Rating
HD.01	Fire in machinery space	Z	2	T	Training, detector placing	H
HD.02	Fire on car deck	Y	2	T	Training, detector placing	H
HD.03	Fire in accommodation	Z	2	T	Training, detector placing	H
HD.04	Fire in galley	Z	2	T	Training, detector placing	H
HD.05	Vehicles falling over	Y	3	T	Lashing of vehicles	H
HD.06	Vehicle hits passenger	Y	3	T	Lanes for walking, warning	M
Etc	-	-	-	-	-	-

Cost-effectiveness rating: H (High), M (Medium), L (Low)

Figure D.3d On board activities related hazards

Ref	Hazard Description	C	P	R	Risk Reduction Suggestions	Rating
HE.01	Bomb threat	Y	2	T	Seek intelligence, search drill	H
HE.02	Piracy	Z	2	T	Educate, prevention training	M
HE.03	Rescue boat failure	Z	2	T	Regular testing	M
HE.04	Bridge window damage	Z	1	N	-	-
HE.05	Buzzed by aircraft	W	1	N	-	-
HE.06	Hit by a missile	Z	1	N	-	-
Etc	-	-	-	-	-	-

Cost-effectiveness rating: H (High), M (Medium), L (Low)

Figure D.3e Security related hazards

Ref	Hazard Description	C	P	R	Risk Reduction Suggestions	Rating
HF.01	Integrated bridge system failure	Z	3	I	Regular inspection and training	H
HF.02	Navigation lights failure	X	1	N	-	-
HF.03	Steering gear failure	Y	1	N	-	-
HF.04	Joystick failure	Z	3	U	Regular check, training	H
HF.05	Radio communication failure	W	3	N	-	-
HF.06	Total engine failure	Z	2	T	Planned maintenance	H
Etc	-	-	-	-	-	-

Cost-effectiveness rating: H (High), M (Medium), L (Low)

Figure D.3f On board facilities and equipment related hazards

Component 3: **Risk reduction**

In all the identified hazards, see figure D.2, suggestions for risk reduction are given for all the ones with intolerable, uncertain and tolerable risk levels. Further information is now given to the hazards with intolerable and uncertain risk levels.

HA03: Severe waterjet vibration

Description

Vibration will occur in any machinery having moving items and, provided the amplitude of vibration is low, this will not give rise to any problems. Water jet vibration is caused by uneven loading due to the passage of objects temporarily entrained in the flow and the vibratory levels can become noticeable, leading to the need to lower the level.

Consequence reduction

The entrained objects should be removed and this is usually done when the flow is reversed. When this method is not able to remove the objects, divers will have to be employed.

Probability of occurrence reduction

Some form of filter could be installed at the point of water entrance so as to prevent the objects from being entrained in the intake of water but this would obstruct the flow.

HA04: Water jet blockage

Description

Water jets can be blocked due to a number of reasons. The main one is associated with debris such as fishing nets or lobster pots entering the water intake and leading to the obstruction of the flow.

Consequence reduction

Similar to removing objects in the case of waterjet vibration, the debris can be removed by reversing the flow. In extreme cases, divers may be required to do the removal.

Probability of occurrence reduction

Use of guarding filters would prevent debris from entering the water inlets but would obstruct the flow. Since there are four water jets, there is sufficient redundancy as to ensure safe operation until the ship goes into port.

HB03: Unruly passengers at sea

Description

On some trips, passengers can behave in an unruly manner and these are due to the following main causes:

- Drunkenness.

- Drug abuse.

- Provocation.

In a small scale this is more of a nuisance, but on a larger scale this can have serious consequences.

Consequence reduction

It is important to have trained staff who can recognise the main causes and take action to minimise their effects. The training involves methods of calming people and isolating individual troublemakers.

The master of a passenger ship has a number of legally approved powers in certain circumstances to act for the safety of ship and personnel, e.g. detention and restraint of an individual.

Probability of occurrence reduction

Devise efficient communication procedures to ensure that staff at the arrival port are informed in advance and that local police are alerted to deal with troublemakers on the ship's arrival.

HC04: Wake wash

Description

When a ship is travelling forward in a seaway, waves are generated from the bow and stern of the ship. These waves are divergent and produce triangular patterns on both sides of the ship. These waves can travel a long distance before the amplitude is greatly reduced. Generally, these generated waves do not cause problems to small boats or shorelines because the amplitudes are small. However, for high speed craft, some combinations of speed and water depth or critical speed range can lead to resonance effects when the natural and encounter frequencies have the same value and this can result in high wave amplitudes. This in turn can cause damage to shorelines due to the wake wash and endanger the lives of those in small boats.

Consequence and probability of occurrence reduction

The effects of wake wash can be minimised as follows:

* Educate the crew on the wake wash phenomenon.

* With the aid of a speed-depth chart, information on the critical speed range can be made available and this can assist the crew to avoid operating in that range so as to minimise the effects.

* Support the use of the speed-depth charts with training.

* Educate the public and those living on shorelines where high speed craft operate on the effects of wake wash phenomenon so that actions can be taken to minimise the consequences.

HC05: Unexpected extreme weather

Description

The weather on the routes across both the Irish Sea and the North Sea can change rapidly from a fresh wind to gale conditions with little notice. When the HSS1500 is in port, a decision can be made whether or not to sail. However, the problem is less straightforward when HSS1500 is at sea.

Consequence reduction

To reduce the ship's motion for the comfort of passengers and to minimise potential structural damage, the ship requires to change heading. It will be noted that the HSS 1500 has a special hull form which results in the vertical acceleration (associated with sea sickness) being reduced with speed. Indeed, should the speed be increased from 20 to 40 knots the vertical accelerations are reduced by 50%! The best action to take should be based on the operational experience of all three ships gathered over the years of operation.

Probability of occurrence reduction

A valid weather forecast is a requirement of the permit to operate and no voyage can be undertaken without one. Any extreme weather can generally be planned for. Special forecasting arrangements have to be put in place if the HSS 1500 is to travel outside its designated route. Since the forecast may not be very accurate, when unexpected weather occurs, it is useful to use additional sources for gathering data simultaneously so as to assist in decision making. The approach would involve:

•   Acquiring weather data continuously.

•   Comparing data obtained from forecasts with operational conditions.

•   Making direct personal contact with duty weather forecasters.

HC06: <u>Integrated bridges system failure</u>

Description

The HSS1500 is designed using an integrated bridge system and failure would incapacitate the ship. The HSS 1500 was built in such a way as to ensure that there is double redundancy for all critical systems.

Probability of occurrence reduction

The most effective method of reducing the likelihood of failure is by regular and well-organised maintenance using reliable operational data. There is a weekly incident report on the operation of the integrated bridge system from all three HSS1500 and the information is circulated and shared. The information from these reports provides inputs to the maintenance programme. Additionally all operating staff were trained by the makers of the integrated bridge system before taking up their duties.

HF07: <u>Joystick failure</u>

Description

In HSS1500, the vessel's manoeuvring is done using a joystick in place of the traditional wheel. The joystick therefore takes on a sensitive and important role. For this reason, failure of the joystick can affect the operation of the ship.

Consequence reduction

Have a backup system installed, so that when one joystick fails, it is still possible to operate the ship with the backup system.

Probability of occurrence reduction

Likelihood of failure can be reduced by regular maintenance and regular training for staff with alternative (backup) manoeuvring methods.

Component 4: **Emergency preparedness**

The emergency plan of HSS1500 is based on the guidelines given in IMO's International Code for the safety of high speed craft, called the HSC Code. The relevant chapters for HSS1500 are Chapters 4, 7, 8 and 18 and brief comments are given below:

(a) <u>HSC code Chapter 4: Accommodation and escape matters</u>

The regulations laid out in this chapter are comprehensive in their approach to the designs of a vessel but little attention is paid to crew and passenger actions and responses to emergency situations. For this reason the safety management system will need to include responses appropriate to HSS1500.

(b) <u>HSC Code Chapter 7: Fire safety</u>

This chapter is concerned with the provision of appropriate measures to minimise risk of fire, fire spreading, damage to both crew and passengers and fire containment, prevention and detection and extinguishing systems. Fire is a hazard identified for HSS1500 and effective crew procedures or actions to be taken in a fire emergency scenario are devised, e.g. galley fire requires shut down and close up, vehicle deck fire to be dealt with by foam application and fire extinguishers.

(c) <u>HSC Code Chapter 8: Life-saving appliances and arrangements</u>

This chapter is concerned with the provision of life-saving appliances and arrangements such that abandonment of the craft can be achieved safely in the evacuation time of 18 minutes. In practice, well trained and designated crew members are in charge of the launching of survival craft as a part of the ship's established evacuation procedure.

(d) <u>HSC Code Chapter 18: Operational requirements</u>

This chapter is concerned with the safe operation of a craft in all conditions under which it will be operated and the prevention of operation in dangerous conditions. The most important section of this chapter refers to the training and qualifications of the crew, with information on training requirements and type-rating certification for HSS1500. The latter can be achieved using computer based training with the aid of dedicated CD-ROMs. Other crew training sessions provided include fire-fighting methods, fast rescue boat training, crew management training and car deck management.

For HSS1500, additional steps were taken to determine scenarios in which emergency procedures need to be prepared. These emergency scenarios usually stem from hazards located on the boundary between the intolerable and tolerable risk regions. To be effective, emergencies have to be managed and each of these emergency scenarios need to be examined so as to derive appropriate responses. For example, typical actions include the master being informed of an accident, the master ordering an investigation, and giving first aid to passengers. These actions can be grouped and form various generic action modules. In this way, all the emergency scenarios can be assigned with the relevant generic action and it can then be possible to give focused training to the crew based on specifically safety training modules. This, in turn, greatly enhances the effectiveness of emergency preparedness.

Stage 3: The status

After making trips on all three HSS1500, and discussing with the key personnel responsible the vessel's safety matters, all the supporting information was gathered together as outlined in Stage 2. On completion of the investigation, a safety case report was prepared and given the name Stena Line's HSS1500 – The Safety Case 2001, in June 2001. The report gave the safety status and has three parts:

Part 1:   An executive summary with concise statements concerning the safety information and conclusions.

Part 2:   The main report began with an introduction, followed by the approach adopted to prepare the safety case. The HSS1500 was then described, together with the operating environment. A section on safety assessment involved hazard identification, risk assessment, risk reduction and emergency preparedness. The safety management system was then given, together with recommendations and conclusions, the total length being 30 A4 pages.

Part 3:   The details were given in 12 appendices which provided expansion on the items considered in the main text.

D4 Conclusions

The main conclusions to be drawn from the given example are:

a) The safety of a ship based on a novel design with little operational experience can be treated using the concepts associated with the safety case approach.

b) The safety case can be prepared systematically using the GMS for safety approach to identify the three stages concerning the need, the safety information and the safety status.

c) By monitoring and comparing the safety performance on sister vessels and by comparing relevant information with other ferry operators, e.g passenger behaviour, security, etc. the management process for safety can be improved.

GLOSSARY OF SAFETY TERMS

Absolute: The term is used to describe something which has a unique meaning or value that would be uniformly interpreted by everyone.

Acceptable: Agreeable to a decision or outcome of a situation based on the available information.

Accident: The unexpected, unplanned and usually harmful outcome of an activity.

Action: The practical implementation of a decision.

AHARP: As High As Reasonably Practicable.

ALARP: As Low As Reasonably Practicable.

Attitude: A way of thinking or the opinion held on an issue by individuals or a group of people that is reflected in their approach to dealing with people, things or situations.

Audit: A formal examination of all, or parts, of an activity, situation or system in order to check that the performance meets the pre-defined specification.

Behaviour: The manner in which individuals act as seen by others. (Sometimes this human attribute is applied to equipment).

Brainstorming: An ideas generation technique suitable for use by a group of people in identifying hazards in a system, situation or activity.

Catastrophic: A situation which involve a very significant failure such as loss of life, great financial damages or extensive pollution of the environment.

Cause: The origin of an occurrence that leads to an effect.

Cause-Consequence analysis: The process for understanding the relationships between a cause and the consequences of an incident or accident.

Communication: The interaction between humans or humans and machines or machines to machines in order to exchange information.

Consequences: The results deriving directly or indirectly from an action or a combination of actions.

Containment: Restriction of an activity or occurrence within a set of pre-defined boundaries.

Cost-Benefit Analysis: The process of identifying and understanding the relationship between the cost and the potential benefits in a system or service.

Culture: A belief, philosophy or faith held by groups or individuals which is demonstrated in practice through the attitudes, actions and behaviour adopted by individuals, an organisation or a nation.

Danger: A situation which is perceived by humans to be harmful.

Define: The process of establishing the objective and performance criteria for carrying out an activity or task.

Discounting: The term refers to a procedure for comparing cost items arising from different time periods by adjusting all the values to a specific period, such as the first year, before making the comparison.

Duty holder: The senior person in an organisation with the prime responsibility for the safety of a project, an installation or a system.

Emergency: A situation in which action must be taken within an extremely short time to minimise or prevent injury to human beings, damage to property or harm to the environment.

Environment: The term is used to refer to the surrounding media in which the ship is operating such the sea and the atmosphere.

Ergonomics: The science of matching environment and hardware facilities to a specific task in the way that most closely meets the needs of the user.

Escape: Getting away from a location exposed to a hazard with a high risk level (e.g. a building on fire) to a location with a lower risk level (e.g. outside of the building).

ETA:	Event Tree Analysis: a tree structure for relating a "top event" to its component using binary logic.
Evacuation:	The process of moving a group of people away from a location in which they are exposed to danger.
Failure:	The malfunction of the whole or part of a system, as a result of which its specified objective is not being met.
Fault:	The failure to meet a specification by humans in doing a task or by components of a system, resulting in failure or malfunction.
F-N curve:	A popular graphical presentation of the frequency of occurrence (F) against the number of outputs of the occurrence (N).
FMEA:	Failure Mode Effect Analysis. A method for identifying ways of failure and examining their effects.
FSA:	Formal Safety Assessment. A systematic way to approach the development of new saftey regulations.
FTA:	Fault Tree Analysis. A tree structure for relating the outcome of a critical situation, known as the 'top event', to its components, using a logic based on "AND" and "OR" gates.
Hardware:	The term is used to describe a piece of equipment, either complete or any of its components.
Harm:	A situation which can lead to injury to people, damage to property pollution of the environment or a combination of the three.
Hazard:	Something which can lead to an undesired outcome in the process of meeting an objective. These can involve injury to human beings, damage to property, or harm to the environment, or a combination or some or all of these three.
Hazard log:	The term is used to describe the list of hazards which has been identified during the implementation of an activity or the operation of a system.
HAZOP:	Hazard Operability. A technique for identifying the hazards of a system and is popularly used in the process industry.

Human capital:	A method of doing analysis of the cost of human injuries and fatalities which treats human beings as having a capital value.
Human error:	Unintentional action or outcome of a decision caused by such factors as momentary loss of concentration, following incorrect procedure or a lack of specific knowledge for doing a specific task.
Human factors:	The interfacing of a set of personal capabilities and characteristics with hardware, software, ergonomics and the operational culture in the effective performance of a task.
Human violation:	A deliberate action stemming from such factors as routinely ignoring regulations or good practice, self indulgence or making inappropriate choices in critical circumstances.
IMO:	**I**nternational **M**aritime **O**rganization.
Implement:	The process of applying organised resources and activities to ensure that the objectives are met.
Incident:	The unexpected and unplanned outcome of an activity which usually does not involve injury to people or damages.
Intolerable risk:	A risk of a hazard which has been estimated to be very significant due to a combination of high consequence and high likelihood of occurrence.
ISM Code:	International Safety Management. It is a code adopted by the International Maritime Organisation.
Leadership:	The term is used to describe the role of an individual or a group of individuals who have the authority to act in an appropriate manner and to make decisions in order to ensure the assignment or project objective can be achieved effectively.
Measure:	The use of various methods and information for verifying and checking to what extent performance criteria have been satisfied.
Negligible risk:	A risk of a hazard which has been estimated to be insignificant due to a combination of low consequence and low likelihood of occurrence.

Organise: The process of preparing and planning to enable the defined objectives to be implemented.

Policy: The objectives and approach of the organization in a functional area such as safety together with the criteria and principles on which actions, decisions and responses are based.

Port State Control: A set of regulations from IMO that gives a coastal State the right to inspect visiting foreign ships in national ports to verify that the condition of the ship and its equipment comply with the requirement of appropriate international regulations.

Prescriptive: The laying down of rules or instructions which must be adhered to.

Prevention: A defensive measure in anticipation of a likely occurrence in order to minimise its effect.

Probability: The likelihood of occurrence of an event or activity.

Process: A series of logical steps linked together to ensure the end result is achieved.

Regulations: A set of instructions, formulated by a body with authority, which must be adhered to by the providers of products and services to the public or other third parties.

Reliability: The quality that determines the trustworthiness of information provided or results obtained.

Remote: A situation with little chance of occurring.

Rescue: To recover some one or something from a situation that can cause harm to people and equipment.

Review: The process of judging and comparing the result achieved and lessons learnt with the intention of improving future performance.

Risk: A measure of a hazard's significance involving simultaneous examination of its consequence or severity of the outcome and the probability of occurrence.

Risk assessment: The process that determines where to place a hazard according to its significance on a risk scale which normally has the intolerable, tolerable and negligible regions.

Risk level:	The standard that determines the significance of risk.
Risk mitigation:	This is the process which makes the risk less severe or intense.
Risk reduction:	This is the process which uses various methods to lower the risk level of hazards for an activity, situation or system.
Risk region:	The area to which a hazard is classified based on the magnitude of its risk.
Rules:	The code of conduct, established usually in a written form, for the implementation of an activity and which is expected to be observed by those directly concerned.
Safe:	A situation in which the harm is perceived to have little likelihood of occurrence and the consequence is regarded as very low.
Safety:	A human perceived quality that determines to what extent the management, engineering and operation of a system is free from danger to life, property or the environment.
Safety case approach:	An approach which meets the safety requirements or standard with an appropriate method supported by a structured argument or case using the available evidence while taking into account the nature of safety.
Safety case:	The collection of all relevant evidence to enable the safety case approach to be applied.
Safety case report:	This is a term used to describe a report which highlights the safety status, using the appropriate evidences of an activity, situation or system at a given point in time or stage of the development.
Safety culture:	A belief, philosophy or faith held by groups or individuals on safety matters which is demonstrated in practice through the attitudes, actions and behaviour adopted by the people, an organisation or a nation.
Serious:	A term used to describe reasonably high risk significance.

Software:	The term used in the safety context covers management decisions and policies, standards and procedures.
Stakeholder:	A person with interest in or can be affected by the outcome in the performance of an activity, task or system.
Standard:	A measurable reference for comparing the performance of different individuals, pieces of equipment or forms of software.
System:	A general term used to refer to a structured arrangement of common items which can be co-ordinated to meet a specific objective. It can be applied to equipment and human activities.
Teamwork:	The term is used to describe a group of people working together to meet a common goal.
Tolerable risk:	A risk of a hazard which has been estimated to be moderate from appropriate assessment of the seriousness of consequence and the likelihood of occurrence.
Unacceptable:	Not agreeable to the decision or the outcome of an activity or situation based on the available information.
Uncertainty:	The outcome of an activity, situation or system which is not well defined.

REFERENCES

ABS (1996) *The Human Element*. American Bureau of Shipping. Survey. Vol. 27, No.7, September 1996.

ABS (2003) Guidance notes for the Application of Ergonomics to Marine Safety. http://www.eagle.com

ALERT (2005) *The International Maritime Human Element Bulletin*. Issue No. 7, The Nautical Institute, http://www.nautinst.org

Anderson, P.(1999) *The Mariner's Guide to Marine Insurance*. The Nautical Institute,1999, ISBN 1-870077-48-2.

ATSB (2003) *Reports of Marine Accidents*. The Australian Transport Safety Board, http://www.atsb.gov.au/marine/incident/index.cfm

Baker, C.C. and McCafferty, D.B. (2005) *Accident Database Review of Human Element Concerns: What do the results mean for classification?* Royal Institution of Naval Architects' Conference, London, February 2005.

CIMAH (1984) *The Control of Industrial Major Accidents Hazard (CIMAH) Regulations*. 1984. Statutory Instrument No. 1902. Revised version 2002.

Cox, S., Cleyne, A. (1998) *Meiburn Safety Culture in Offshore Environments*. HSE Offshore Technology Report.

CTSB (2003) *Reports of Marine Accidents*. The Canadian Transport Safety Board, http://www.tsb.gc.ca/en/publications/index.asp

Cullen (1990) *The Public Inquiry into the Piper Alpha Disaster (The Cullen Report)*. HMSO Cm: 1310. November 1990.

DEn (1965) *Nuclear Installation Act*. UK Department of Energy, HMSO, 1965.

DTp (1986) *Lifesaving Appliances Regulations*. UK Department of Transport, HMSO.

DTp (1987) *MV Herald of Free Enterprise – Fatal Accident Investigation (Sheen Report)*. Report of Court No.8074, UK Department of Transport, HMSO.

DTp (1990) *Report on the Accident to Boeing 737/400, G-OPME, near Kegworth, Leicestershire*. Air Accident Branch, UK Department of Transport, HMSO, 4/90.

Dogliani, M., Vassalos, D., Strang, T. (2004). *Evacuation Notation — a new concept to boost passenger evacuation performance in the cruise industry*. COMPIT 04, Iguenza, Spain, May 2004.

Fairhall, D.J, Jordan, P. *Black Tide Rising: Wreck of the Amoco Cadiz*. Deutsch, 1980.

Fleshman, A.B. and Hogh, M.S. (1989) *Cost Benefit Analysis in Evaluating the Acceptability of Industrial Risk: an Illustrative Case Study*. 6th International Symposium on Loss Prevention and Safety Promotion in the Process Industries, Oslo, June 1989.

Flint, R.H., and Slaven, G.H. (1992) *The Selection and Training of Offshore Installation Managers*. Report 92-011. Robert Gordon's University, 1992.

Gavin, A.G. (1997) *Bulk Carrier Structural Safety*. Joint Branch: Royal Institution of Naval Architects/ Institute of Marine Engineers, December 1997.

Gill, C et al (1967) *Wreck of the Torrey Canyon*.

Harris, D et al (2005) *Using SHERPA to predict design-induced error on the flight deck*. Aerospace Science and Technology, Elsevier.

HSE (1989) *Human Factors in Industrial Safety*. UK Health and Safety Executive, HMSO.

HSE (1991) *Successful Health & Safety Management*. HMSO, Health and Safety series booklet HG(G)65, ISBN 0-118859-88-9.

HSE (1992-1) *The Tolerability of Risk from Nuclear Power Stations*. UK Health and Safety Executive, 1992 edition. ISBN 0-11-886368-1.

HSE (1992-2) *A Guide to Offshore Installation (Safety Case) Regulations*. UK Health and Safety Executive, HMSO, L30. November 1992.

HSE (1999) *Reducing Errors and Influencing Behaviour*. Sudbury, UK Health and Safety Executive Books, HSG 48.

HSE (2001) *Safety Culture Maturity Model*. UK Health and Safety Executive Offshore Technology Report 2000-049.

HSE (2002) *Techniques for Addressing Rule Violation in Offshore Industries*. UK Health and Safety Executive, Offshore Technology Report 2000/96.

House of Lords (1991-1) *Safety Aspects of Ship Design and Technology*. House of Lords' Paper 75. HMSO, September 1991.

Iarossi, F.J. (2003) *Marine Safety: Perception and Reality*. 17th Chua Chor Teck Memorial Lecture, Singapore 2003.

IMO (1994) *International Safety Management Code (ISM Code)*. IMO Publication – 186E. 1994.

IMO (1995) *Formal Safety Assessment*. Submitted by the UK Government to the 65th Session of IMO's Maritime Safety Committee, Agenda Item 24, February 1995.

IMO (1996) *International Code of Safety for High Speed Craft*. International Maritime Organization, 1996.

IMO(2002) *Interim Guidelines for Evacuation Analysis of New and Existing Passenger Ships.* MSC/Circulation.

IMO (2004) *Safety of Life at Sea (SOLAS)*. International Maritime Organization Publication ID110E, ISBN 9-280141-83-X.

IMO (2006) *MARPOL.* International Maritime Organization Publication IC520E, ISBN 9-280142-16-X.

IMO(2007) www.imo.org *Information on the background to the International Maritime Organisation.*

Jones, S. *Maritime Security*, The Nautical Institute, 2006, ISBN 1-870077-75-X.

Kletz, T.A. (1991) *An Engineer's View of Human Error*, 3rd edition. Institute of Chemical Engineers, 1991.

Kletz, T.A. (1992) *HAZOP and HAZAN.* Third edition. Institute of Chemical Engineers, 1992.

Kuo, C. (1990) *A Preventive Framework for Achieving Effective Safety.* Invited Address, 4th International Conference on the Stability of Ships and Ocean Vehicles, Naples, Italy. September 1990.

Kuo, C. (1992) *A Preventive Treatment of Offshore Safety.* Proceedings of ISOPE-92-(International Society of Offshore and Polar Engineers), San Francisco, June 1992.

Kuo, C. (1993) *The Role of Human Factors in the Safety of Marine Systems.* Proceedings of ISOPE-93, Singapore. June 1993.

Kuo, C. (1996) *Introducing Human Factors into the Maritime Safety Framework.* Keynote Address, Symposium on Human and Organisational Error in Marine Situations. SNAME, Arlington, Virginia, USA. November 1996.

Kuo, C. et al. (1997) *A Safety Case Approach for Stena Line's High Speed Craft HSS 1500.* Royal Institution of Naval Architects' Spring Meeting, 1997.

Kuo, C. and Houison Craufurd, S (2000) *Managing Human Errors in Maritime Activities.* Royal Institution of Naval Architects' Conference London, September 2000.

Kuo, C. Smith, A. and Cain, C. (2001) *Interactive Multi-media Technology for Safety Training on Stena Line's HSS 1500.* FAST 2001 Conference, Southampton, September 2001.

Kuo, C. and Sukovoy,O. (2004) *The Generic Management Systems (GMS) Approach to Fire Safety of Composite Materials.* INTERFLAM conference, Edinburgh, July 2004.

Lees, F.P. and Amy M.L. (1989) *Safety Cases within the 'Control of Industrial Major Accident Hazard' Regulations 1984.* Butterworths, 1989.

Leiden, K et al (2001) *A Review of Human Performance Models for the Prediction of Human Error*. Report for National Aero Space Admin by AMES Research Centre.

Liu, Y.G. et al (2000) *Human Error Analysis in Ship Operations*. Proceedings of Foresight and Precaution Conference, Edinburgh, May 2000.

MacLachlan, M. (2005) *The Shipmaster's Business Companion*. The Nautical Institute, 2005 ISBN 1-870077-45-8.

MARPOL (2006) *Marine Pollution Conventions*. Consolidated edition, IMO publications, ISBN 92-801-421-6-X.

Means, K. et al (1997) *Human and Organisational Factors in Offshore Safety*. Offshore Technical Report 543, HSE books.

O'Neil, W.A. (1996) *Responsibility to the Human Element*. American Bureau of Shipping, Survey. – Vol. 27, No.3. September 1996.

O'Neil, W.A. (1997) *The Quest for Safety – the Limits to Regulation*. The Wakefield Lecture, UK March 1997.

OREDA (1982) *Offshore Reliability Data Handbook (OREDA)*. Penn Well Books, 1982 onwards.

Rasmussen, J (1982) *Human Errors: a Taxonomy for describing Human Malfunction in Industrial Installations*. Journal of Occupational Accidents, No.4,1982.

Re, A.S., Lam, E., Veitch, B., Igloliorte, G.(2003) *Quantitative Assessment of Escape and Evacuation*. International conference of the Royal Institution of Naval Architects, London.

Reason, J. (1990) *Human Error*. Cambridge University Press, 1990.

Reason, J. (1991) *How to Promote Error Tolerance in Complex Systems in the Context of Ships and Aircraft*. Proceedings of Safety at Sea, The Nautical Institute, London, 1991.

Reason, J. (1997) *Managing the Risks of Organisational Accidents*. Ashgate Publications,1997.

Reason, J. & Hobbs(2003) *Managing Maintenance Error*. Ashgate Publications, 2003, ISBN 0-754615-91-X.

Reben, A.S. (1985) *The Penguin Dictionary of Psychology*. Penguin Books. 1985.

RINA (1992) *Guidance to Members on Safety Matters*. Royal Institution of Naval Architects, London, 1992.

Sanders, M.S. and McCormick, E.J. (1987) *Human Factors in Engineering and Design*. McGraw-Hill Books. P.5. 1987.

Statt, D.A. (1990) *The Concise Dictionary of Psychology*. Routledge, London, 1990.

Stockbridge, H.C.W. (1975) *Behaviour and the Physical Environment*. Batsford, London, 1975.

UK P&I Club (2000) *Analysis of Major Claims to 2000*. UK Mutual Steam Ship Association (Bermuda) Ltd. Publication, 2000.

UK P& I Club (1999) *Human Elements*, Publication of the UK P&I Club, London.

UK MAIB (2003) *Annual Reports of Marine Accidents Investigation Branch (MAIB)*, UK MAIB, Southampton.

Vassalos, D. et al (2004) *Effectiveness of Passenger Evacuation Performance for Design, Operation and Training using First Principles*. Lloyd's List Events, March 2004.

Vassalos,et al (2001) *A Mesoscopic Model for Passenger Evacuation in a virtual ship-sea environment and performance-based evaluation*. Pedestrian and Evacuation Dynamics, April, Duisburg, Germany.

WOAD (2004) *Worldwide Offshore Accident Databank*. User manual, Det Norske Veritas.

INDEX

R

S

Maritime  Futures

Maritime Futures is the concept behind a new series of books which are designed to expand the horizons of the possible, and explain how the work of innovative technologies will impact on maritime industries. The series aims to demonstrate how management strategies can be aligned to take advantage of new opportunities.

Each book makes a ground breaking contribution to the understanding of new technologies and the way they can be applied to improve performance.

:/ Waves of Change — inspiring maritime innovation

This book explains how conflicting expectations arise between those who hold traditional values and those who see innovation as the way forward. Sooner or later, shipping will have to embrace the wider opportunities created by new developments in information technology. The book sets out to demonstrate how managers, and that includes sea staff, can transform this potential into results. Dr John Robinson, himself an experienced senior executive, provides an enlightening account of how to implement innovative strategies A truly scene-setting book for the series that will change perceptions forever.

:/ The Management of Maritime Safety

This book explores the ways that different industries have adapted to ensure their operations are safe. The author Professor Chengi Kuo, a ship technologist, explains the difference between traditional prescriptive regulations and the discipline behind the safety case approach. In an innovative environment the past is not necessarily an infallible guide to the future, but ways have to be found to protect the public, workers and the environment from unsafe practices. Ultimately, whichever system is used has to be managed and the author encourages readers to question whether it is now time to rethink our priorities.

:/ Integrating ship bridge systems — Vol 1 Radar and AIS

Marine equipment has been designed and produced as separate units, but the availability of fast reliable data processing now enables individual items to he integrated into more flexible and applicable work stations. Linking Automated Information Systems to radar (compulsory on all new radars post 2008) provides new opportunities for presenting ship data so that more informed navigational decisions can he made. With integration comes more variations of possibilities. Dr Andy Norris, a leading equipment designer, shows how to avoid the clutter of spurious information by concentrating on the navigational tasks for which the equipment will be used.

:/ Integrating ship bridge systems — Vol 2 Positioning

Although all ships use GPS, there is still no alternative system at sea to take over if the GPS satellites are disabled. For reliability there need to be three systems available. With only two it is not possible to know which system has failed: so the search is on for a three-way electronic solution to this age old maritime problem. Dr Andy Norris explores the viability and benefits to the industry of making that crucial step into the electronic age. At this stage the sextant will surely follow the example of Mr Morse's communication code. Further volumes are being planned.

:/ Leadership Throughout

Who is going to win the tug of war between those who have their feet firmly on the ground supporting traditional maritime values or their more cerebral adversaries who see opportunities for mobilising support through new alliances to capitalise on the opportunities presented by powerful information technology networks.

It is an intriguing question which all managers and sea staff will have to address as change gathers momentum amplified by the economics of competition. Leadership in this context assumes new meaning with respect to organisational development. However, there can be no point in being out in front if everybody else is sailing in a different direction.

The author is a mariner, with an MSc from Exeter University, and is a personel development consultant active in the multi-cultural Middle East. He doesn't say leading is easy but he does demonstrate how to acquire the skills to succeed.

:/ Other subjects being planned

Educational access, the key to success in taking computer based systems to sea — Expanding the economic horizons of sea transport — Redefining Maritime Policy.

Maritime  Futures

are published by   and supported by

The series is supported by the UK Maritime Forum
which includes the following professional associations:

The Royal Institution of Naval Architects
The Royal Institute of Navigation
The Institute of Marine Engineers, Science and Technology
The Institute of Chartered Shipbrokers
The Nautical Institute
The Society for Underwater Technology

If you would like to be kept in touch when new titles appear,
please simply record your e-mail address by sending it to
maritime.futures@nautinst.org

For further information contact
www.nautinst.org
The Nautical Intstiute, 202 Lambeth Road, London SE1 7LQ
Tel: +44 (0)207 928 1351

NOTES